Coyote Country

D1562267

New Americanists *A series edited by Donald E. Pease*

Coyote Country

Fictions of the Canadian West

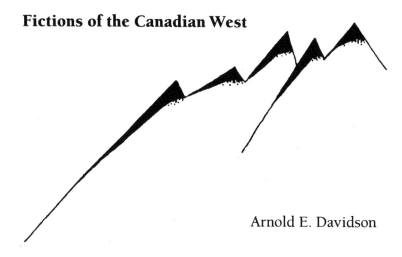

Arnold E. Davidson

DUKE UNIVERSITY PRESS   *Durham and London 1994*

© 1994 Duke University Press
All rights reserved
Printed in the United States of America on
acid-free paper ∞
Typeset in Berkeley Medium by
Tseng Information Systems.
Library of Congress Cataloging-in-Publication Data
appear on the last printed page of this book.

For Charles and Susan

Contents

Acknowledgments

Any book entails more debts than can be disposed of in an acknowledgment. To name just a few, I would like to thank, first, my father and my grandfather for teaching me much that I once knew about living on an Alberta ranch: the structure of haystacks, the poetry of fences, the reading of land and livestock. I also thank my mother, one of the best teachers I ever encountered, for aiming me at other reading, reading that took me away from Alberta to university and eventually university teaching in the United States. Another teacher to whom I am particularly indebted is Robert Kroetsch, who not only directed my Ph.D. dissertation, but also, more important, directed me, through his own fiction, back to the Canadian West.

I am also especially grateful to the National Endowment for the Humanities for awarding me a fellowship that supported much of the early research on which the book is based; to the Canadian Embassy in Washington, D.C., for granting me a Senior Canadian Fellowship Award that allowed me to complete most of the manuscript; and to the Association for Canadian Studies in the United States for awarding my completed manuscript the association's Canadian Studies Publication Grant. Thanks are due, too, to *ARIEL* (and the Board of Governors, the University of Calgary), *Canadian Literature, Journal of Canadian Fiction,* and *Studies in Short Fiction* for allowing me to incorporate into my book material that first appeared in essays I published in those journals. I also thank Columbia University Press for allowing me to draw on my essay, "Canada in Fiction," in *The Columbia History of the American Novel* and the Modern Language Association for allowing me to include in the book a much expanded and revised version of my "The Reinvention of the West in Canadian Fiction" published in *Studies on Canadian Literature: Introductory and Critical Essays.*

Along the way to a completed study valuable counsel and encouragement has been offered by family, friends, and colleagues, particularly my sister and brother-in-law, Karen Davidson and Roy Cunningham; my son and daughter-in-law, Charles Davidson and Susan Brown; my former colleagues, Ken Bidle, George Cornell, and Linda Wagner-Martin; my present colleagues, Clark Cahow, Thomas Ferraro, Frank Lentricchia, Michael Moon, Eve Sedgwick, Barbara Herrnstein Smith, John Thompson, and Jane Tompkins; and, finally, my fellow students of Canadian fiction, Linda Hutcheon, Lorna Irvine, W. J. Keith, Camille LaBossière, Shirley Neuman, W. H. New, and Robert Thacker. For all of your advice, thank you. For not always following it, my apologies. Thanks are also due to my typists, Jennifer Huntly and Kathryn West; to my research assistants, Susan Lynch, Glenn Willmott, Julia Dryer, and, again, Kathryn West; and to my editor at Duke University Press, J. Reynolds Smith. Last and mostly, I here thank Cathy N. Davidson for her contributions to the writing of this book.

Coyote Country

Introduction: Coyote Country

Early in the twentieth century a young "colored" man from Winston-Salem, North Carolina, went west to Southern Alberta and reinvented himself as Buffalo Child Long Lance, a chief of the Blackfoot. In that capacity he returned to the United States and gained considerable renown, associating with the rich and famous in Hollywood and New York, producing and starring in one of the first movies to treat Natives seriously, writing and speaking on behalf of Native causes.[1] It is an odd success and hard to evaluate. His achievement is undeniable but so is his fraud. His fraud is also understandable, especially when we consider that he was of mixed white, Native, and perhaps black ancestry, yet, for him, what signified mostly in the United States of his time was black. His family denied being part Negro but was still officially deemed colored. He himself departed from West Point (where he had been admitted as a full-blooded Cherokee) when an army investigation threatened to expose his passing. In this context the Freudian implications of the name he assumed are particularly suggestive. "Long Lance" is a definite claiming of a potency that America preferred to deny black men. Yet Natives early recognized that Long Lance could not really act or speak for them, for he simply did not know their ways. Disputing a false definition of the "Negro," he falsely inscribed himself as a Native, as simply another (although preferred) "Other."

It is tempting to go west and play Indian. Numerous people have done so and most without the impetus of racism. Archibald Stansfeld Belaney, for example, although born and raised in Hastings, England, could come to Canada to become Grey Owl, ostensibly a half Apache adopted by the Ojibway and taught by them the ways of the woods.[2] On two book tours back in England, in braids, buckskin, and wampum belt, he could pass as Canada's most famous Indian. In that false guise he also became one of Canada's more popular writers and greatest conservationists, two successes that went together. After Grey Owl, encouraged by Anahareo, his Iroquois "wife" (Belaney was legally married to someone else), adopted two orphaned beaver kittens, he gave up trapping to work on beaver conservation in western Canada and to write movingly about these "little people" in books such as his *Pilgrims of the Wild* (1935). He thereby fostered "environmental consciousness" to the degree that, "in the pantheon" of nature writers, one recent commentator has claimed, "Grey Owl belongs with Henry David Thoreau, John Muir, Aldo Leopold, and Rachel Carson."[3] A very real accomplishment for a fake Indian.

One could also go west and play author without playing Indian but with much the same reasons as those who did. The space and heritage of the West precluded too careful an inquiry into just who you were and who your ancestors had been for the last several generations. There were more opportunities for improvisation, even of the self. Ernest Nephtali Dufault, a Francophone Canadian, could travel to Montana to pass himself off as an orphan from Texas raised by a kindly French-Canadian trapper (thus that accent) and thereby become Will James, one of the major American Western writers.[4] Or a young man, Felix Paul Greve, afoul of the law in Germany, fakes a suicide and emigrates to Canada where he becomes Frederick Philip Grove, ostensibly the illegitimate son of a Swedish baron. Grove claimed a long romantic history behind him but had, more validly, a long future ahead of him as one of the first major Canadian Western writers.[5]

I invoke these four historic characters as my imagined muses because, briefly, between them, they embody much of the freedom and the possibility, the fictiveness and the bricolage implicit in any construct of the West. They are all also versions of Coyote, "perhaps the most conspicuous figure in the oral literature of the Native American peoples" of Western North America and the figure of New World Native mythology "who creates and is destroyed, who cheats and is ultimately cheated—who surpasses all others in intelligence but finally 'outsmarts himself.'"[6] But this is just one reading of Coyote and perhaps too dualistic. For Gary Snyder, in his aptly titled article, "The Incredible Survival of Coyote," "the most interesting psychological thing" about Coyote is "that there wasn't a clear dualism of good and evil." Coyote sometimes "clearly manifested benevolence . . . and had a certain dignity; and on other occasions he was the silliest utmost fool, and at the same time . . . he's just always traveling along, doing the best he can."[7] It is hard to get a fix on Coyote and for that reason he/she and his/her avatars (Long Lance et al.) especially fit my purposes and the Canadian Western.

Although I will discuss Canadian Westerns largely in terms of their departures from the preestablished patterns of the traditional American Western, such cross-border comparisons should in no way suggest that north of the border we can expect artistic innovations in content and form, while south of it there is only convention and cliché. There are, of course, Canadian Westerns as dubiously formulaic and as artistically dead as the shallowest, Eastern-titillating American "dime" Westerns. Indeed, one of the first Canadian Westerns, J. E. Collins's *Annette the Métis Spy* (1887), with its title featuring of the Other woman, suggests the first American dime Western, Ann S. Stephens's *Malaeska: The Indian Wife of the White Hunter* (1860), and if the exotic heroine in the Canadian novel is somewhat domesticated by her familiar name, she is also made more dangerous by being an active agent for the enemy. Or in his first novel, *The Story of Louis Riel* (1885), Collins "explains" that the Riel Rebellion was not an attempt of the Métis to retain their land and traditional way of life, but was Louis Riel's attempt to steal the white girlfriend of Thomas Scott, an outspoken Ontario Protestant executed early in the rebellion. As Dick Harrison points out, Collins made the mistake of filling out this slight and quickly written novel (in seventeen days, to take advantage of the interest in the rebellion of the same year) with "newspaper accounts of Riel's trial bound in at the end of the book," and, "in striking contrast to Collins's own writing, the bare journalistic accounts are so much more moving than Collins's sensationalism that they expose the flimsy contrivance to which they are appended."[8] Suffice to say that Collins is no James Fenimore Cooper; he is not even a Ned Buntline (one of the populizers of Buffalo Bill) who at least competently constructed the formulaic fictions he so abundantly produced. Nor does a metafictional pedigree attest to a Canadian Western's artistic excellence. Geoffrey Unsell's *Perdue or How the West Was Lost* (1984) is as woodenly postmodern as *The Story of Louis Riel* is programmatically pro-Protestant.

Neither is the American Western a monolithic deployment of narrative conventions for claiming a new land—Fenimore Cooper's ethnocentric offenses raised to the level of genre. If one version of the American Western can be seen as originating in *The Last of the Mohicans* (1826), another rather different one is concurrently well launched with Lydia Maria Child's *Hobomok* (1824) and Catharine Maria Sedgwick's *Hope Leslie* (1827), both of which portray a white woman's marriage to an Indian without demonizing the husband. As Dana D. Nelson notes, the different "vision" of "female frontier novelists" such as Child and Sedgwick "counters the 'Adamic myth' and its valorization of white-male conquest."[9] And Sedgwick herself observes in her preface how an Indian perspective might counter the prevailing perspective of white representations of the Indian: "In our histories, it was perhaps natural that [the Indians] should be represented as 'surly dogs,' who preferred to die rather than live, from no other motive than a stupid or malignant obstinacy. Their own historians . . ., if they had such, would as naturally, and with more justice, have extolled their high-souled courage and patriotism."[10]

Deriving from different Eastern beginnings, the American Western continues to accommodate diversity, as can be suggested by even a brief catalog of titles: Edward Abbey's *The Monkey Wrench Gang* (1975), Thomas Berger's *Little Big Man* (1964), Richard Brautigan's *Trout Fishing in America* (1967), Willa Cather's *Death Comes for the Archbishop* (1927) and *My Ántonia* (1918), Sandra Cisneros's *Woman Hollering Creek* (1991), E. L. Doctorow's *Welcome to Hard Times* (1960), Richard Ford's *Wildfire* (1990), Jack Kerouac's *On the Road* (1957), Ken Kesey's *One Flew Over the Cuckoo's Nest* (1962), Norman Maclean's *A River Runs Through It* (1983), Cormac McCarthy's *Blood Meridian* (1985), Larry McMurtry's *Buffalo Girls* (1990), Wright Morris's *Plains Song* (1980), Tillie Olsen's *Yonnondio* (1974), Tom Robbins's *Even Cowgirls Get the Blues* (1976), Marilyn Robinson's *Housekeeping* (1981), Wallace Stegner's *Angle of Repose* (1971), John Steinbeck's *The Grapes of Wrath* (1939), and, by Native American writers, works such as Louise Erdrich's *Tracks* (1988), N. Scott Momaday's *House Made of Dawn* (1968), Leslie Marmon Silko's *Ceremony* (1977), and James Welch's *Fools Crow* (1986) and *Winter in the Blood* (1973). These novels—and many more could be listed—do not fall under one rubric and certainly not the rubric of the popular Western.

Even that last rubric is problematic. "Generalizations about popular Westerns should be suspect," James H. Maguire warns, "partly because it is unlikely that any critic could read them all, but mainly because all sorts of popular writers have varied the pattern, and some have occasionally broken out of the formula."[11] The warning, however, is suspect too. Somehow the generalizations are dubious although the pattern is there to be varied and the formula to be broken out of. Why not formulate the formula? And, indeed, two pages later, Maguire refers to "the stereotypes of the standard 'horse opry.'"[12] Are we, with this form that both is and isn't, already well into the realm of Coyote?

One way out of the impasse of the Western as both thoroughly formulaic and formally diverse is to admit that the term now applies to more than novels. Throughout most of the twentieth century the Western was a Hollywood staple and as such was highly standardized, particularly with respect to its portrayal of women and of Natives. As Jon Tuska observes: "All we can learn about women from the vast majority of Western films is what roles the patriarchy felt they ought to play, and nothing at all of the roles they actually did play on the frontier."[13] With Natives as well, Westerns are "guilty of vicious stereotyping" and give us Indians constructed only for the killing, which is "only so much 'newspeak' for enjoying genocide."[14] The Hollywood Western, Tuska concludes, has pandered "for so long" to "illusions and comforting fantasies" about an imaginary West, it has made so many films "mired in . . . rigid, formulary convention" and replete with "stereotypical characters" that any attempt "to tell [in a movie] of the actual history of the American West" would seem "depressing and subversive: in a word, unAmerican."[15] Moreover, this movie rendering of the American West has long been recycled, first, in the thirties and forties, as radio Westerns, and, then, "since the 1950s, television series such as 'Gunsmoke,' 'Wagon Train,' 'Bonanza,' and 'The Young Riders' [and still more recently, 'Doctor Quinn, Medicine Woman'] have brought 'the West that wasn't' to millions of living rooms."[16]

That quadruply inscribed—in fiction, movies, radio, and television— "West that wasn't" gives me my starting point. If this "West" wasn't the American West that it purported to be, even less was it the Canadian West. Western Canada, it must be emphasized, has a history substantially different from that of western America and radically different from the American Western. To begin with, the land was settled in a later and far more orderly fashion than was the case in the United States. For the most part, the North West Mounted Police were there first, before the settlers. They were deployed to prevent "the gun-fighting, the lawlessness, and the bloody clashes with Indians [characteristic, at least in Canadian eyes, of] the American frontier," and the fact that "six weeks after the act [establishing the North West Mounted Police] was passed, a group of American wolf hunters, claiming they were looking for some stolen horses, massacred a camp of Assiniboines in the Cypress Hills . . . merely accentuated the need for rapid action."[17] Western Canada didn't want Indian wars and except for two "brief and relatively bloodless" encounters, the Louis Riel uprisings of 1869 and 1885, didn't have them.[18] The Mounties, moreover, were vested in a red-coat authority of empire intended to preclude the need for shoot-outs, for being fastest on the draw. Whereas the typical "Western hero resolves the conflict between civilization and savagery by a salutary, almost surgical, application of violence which tilts the balance of power in favour of civilized law," the Canadian Mountie hero (in contradistinction to the U.S. Mountie hero who, in American novels and movies, soon became mostly a northern marshal) resolves the same conflict to the same end "but in a different way—not by using violence but by denying it."[19] The settlers, I would also note, came west more by steam locomotive than by wagon train. A conductor's "All aboard" just does not ring with the same fictive possibilities as the wagon master's "Roll 'em west." In short, the whole subject matter of the traditional Western—wagon trains and Indian wars, cowboys and rustlers, shoot-outs and stampedes—has almost no place in the Canadian West.

The departures of Western movies from historic truth (whatever it might have been) are programmatic and, as Tuska notes, provide directives that "prescribe to viewers what they ought to believe, think, and how they ought to behave"—recipes on how to be unproblematically American.[20] This is a program that the popular Western has followed from its start. Thus Nelson can point out how Robert Montgomery Bird's *Nick of the Woods* (1837), Cooper's *The Last of the Mohicans,* and William Gilmore Simms's *The Yemassee* (1835) all "work to repress class and social discrepancies under the rubric of a larger and fundamentally 'white' American identity" and thereby posit "a unified front whose internal social and material conflicts are displaced onto a conflict fictionalized as Progress versus Nature, or White versus Red."[21] Here, too, we have a recipe on how to be unproblematically American.

Canadians, however, are going to have problems with such recipes. They, too, are inundated with versions of a mythic West, a mythically American West that leaves them out. From Georges Bugnet, Frederick Philip Grove, Martha Ostenso, Sinclair Ross, Laura G. Salverson, and Robert Stead to M. Allerdale Grainger, Margaret Laurence, Edward Alexander McCourt, Gabrielle Roy, and Ethel Wilson to, still more recently, Sandra Birdsell, Sharon Butala, Gary Geddes, Patricia Joudry, Fred Stenson, W. D. Valgardson, and Guy Vanderhaeghe (and many others could be named), Canadian Western writers have resisted the mythic American West with a more realistically portrayed Canadian one. Or sometimes with a comically portrayed Canadian one, as in Paul Hiebert's *Sarah Binks* (1947) that celebrates the accomplishments of "the Sweet Songstress of Saskatchewan" by recording such verse as "The farmer leaps from bed to board,/And board to binder on the land;/His wife awakens with shouts of joy,/And milks a cow with either hand."[22] This "West that wasn't"—both the novel and the poetry—isn't the American West that wasn't either. And a few contemporary Canadian authors, particularly Nicole Brossard in *Le Désert mauve* (1987), Jane Rule in *Desert of the Heart* (1977), and George Ryga in *In the Shadow of the Vulture* (1985), have even assayed the large task of rewriting and remythicizing the American West itself.

Still other Canadian writers, from Howard O'Hagan and Sheila Watson to Thomas King, Robert Kroetsch, and Aritha van Herk, have been intrigued by the possibility of forging a Western Canadian mythic fiction different from the prevailing American version. In good Canadian fashion (we may not know who we are but we certainly know who we are not), they counter programmatic myths of American identity with a counter discourse on the problematics of mythic identity. The fiction of these writers, the ploys whereby they invert and parody, unwrite and rewrite the popular American Western is the subject of my study, and the fact that a number of them, from Watson to King, make extensive use of Coyote as the Native trickster—and another countering of American myths of achieved identity in the West—gives me my title.

In this book, then, I do not assay the kind of cross-border comparisons of specific Canadian and American literary texts that such scholars as Carol Fairbanks in *Prairie Women: Images in American and Canadian Fiction* or Robert Thacker in *The Great Prairie Fact and Literary Imagination* have already advanced. Instead, I am concerned with the ways in which a number of Western Canadian fiction writers make use of the paraphernalia of the classic U.S. Western. Given the extraordinary delineation of cultural values by the mass-produced Western (by definition, "American") since the 1890s, how have experimental Canadian writers inverted and subverted the basic tropes, metaphors, ideologies, gender contracts, and racial hegemonies within their own fabulations? And how have the ruling myths of colonial expansionism in the United States—as embodied by the classic American Western—been appropriated, transformed, and parodied as part of the "paracolonial" project of a number of Canada's (and North America's) most interesting, experimental, oppositional, and metafictional writers?[23]

To partly answer those large questions, I first trace out how a genealogy of different myths leads to one myth that particularly differentiates the Canadian Western from the American and provides thereby the basis for Canada's most impressive Westerns. This myth is, at its simplest, a search for myths of origin, and, as such, it insists on the Canadian grounding of Canadian Westerns, on their calculated difference from their American predecessors and counterparts. In the next section of the study, I assess in detail three mythic Canadian Westerns, two founding novels and one more contemporary text that, for me, best illustrate the accomplishment of this form. Then, in two final sections, I look more closely at the ongoing questioning of gender and race (the portrayal of the Native) in this fiction that begins by insisting on the need for narratives other than the male monologues of the traditional Western that are as straight and white as a Texas highway. The project of the Canadian Western is, after all, to tell different stories of a different West.

The popular American Western casts its tall, lanky shadow over the Canadian West, and the challenge of that presence must be answered. The Canadian response, however, is not simply a Bloomian battle with one's literary progenitors. Instead, it is as if the gunfight at the OK Corral were restaged with the Matt Dillonish U.S. marshal facing not some outlaw or renegade, but Coyote himself. The question of who will be the winner in such a shoot-out is hardly the issue; the point is that the whole *form* of the encounter is altered from shoot-out to melee. The subversive imperatives driving the Canadian Westerns that are the subject of my study transform and transmogrify the mythology of the classic American Western. That is the point of Coyote, with his tricks and transformations, and the terrain of *Coyote Country.*

Part I Overview

1 Reinventing the West

For almost all North Americans—Canadians as well as Americans—the term "Western" immediately evokes a certain narrative structure that John G. Cawelti, in *The Six-Gun Mystique*, has cogently analyzed in terms of a frontier conflict between advancing civilization and retreating savagery (the civilization defining, of course, the savagery). This structure dramatizes, for those on the defining side of the dividing line, the opposition between, on the one hand, the need for a stable social order with an enforced morality and, on the other, the appeal of individual freedom and irresponsibility pursued to the point of lawlessness and moral chaos. Despite the temptation of the latter, the issue is regularly resolved in favor of the former through the actions of a hero who makes the right judgments and who, as "a man with a gun," makes those judgments stick.[1] As Cawelti points out, the ambivalent moral stand of the traditional American Western is reified by the ambivalent hero who employs violence to counteract violence. Like the frontier, this protagonist, too, is poised between a feared and desired freedom, a required but resented order. His action suspends his indecision. Small wonder the imperatives of heroism—and of violence—in the American frontier mythos are seldom resisted.[2]

This Western formula is so established that it can substantially shape even fictions intended to transcend it. Thus John R. Milton, in *The Novel of the American West,* distinguishes between the "subliterary genre" of "the western of the lowercase *w* [with] its popular appeal to mass audiences" and "a higher form of literature" (the "Western" in the uppercase mode) that "strives to become significant in both theme and form."[3] As this critic acknowledges, however, "the legendary cowboy . . . has in the past seventy-five years ridden through an amazing number of bad novels" but only "a few good ones."[4] I would suggest that even the few "good ones"—novels that

Milton assesses in some detail—such as Walter Van Tilburg Clark's *The Ox-Bow Incident* (1940), Frank Water's *The Man Who Killed the Deer* (1942), A. B. Guthrie, Jr.'s *The Way West* (1949), or Frederick Manfred's *Lord Grizzly* (1954)—are still close to the formula Western largely because that cowboy still rides through them.

The very way in which Milton's capitalized Western critically examines what the other more subliterary form mostly assumes still conjoins the two forms as explorations of basically the same mythos of the West. For example, in *The Ox-Bow Incident* the three lynched "outlaws" are not guilty of the rustling and murder for which they are put to death, a state of affairs seldom envisioned in standard Westerns in which lynchings abound but the vigilantes generally manage to get the right man. So what is normally an example of rough-and-ready frontier justice turns out to be the real crime. As such and as one of the conscience-stricken actual killers subsequently attests, it could have and should have been prevented—prevented, indeed, by the very code that underwrote it. As Milton notes, "what characterizes *The Ox-Bow Incident*" as serious literature "is the lack of the strong will and the fast gun."[5] Yet that absence serves to validate the ethos affirmed by the presence of the hero and his trusty Colt .45 in more standard Westerns (Milton's smallcase category). In short, both forms occupy very much the same American frontier. Neither do recent parodic Westerns substantially controvert the Western formula. As Dick Harrison observes in "Fictions of the American and Canadian Wests," "even [the highly praised Western] satiric writers such as Thomas Berger in *Little Big Man* and Ken Kesey in *One Flew Over the Cuckoo's Nest* are ultimately less concerned with criticizing frontier values than with lamenting their passing."[6]

Canadian writers, however, have not produced authentic all-Canadian-content versions of American Westerns because a key ingredient is missing. Harrison, in *Unnamed Country: The Struggle for a Canadian Prairie Fiction,* emphasizes that the first Canadian settlers, like the early settlers of the United States, encountered great difficulties, but they viewed their experience differently. "They had the sense of a plain patrolled by the North West Mounted Police, surveyed for settlement, with a railroad stretching out to cross it. They were not on the edge of anything; they were surrounded by something, and they took it to be the civilized order they had always known."[7] The land was all surveyed and neatly divided before it was occupied by families who moved west mostly on the new railroad. Consequently, "nineteenth- and early twentieth-century Western Canadian literature is different from traditional Western American literature because there never has been a [Canadian] frontier literature."[8] There was no frontier literature because there was no frontier, and that lack freed the novel for a different task—"to create," in the words of Rudy Wiebe, "a past, a lived history, a vital mythology."[9] There is little place in either that history or mythology for the construct of the frontier as originally formulated in the United States in the fiction of James Fenimore Cooper and then massively popularized by Zane Grey and others in the early decades of the twentieth century.

Neither is the frontier a main feature of what we might call the Canadian literary imagination, as Robert Kroetsch points out in one of his early interviews, significantly titled "The American Experience and the Canadian Voice": "In the United States, the Freudian metaphor has swept the boards, the superego versus the id kind of thing. The id is the good guy trying to free himself . . . youth or the frontiersman, the man in the ten-gallon hat." Canadians, in contrast, are "more Jungian"; they are "fascinated with problems of equilibrium," whereas "Americans are interested in expansion. This difference," Kroetsch concludes, "has to have an effect on our literature, on our language."[10]

That "effect," I think, can be seen especially in recent Canadian Western writing. Inundated by fictional Indian attacks and cavalry rescues, outlaws and marshals and high-noon duels in the sun—inundated despite a history different from the American experience, in which such elements are at least loosely grounded—Canadians can feel a certain anxiety of influence. A number of authors have responded with fictions setting forth mythologies of the Canadian West conceived in a new vein best characterized as the conscious deconstruction of the mythologies of earlier Canadian prairie fiction as well as of the mythology of Manifest Destiny perpetuated by the American Western. As authors dispense with in fiction the frontier they never had in fact, they free themselves and their readers into a play of textuality and intertextuality. That play, moreover, serves to subvert the standard Western dialectics of power, the established relationships between the pioneer and the prairie, the cowboy and the Indian, the masculine and the feminine. The result, on the largest level, is the reinvention of the West and the Western, the creation of a literary landscape in which both author and reader are invited to work out other possibilities of being.

For example, in the conclusion of George Bowering's *Caprice,* all the old Western verities can be blatantly reversed. When the eponymous *heroine,* after avenging the death of a *brother,* rides off alone, *she* leaves her lover behind. *He* cannot come with her, because he is a teacher, "the school year" has "just begun," and, as she insists, his "place is already made."[11] Hardly the usual Western version of "a man's gotta do what a man's gotta do!" She rides off, moreover, "into the sunrise," not the sunset (that cheaply elegiac evocation of the passing of a whole way of life) and she rides not just eastward, but "eastward through the west that was becoming nearly as narrow as her trail."[12] In those last words of the novel, the Western itself circles back to the East that ever defined it, and what was cast as limitless panorama and possibility self-deconstructs to trail, to the delimiting text of the Western that has always been both larger and smaller than the landscape it would contain.

Or in a more serious vein, the protagonist of Margaret Laurence's *The Diviners* (1974) is Morag Gunn, an orphan girl who reads in the ranting of her foster-father, Christie Logan, the outcast, shell-shocked, town garbage collector, the possibility of both escape and vocation; who leaves the small town of Manawaka, Manitoba, to become a major writer; and who also discerns—another reversal—that contrary to Thomas Wolfe's "You Can't Go Home Again . . . it may be the reverse which is true" and sometimes "you have to."[13] She does not find her "roots" in Scotland but in returning to Canada and settling in a log cabin near a small Ontario town the equivalent (a hundred years earlier) of the Manawaka she left behind. This is the East as the West, the "West" particularly of Catherine Parr Trail (a nineteenth-century pioneer Ontario woman writer) who is regularly invoked in the novel, a sort of Ariel, as Barbara Godard astutely notes, to Morag's Prospero.[14]

Morag, moreover, has her Miranda too. The mother's retrospective quest is balanced in the novel by the daughter's prospective one. Furthermore, the daughter herself represents a rebalancing of Western Canadian history. Christie had told Morag mythic tales of the Scottish settling of Western Canada and of the settlers' wars with the Métis. Jules Tonnerre, a Métis schoolmate, told her equally mythic tales of heroic Métis resistance to the taking of their land. Morag re-equates those different and parallel actions when she leaves her dominating English husband (himself a product of British rule in India) for an extended affair with Jules, who rigorously does not try to play the patriarchal authority to either Morag or Pique, the daughter born from their union. But only at the end of the novel can Morag fully release Pique to find her own vocation as an artist and her own relationship to her mixed heritage. The Western as Eastern (Morag's Eastern journey) becomes Western again as Pique sets out for Manitoba and her Métis relatives.

Behind these reversals is a still larger reversal, a rewriting of Shakespeare's *The Tempest* (the Ur-Western in its claiming of authority over an Other and an Other's land). As Godard points out, Laurence's deceptively simple novel first reverses, on the level of the protagonist's private life, the resolution of Shakespeare's *Tempest* in which the woman can be elevated only "by being chosen as wife of the hero." In vivid contrast to that standard ending and its implicit social order, "Laurence's new order is an order of one in which the shero [sic] makes the choice and works hard for her own success."[15] That resolution is also metafictionalized when one of the books Morag writes is *Prospero's Child*, and the novel within the novel must be read back into our reading of the containing novel. As Godard concludes: "Laurence rewrites Shakespeare's Prospero/Miranda story to show [what] the relationship between parent/child, author/creator, writer/reader [and, I would add, colonizer/colonized] is like when the magician abdicates his power over the word and the knowledge it permits, ceases to be an *authority* and lets everyone tell or write their own story."[16] Such "Othering [of] the text" is a "violation of hierarchies and boundaries." It is a "breaking [of] Prospero's wand of power and along with it the enchanted spell over Caliban and Miranda so that they too can tell their stories, those of the aborigine and the daughter."[17] Again we see the Canadian Western's preference for Other stories.

Gabrielle Roy's *Where Nests the Water Hen* (1951) also features a Manitoba mother as Western hero. Luzina Tousignant's heroism is her endurance on the harsh western margin of the French settlement of Canada and her determination that her French heritage shall endure too. More specifically, it is her almost yearly journeys from her isolated island settlement to the nearest town to bear a new baby (as well as to see something of the larger world) and then her labor to bring teachers to the island to educate her children and to send them out into that larger world:

> To think, though, that [Edmond] was finishing his medical studies at Laval University. . . . Could they even have suspected, in the days when they heard about Frontenac at the Water Hen, that Edmond would one day with his own eyes see the citadel of French resistance! And thus Luzina glimpsed, at times, her own strange greatness through this ultimate distance separating her from her children.[18]

We have here the settling of the West as the unsettling of it, and both as acts—in Manitoba and Quebec—of French resistance to Anglo domination.

Or set in the far North, Roy's *Windflower* (1970) reverses both Hollywood romance and the Western. After she has just seen a Clark Gable movie and "had found Gable himself extremely ugly but, to make up for this, incomparably funny when he kissed the heroine," an adolescent Inuk girl meets and makes love to a young American soldier stationed in the Arctic.[19] Their brief and mosquito-ridden encounter is hardly the stuff of Hollywood romance, nor is its aftermath, the Native girl left pregnant to raise her blond and blue-eyed son alone as best she can, as part-Inuk and part-white. Furthermore, the white ways she tries to make part of his experience are not validated in the novel. The playpen she early provides is, from the perspective of her people, an intolerable prison, and, on a larger level, she later realizes she enslaved herself in her efforts to provide him with the white accouterments she thought he should have and, furthermore, only lost him in the process when he, again inverting the Western, lights out *from* the territories and opts for "civilization."

This novel also self-consciously "repeats itself" (139) at its end. Elsa Kumachuk suspects her son has become an American soldier sent to Vietnam. She studies the faces of the pictured Vietnamese in "newspapers that reached Fort Chimo" and "found them much like the faces of the people here" (139). She even imagines him doing as his father had done. "The dense reeds must provide good hiding-places and the insatiable insects would swarm there also." Thus "a grandson might have been born to her at the ends of the earth that she had not the slightest chance of ever seeing." In short, "life was proving to be more preposterous and surprising than the movies had ever shown in the old days" (139). But the relationship is not that simple either and is more than a long lesson in colonial subjecthood as a corrective to the colonizer's myths of achieved selfhood:

> So she would not for anything have missed the tragic news of the world that was the source of her pleasant make-believe. She was as faithful to the news broadcasts as she was to the sunset at the edge of the immense horizon or to the river, waiting patiently for bulletins to begin, sitting at the back of the hut, her hands folded and her face open and expectant, rather as if she were at the movies or in church. (139–40)

Green Berets and Riders of the Purple Sage, faith and fantasy, transitory human action and abiding landscape are all somehow here mixed and merged.

The fictional inversions just noted, the questioning of the Western by the Western, is a well-established Canadian literary tradition with its own national history. Abstracting from the three major studies of the Canadian Western (Edward McCourt's *The Canadian West in Fiction,* Laurence Ricou's *Vertical Man/Horizontal World,* and, most important, Harrison's *Unnamed Country*), we can note how, in this fiction, one mythos has succeeded another. As Harrison especially emphasizes, early Canadian writers developed their own myth of the West, a myth of a garden to be cultivated in the name of empire. Such authors as Ralph Connor or Nellie McClung evolved that mythic Canadian West from a strong sense of self and an even stronger identification with the empire, whose comforting presence they felt—or strove to envision. But their literary West was achieved more through expectation than observation, and the garden myth foundered on the inescapable fact that even the most sustained effort of creative imagination could not put much bloom on a forty-degree-below-zero prairie blizzard (a lesson that became even more obvious with the advent of the "dirty thirties"). So, starting in the 1920s, Canadian writers replaced this early fiction of the Canadian West with grimly realistic novels—most notably Frederick Philip Grove's *Settlers of the Marsh* (1925), Martha Ostenso's *Wild Geese* (1925), and Robert J. C. Stead's *Grain* (1926)—that documented the limitations of prairie life instead of extolling its promise.

The stark realism of the late 1920s and early 1930s, with its dark portrayals of drought and depression, found fullest expression in the prairie patriarch striving to impress his will on all around him in a futile effort to achieve the garden of his imagination. His failures to dominate either his family or the land and his consequent dispossession in the text, despite his self-proclaimed central role, anticipated his virtual exclusion from subsequent texts. Saddled with this fictional father, his author sons and daughters soon had an easy oedipal revenge and simply wrote him out of existence. Stand-ins were occasionally provided—for example, the kindly hired hand in W. O. Mitchell's *Jake and the Kid* (1961). But even better, the displacement of the father could itself become a ground of origin and being, leaving the protagonist as well as the author and the reader all true orphan heirs to their previous prairie placelessness. Realistic portrayals that tended to tragedy thereby gave way to mythic visions tinged with comedy, but the myth now was a myth of lost origins and a consequent reconstruction of imagined history and/or genealogy whereby past, present, place, and protagonist might all be conjoined.

The third myth is thus in opposition to the first as well as to the second. The garden myth was, as noted, a simple, straightforward hope for the future, a vision of what the garden might be when it had become the garden it should be. Contemporary mythic fiction is more complex and subtly paradoxical. It gives us mythic portrayals of the need for myth, and the myth most needed is a mythic picture of the past—"contrive[d] authentic origins" in Kroetsch's phrase.[20] Furthermore, the search for the missing myth is regularly mocked and parodied in the very works that also portray that same search as essential. And there is still another structuring polarity to this new mythic fiction. In "Unhiding the Hidden," Kroetsch observes that he once "considered it the task of the Canadian writer to give names to his experience, to be the namer," but "now suspect[s] that, on the contrary, it is his task to un-name."[21] More and more, this author, and others too, have insisted on unnaming, on the need to free experience from the constraining term or label. Words must take us beyond the import of those words, just as myth must provide us with an imaginative pattern that gives to the facts of experience a depth and dimension that those facts do not necessarily possess in themselves.

The garden myth as a myth was far too limiting and served mostly to reduce Western Canada to England's and Toronto's back forty—the wheat fields out there that helped to support the rest of us back here. At least as constraining, and as colonial, was the far more pervasive North American myth of the frontier West that well might have consigned Western Canada to Ponderosa North—an extension of Hollywood instead of empire. But in this case too, the facts of the land helped to refute the myth whereby the land might have been falsely imaged out of its own authentic existence.

The best contemporary Canadian Western writers undo the preexisting models that I have just discussed in order to achieve their different mythic models that are mostly an amorphous and thus unlimiting search for a model. For example, Sheila Watson's *The Double Hook* (1959) begins with the father missing and then disposes of the mother too. That mother's matricidal son frees himself into life but his sister into death (everything is doubled in this novel), while Coyote, conjoining attributes of the Christian God and the Indian trickster, presides over the action. Tricky action: "when he meets on page one Coyote and his twelve apostles, the reader should recognize that he has met the novelist as jester."[22] Similarly, Jack Hodgins's *The Invention of the World* (1977) "is about the process of uninventing narrative worlds," and, as Robert Lecker assesses in some detail, the novel "distorts, corrupts, and truncates precisely the structures and patterns [particularly those of myth and history] around which [it is] built."[23] And in much the same vein Robert Kroetsch in all of his novels—from *But We Are Exiles* (1965) to *The Puppeteer* (1992)—plays with the constructs out of which they are formulated to highlight their fictionality, the fact that they are the invention of themselves and their world.

Kroetsch's *Badlands* (1975), for example, begins with Anna Dawe retracing, some fifty years later, her father's 1916 expedition after dinosaur bones down the Red Deer River and through the Alberta Badlands. She would recover the father missing in her life by uncovering his story, and in that story, too, there is a significant absence. Its potential hero early went AWOL. "In the western yarn those men were trying to tell each other," Anna observes, "he was the only one with the ability to become a hero, the wisdom not to. Home was a word he understood, and heroes cannot afford that understanding."[24] "He" is Claude McBride, and even his name has the right heroic ring—like Kit Carson or John Wayne, as direct and forceful as the thunk of an axe. But how can this auspiciously named character desert the task at hand and how can the novel get along without him?

Very well, it seems, for Kroetsch's Western is working with a new mythology, one that dispenses with the older central figure and his potential for heroic selfhood. McBride is replaced, on the first expedition, by Anna Yellowbird, a fifteen-year-old Indian girl, a child-widow whose husband has gone off to be killed in World War I. Because she has her own mythologies, because a shaman has told her that a hunchback will lead her to the spirit of her husband, she joins the bone-hunting venture and becomes its guide. She becomes, too, the lover of its leader as well as of most of his crew. And William Dawe's dinosaur-hunting expedition is itself replaced by a subsequent expedition—his daughter searching first for her missing father and the places where he may have gone wrong but also for herself, her country, her fiction, her myth, none of which is to be found in the patriarchal pieties of the conventional Western.

Kroetsch's redefinition of traditional mythic values and structures controverts the six-gun mystique with its attendant assumption of Manifest Destiny on two different levels. First, manifest to whom? The vacillating narrative stance of *Badlands* undermines the authority of all the voices whereby the text is rendered. Second, whose destiny? By confuting the standard mythic teleologies, particularly the final ascendancy of the—by definition, male—hero, the novel raises ontological questions about the validity of any pursuit of the signs and symbols of transcendence, whether the bodies of recently vanquished enemies or the bones of long-dead dinosaurs. Destiny is hardly manifest. On the contrary, it is a concept as dead end (and particularly so in a postmodernist context) as William Dawe's tedious field notes or the skeleton he found at the cost of his surrogate son.

Such Canadian Westerns as Kroetsch's *Badlands* simply do not take their place as literary markers of and monuments to what Walter Prescott Webb could grandiloquently designate *The Great Frontier*. Although recent revisionist Western histories, particularly Patricia Nelson Limerick's *The Legacy of Conquest* and Richard White's *"It's Your Misfortune and None of My Own": A New History of the American West*, have questioned the long tenure of Frederick Jackson Turner's "frontier thesis" (first enunciated in his 1893 essay, "The Significance of the Frontier in American History") as a historical paradigm, it certainly continues as a literary one. Indeed, Webb's own *The Great Frontier* aptly exemplifies how much the frontier thesis is itself a literary deployment of myth rather than a synthesis of historical data.

To illustrate the envisioned working of that frontier, Webb, in his chapter "The Emergence of the Individual" and in a section titled "Jim Brown Knows the Way," asks us to imagine five men setting out on a forest journey into hostile Indian country. Four of these adventurers—a general, a banker, a professor, and a preacher—"have risen to high position in their respective occupations"; they "represent civilization at its best"; but the fifth, a frontier roustabout Webb names Jim Brown, has "not so distinguished himself."[25] Nevertheless, Jim Brown turns out to be the natural leader of the expedition. He can read the lay of the land, find game, tan leather to make them all new clothes when the civilized costumes of the four "tenderfoot" travelers soon wear out; he can also bring down the Indian leader when the white men are, predictably, attacked.

This whole narrative is, for that matter, so predictable that it does not at all serve, as Webb intends, to demonstrate "how natural political democracy . . . in the truest sense of the word" comes into being on the frontier through the agency of men, like Jim Brown, who had already freed themselves from "civilization's stamp of human inequalities" (45, 39). Civilization's inequalities are simply replaced by "Nature's," and Brown is portrayed as superior to the general who prepares for a wilderness excursion by donning his uniform and medals or the banker who stuffs his moneybelt. Making much the same point, the professor "who has studied so hard that he has ruined his digestion" (37) soon recovers it with campfire cooking. All four of these professional successes, we are shown, come to be substantially better men by virtue of their venture in the wilderness, so much so that one wonders how they could have been so incompetent in the first place. We also notice that none of them had any reason for their excursion other than the fact that Webb's parable requires it, just as all of them (Brown included) are, as characters, mere clichés.

The way in which this wilderness fantasy ostensibly functions as a civic lesson illustrates how deeply the myth of "the great frontier" and the supposed effects of that frontier are ingrained in American thought and literature. Moreover, this myth, even in Webb's idealized redaction, has its distinctly pernicious elements. The largest change recorded in the narrative is that of the Reverend Henderson Fowler, who learns first to hunt and then to hunt Indians; who feels, with his first human kill, a "sense of exaltation . . . he had never known before" and who realizes that (the last words of the story) "in the new theology of the forest, the Sixth Commandment does not apply to Indians" (44). How convenient that the forest allows a conjoining of religion and genocide in the name of nature.

Webb's frontier fantasy sets forth a metaphysics of Indian killing as much as a politics of natural democracy—as if the fostering of white equality more than compensates for the suppression of Native rights and the extermination of Native peoples. Standing mostly outside of that politics and metaphysics (and America's long history of Indian wars), a number of Canadian authors have critically examined this American construct. Admittedly, Canadian writers can hardly take much pride in their country's historic treatment of Native tribes, even though most of the treaties were kept. Most of the land was still taken away, and if the federal government continues to pay the promised treaty money, it also must be acknowledged that the always token sums went rather further in the 1890s than they do in the 1990s. Nevertheless, there were very few military encounters between whites and Natives. As in Kroetsch's *Badlands,* the natural hero can be consigned to the more natural business of attending to his family and farm instead of playing deadly games of cowboys and Indians in the wild.

Native characters also typically have a different symbolic function in the Canadian Western than they do in the American. As Margery Fee astutely observes, a marginal culture such as Canada cannot afford to dispense with the marginal literary figure of the Native because "we are afraid if we don't believe in Indians, we will have to become Americans."[26] Thus, and as Fee also points out, Native protagonists such as Howard O'Hagan's Tay John and Rudy Wiebe's Big Bear do not so much die but more "metamorphose into the land" to be, somehow, still there at the end of the novel and beyond, "available when needed."[27] This white agenda does, admittedly, hold Natives in reserve but it does not hold them in contempt or in abeyance. Another common Canadian ploy is to view the Indian more as an imagined alternative than an implacable enemy. In Mitchell's *Vanishing Point* (1973), for example, the protagonist, a teacher at an Indian school, sets out to civilize his prize pupil, Virginia Rider, but she ends up "Indianizing" him. Or in Kroetsch's *Gone Indian* (1973), Jeremy Sadness, an American graduate student, goes to Canada to discover (comically, of course) his real life as a fake Indian.

The operative word here is fake. Critics such as Terry Goldie and Jane Tompkins have emphasized that any concept of "Indian" is always, in white discourse, a construct that serves white interests. Furthermore, as Tompkins points out, "an Indian account of what transpired when the European settlers arrived here [wherever "here" is] would look nothing like our own," and "their (potential, unwritten) history of the conflict could bear only a marginal resemblance to Eurocentric views."[28] Yet it is precisely that "potential" and hitherto largely "unwritten" Indian history of Western Canada that Rudy Wiebe assays in his major novel *The Temptations of Big Bear* (1973). Wiebe is well aware of the contradictions at the heart of his enterprise. Indeed, what we well might term the two temptations of Rudy Wiebe, temptations out of which his best fiction comes, are, first, a desire to learn Cree and, second, a desire not to. The temptation to learn Cree stands in, of course, for another and admittedly impossible authorial desire, the dream of entering fully not just into the fictional life of created characters, but into a whole different culture. One might then shed the burden of being white and join in the Indians' radically different mode of being. The countering temptation is to remain fixed in one's own experience and language, to admit the romanticism at the heart of any desire to escape. It is a recognition of the limits of the self, of the world, but a recognition partly transcended by the other desire that it contradicts. In short, the two temptations are inextricably linked, and the resonance between the two sounds persistently in the fictions of this complex and comprehensive artist.

Sustained by that first resonant relationship is another, related one, the interconnections, for Wiebe, between history and story. History is what we already have, our accepted version of what we did and of who, consequently, we are. It is a collective language of a collective self reified by repetition, by the particular stories we choose to retell to one another—stories, for the most part, already chosen for us. Thus the potential of story, for Wiebe, is always larger than the particulars of history, since history selects some possible stories and suppresses others. Wiebe himself, in an interview with Shirley Neuman, sums up this relationship in terms that also implicitly premise his fictional agenda: "I doubt the *official* given history. . . . You know there is another side to the story and maybe that's the more interesting side. Maybe even truer."[29]

Wiebe seeks to recover something of that "more interesting" and "maybe even truer" other side. To do so, he casts history into a kind of alembic to see if a certain applied creative force might not yield up the very story that it has programmatically concealed—to make it, in a sense, talk Cree. Thus, in *The Temptations of Big Bear* and, similarly, in *The Scorched-Wood People* (1977), Wiebe casts the expected antagonist (Big Bear in the former, Louis Riel in the latter) as the protagonist. The result is a deconstruction of the standard Western novel. An expected epic of victory (How the West Was Won) gives way to an epic of loss—what the Indians lost, what the Métis lost, and what the prevailing whites lost, too, through those two other losses. Both novels thereby contradict established teleologies of Western fiction and Western history. Both are also odd historical fictions in that they effectively controvert the very history out of which they are meticulously made. And if, as W. J. Keith observes, "it is impossible to forget completely [in reading *The Temptations of Big Bear*] that Wiebe is a white striving to reproduce the Indian viewpoint," it is also impossible not to notice that the object of that struggle is to portray Big Bear, in Wiebe's own words, as "an incredibly great man."[30]

Wiebe's major short story, "Where Is the Voice Coming From?", effectively exemplifies his—and the Canadian Western's—penchant for finding the different fiction hidden beneath the official/conventional/accepted one. Based, like the two great novels, on late nineteenth-century Western Canadian history, the tale recounts how Almighty Voice, a young Cree Indian arrested and imprisoned in 1895 for butchering a stray government cow, escaped from jail, killed the Mountie who came after him to rearrest him, and then eluded police pursuit for some eighteen months, killing two more Mounties during that time before he, with two companions, was surrounded by a combined force of approximately one hundred police, soldiers, and volunteers. Fired on by rifles and two cannons, the Indians still made a three-day stand, at the end of which Almighty Voice was the last to die. Wiebe, in an interview, has observed that with such material there is very little "to invent or change." As he notes, "how could you improve on a marvelous name like Almighty Voice?"[31] And, by extension, how could you improve on the known details of his dying or do more than repeat them, more than simply reiterate another version of the official given history.

"The problem is to make the story."[32] With this first sentence in "Where Is the Voice Coming From?" Wiebe brilliantly solves the very problem he here articulates by making it integral to the text. The narrative begins not with Almighty Voice speaking in his own voice or through some more or less omniscient narrator already possessed of the meaning of the tale, but with a would-be narrator vainly struggling to transmute history (the available facts) into story (a meaningful accounting of those facts). This blocked storyteller has tracked down the official records, visited the scenes of the action, seen all the surviving material, but cannot assimilate the assembled evidence into some comprehensive whole. The work is thus both metafictional and antimetafictional—a story about story that is also about the story that isn't there. Even the surviving photograph of Almighty Voice does not resolve this impasse, for it does not fit the story already told that the narrator is struggling both to tell again and to untell. The "Wanted" police poster had noted the "feminine appearance" of the fugitive's visage whereas the face in the photograph is hyperpotently male: "a steady look into those eyes cannot be endured. It is a face like an axe" (84).

Yet even as the narrator cannot apprehend the subject of the photograph and turns away from the best evidence at hand as to who Almighty Voice might have been, he finds himself suddenly transported into that subject's world to "witness" all the details of the other's dying right down to his last wordless war cry. The story concludes with that cry, "a voice so high and clear, so unbelievably high and strong in its unending wordless cry . . . no less incredible in its beauty than in its incomprehensible happiness" (86). More accurately, it concludes with the narrator's recognition of why the cry was wordless: "I say 'wordless cry' because that is the way it sounds to me. I could be more accurate if I had a reliable interpreter who would make a reliable interpretation. For I do not, of course, understand the Cree myself" (86–87).

The narrator ends up in uncertainty and silence again; the text peters out; the reader is not told of Almighty Voice's dying words. Those failures, however, are the story's success. Only Almighty Voice's uncomprehended death cry allows him a voice, a victory, and vindicates his name (which is not Almighty Voice, with all its Christian connotations, but Gitchie-Manitou-Wayo, a name that can be roughly translated, according to my Cree brother-in-law, as Sound of the Great Spirit). Were those last words rendered into some Indian equivalent of "Give me liberty or give me death," they would become rhetoric in the pejorative sense, public speech like the "Wanted" proclamation and, as such, fixed in time. At the end, then, we (narrator and reader) can return to the present-tense title question to see what voice was referred to and from where it comes. Gitchie-Manitou-Wayo's cry exists after and outside the text precisely because it is not rendered in it. That continuing cry "is" and is the story, and Wiebe's art, here as in his major novels, is to make such silence speak.

The dialectic, in Canadian fiction, between white and Indian is different from the more pervasive American Western dialectic. So, too, as already suggested, is the dialectic between male and female. Contemporary Canadian Westerns often exhibit an obvious depriviling of traditional masculine narrative authority along with a concomitant claiming of female narrative authority, or at least a partial recognition of female claims. In *The Temptation of Big Bear,* for example, Kitty McLean, of all the white characters, most understands Big Bear, most recognizes his greatness, and most tells his story. Or in a different vein, Hodgins's *The Invention of the World* contrasts the brutal and self-serving rule of the "Father" (one of Donal Keneally's preferred titles as the leader of an Irish village he transports to Vancouver Island) to the more benign rule of the mother when Maggie Kyle comes into possession of what was Keneally's Revelations Colony of Truth and thereby also inherits and cares for some of the maimed survivors of his self-serving faked and autocratic "Truth." Or by freely adapting "stories from the native people of Vancouver Island," Anne Cameron, in *Daughters of Copper Woman* (1981), portrays Native culture as patriarchalized by the diseases, literal and figurative, that followed white contact but also recounts surviving matriarchal myths, such as how Copper Woman created a "little mannikin," the first man, from her own snot and bits and pieces of various animals.[33] Which is why men remain "imperfect creatures" in comparison to women as "entire person[s]," and why "bringing the [scattered] pieces of truth together" to make themselves and the world whole is more women's task than men's.[34] However, Cameron here gives us (a point I will make in more detail later) more the female inversion of the male Western than a Native inversion of a white one.

A more complicated case of using a Native woman to tell a white feminist story is found in Katherine Govier's *Between Men* (1987). The novel also interweaves an episode from nineteenth-century Alberta history with a frame story that at first seems worlds away. An account of how a young woman university instructor learned self-assertiveness from the new man in her life while divorcing her impossibly spoiled boyish (rich-boy) husband and thereby won back the special course she wanted to teach but that had been canceled by her male department chairman . . . , this does, indeed, sound like it was intended for some woman's glossy such as *Cosmopolitan*. Yet the title of the lost and regained course is "Reinventing the West." As that title suggests, Govier is concerned with the same general issues as I am: the interconnections of different stories, the role of paradigms of race and gender within those stories, the rights whereby stories are disseminated or suppressed. All of this comes out in the history so to speak. The protagonist's preparation for her prospective course is mostly a sustained investigation of a brutal and hushed-up murder of a young Indian woman in Calgary in the late nineteenth-century. Sent from the Indian school to work as a servant for one of the better families in order to learn white ways, Rosalie New Grass is seduced by the husband and then turned, pregnant, out of the house. Seeking an abortionist after the husband has supplied her with the necessary cash, she is sent, as a joke, to a local whorehouse. Taking as the doctor a customer who takes her as a prostitute, she does not cry out when he subjects her to what the historian finally uncovers as the cause of her death: "It became a contest among certain men of ill habits to force their

forearm up inside an Indian woman, just to see how far it would go."[35] After
being brutalized in this fashion, Rosalie is then left to bleed to death.

There are complex resonances between the nineteenth-century narrative
and the twentieth-century one, resonances that are also foregrounded by
the title. "I'm between men" (65), one of the minor contemporary characters early notes, and in that condition she founds "SWARM . . . Single Women
After Rich Men" (66). The members have meetings and wear badges: "Hi. I'm
Hilda and I'm SWARMing" (70). In contrast, later, in the nineteenth-century
narrative, another secondary character, the wife of the man who impreg-
nated Rosalie, comes close to deducing some of the circumstances of the
death but is told to mind her own business (as if this matter wasn't her business): "It's not to do with you," her husband claims, "It's something between
men" (176). Rosalie, too, was between men—between the husband and the
patron of the whore house, the patron and the other men at the same establishment who did not try to save her. In all of these cases, "between men"
is not a viable option. Some other ground must be found, occupied. In this
sense, *Between Men* anticipates relationships "between women" and, as I will
argue later, some of the most intriguing reinventions of the Canadian West.

The interplay of story and history, already noted in Wiebe and Govier, is
a crucial feature in a number of major Western Canadian novels. "This is
a new country," Kroetsch observes in a passage previously partly quoted:
"Here on the plains we confront the hopeless and necessary hope of origi-
nality: constantly we experience the need to begin. And we do—by imitating beginnings, we contrive authentic origins. From the denied Indians.
From the false fronts of the little towns. From the diaries and reminis-
cences and the travel accounts. From our displaced ancestors."[36] On the
West Coast too. George Bowering, in *Burning Water* (1980), refracts George
Vancouver's charting of that coast through the ongoing commentary of two
thoroughly postmodern Nootka Indians and through George the author's
self-conscious telling of George the protagonist's tale. Daphne Marlatt, in
Ana Historic (1988), makes history and fiction out of the nonrecord left by a
woman schoolteacher in early Vancouver and the fact that "the real history
of women," as one of her contemporary characters insists, is still "unwritten
because it runs through our bodies."[37] Marlatt writes this unwritten history in a lexicon of lesbian desire, all of which the last words of the novel
especially illustrate:

we give place, giving words, giving birth, to each other—she and me.
you. hot skin writing skin. fluid edge, wick, wick. she draws me out.

you she breathes. is where we meet. breeze from the window reaching you now. trees out there. streets you might walk down, will, soon. it isn't dark but the luxury of being has woken you, the reach of your desire, reading us into the page ahead. (153)

Even this conclusion, with its deferred ending and promised new beginning, is not that idiosyncratic in the context of the Canadian Western.

The seduction of history and history as seduction is differently fore-grounded in Robert Harlow's *Scann* (1972). Amory Scann, the protagonist, stages a three-day Easter-weekend writing retreat to put together a history of Linden, British Columbia, for the town's fiftieth anniversary and the Linden *Chronicle* he edits. However, he can come up with this history only when it also serves as a ploy whereby he might talk the chambermaid of the Linden House into bed. Nothing, however, comes up but the history. With all that talk, he has not the time and she loses the inclination. The end of this enterprise finally comes when one of the main subjects of the con-structed history, still alive and a resident in the same hotel even, disputes Scann's version by burning it, leaving, after the fire is doused at the sink, "wet ash, scorched paper."[38] The text itself survives parodic deaths by fire and water to remain, at the end, the densely packed novel we have just read as well as a burnt and sodden mess.

The "heroic" protagonists of the history recounted—there are two who almost cancel each other out—are just as incongruous. Scann tells of the struggle between an old trapper Henry Linden, the first settler after whom the town of Linden was named, and a young upstart called only Thrain who accompanies Linden into the bush to engage in covert combat for sym-bolic mastery—mastery of both wilderness and town. But the consequent Oedipal conflict devolves more toward farce than to heroism or tragedy. Far from dominating the wilderness, both men bumble from disaster to worse disaster. At one desperate point, for example, Thrain, "with quick firm slices" (152), pares a frozen and gangrenous Linden down almost to his bare core—the deconstruction of the hero with a vengeance. Later, with the one hand he has left, Linden seizes the knife and plants himself on Thrain's back to force the younger man to carry him back to the town. The endeavor almost kills Thrain even as it images his predicament: "an unnatu-ral double-humped criminal, or a man with his buggering past locked onto his backside" (278)—the deconstruction of history with a vengeance. And Scann, too, has his own personal history that is not left behind when he sequesters himself in the hotel room and that regularly colors the history he constructs in his narrative. If, as Ross Chambers has argued in *Story and*

Situation: Narrative Seduction and the Power of Fiction, "the maintenance of
narrative authority implies an act of seduction," then the character most
seduced in this highly idiosyncratic novel is Scann himself, and from that
tale-engendering fall into narrative (if not into bed) comes a novel not to be
denied even by fire or flood.[39]

The interplay between story and silence—the novel written under threat
of erasure—has a well established Western Canadian pedigree. In Sinclair
Ross's *As For Me and My House* (1941), for example, the blocked life of the
Reverend and Mrs. Bentley in the narrow and restrictive prairie town significantly named Horizon (a here circumscribed by an ever elsewhere) must
be indirectly described in Mrs. Bentley's diary entries because her husband,
a failed artist now a failed minister, can neither recount the family predicament nor administer aid or comfort to it. "Canadian literature," Kroetsch
asserts, "is the autobiography of a culture that insists it will not tell its
story," and its "governing principle" is that Canadian writing "locate itself
as . . . the exciting periphery of a defined and stuffy and self-satisfied center
that is not always locatable," all of which sounds suspiciously like a gloss
on Ross's novel which, indeed, Kroetsch elsewhere deems Western Canada's
"paradigmatic text" because it is a "missing text," a still "unwritten novel,"
surrounding ("Horizon" again) the center of Mrs. Bentley's diary entries
which are another version of the novel that is not there.[40]

The Canadian "dream of origins" can also be a dream of ethnic origins partly
revived as other possible stories in the interplay of story that the Canadian
Western invites. As the narrative voice of Roy's *Where Nests the Water Hen*
at one point observes:

> Here is what happened in the lake country when a son or daughter
> of Ukrainian immigrants scarcely bore any resemblance to them. This
> son or daughter one fine day took notice—in an aesthetic way—of
> the poetry, the warmth, the picturesqueness of the ancient folklore.
> The young people staged an operetta in the Ukrainian language; they
> formed a choral society; they learned from the old people the dances
> of former days now largely forgotten; they put on a great festival, and
> their poor aged parents heard talk to their hearts' content about the
> Ukraine, which they had thought it their duty to forget for progress's
> sake. (120)

Here, too, is a particularly unproblematic example of what Thomas J. Ferraro has recently termed "the return of the culturally repressed."[41] Difference—the Ukrainian-Canadian children from their immigrant parents,

the Ukrainian Canadians from the French Canadians, both from the Anglo Canadians, all three from the Native Canadians also resident in the same wilderness area—is both inscribed and erased. Thus the Capuchin priest at this same Ukrainian festival can find "everything" he is fed "very good" and not at all know "what he had eaten" (117–18).

An excursion into the West to encounter Others already there is not always so innocent, as Arnold Harrichand Itwaru points out in *The Invention of Canada: Literary Text and the Immigrant Imaginary*. More specifically, Itwaru emphasizes that Topaz Edgeworth, the immigrant traveler who comes to Canada and then to Western Canada, is far from *The Innocent Traveller* (1949) of Ethel Wilson's title. Topaz's failures are particularly obvious in her dealings with racial Others, as when she encounters the black porter on the train: "'Ah! Negroes!' exclaimed Aunt Topaz with delight, hastening ahead. 'How do you do! I'm sure I'm very glad to see you! Have you a wife, yes? And family? This is a charming surprise!'"[42] Throughout the novel, Itwaru notes, Wilson portrays "all of the men who are not white" as "emasculated figures, types presented as inferior to the dominant white presence amongst whom a sense of person, as opposed to types, prevails."[43] As Toni Morrison has cogently argued: "Encoded or explicit, indirect or overt, the linguistic responses to an Africanist presence complicates texts, sometimes contradicting them entirely."[44] Topaz's title innocence cannot survive her meeting with a black man and collapses into ignorance and arrogance masked as humanism, a different matter entirely.

Like the black man, the Native, and the Oriental, Nature too is read rather self-servingly in Wilson's novels. "[Her] protagonists who are all Anglo-Saxon in their ethnicity, find no cultural or social hindrances in the new land. For them it is there to furnish their well-being in the ways they see fit. All else is secondary. And everything is understood within the acceptance of the infinite mystery and wisdom of Nature."[45] But Wilson, it should be noted, was a white immigrant from South Africa. A rather different version of the encounter with the new land is provided by other ethnic writers who fall outside the circle of Empire and Eurocentrism that embraced immigrants such as Wilson. Particularly germane in this respect is the different perspective of Joy Kogawa's *Obasan* (1981), a Western novel as an account of life in the new land written from the perspective of those who were not welcome. Considering the anti-Asian laws that long were applied in British Columbia as well as the additional measures whereby Japanese-Canadians were dispossessed and sent into "exile" at the outbreak of war with Japan and then exiled again at its end, no immigrant group was more unwelcome than the Japanese.[46]

At the beginning of *Obasan*, Naomi Nakane and her uncle make their annual visit to the coulee that marks on the "virgin land" prairie the suffering and loss that the protagonist and her family have endured in Canada. Their loss is analogous to that of others. The coulee is near what was once an Indian buffalo jump. Now only "the bones are still there, some sticking out of the side of a fresh landslide." Or "Uncle could be Chief Sitting Bull squatting here. He has the same prairie-baked skin, the deep brown furrows like dry river beds creasing his cheeks."[47] The coulee engraves loss on the prairie and that engraving is reinscribed in Uncle's face, making him a version of Sitting Bull, who also squatted in Canada but was not allowed a real home there. In much the same vein, Naomi's class includes "two Native girls, sisters, twelve and thirteen years old, both adopted" (5). Deprived of their real family and their own way of life, these two could be the young Naomi Nakane as much as Uncle could be Sitting Bull.

The interconnection of the treatment of the Japanese in Canada and the treatment of Indians is especially emphasized by a story that a local character, Rough Lock Bill, tells to the young Naomi and one of her friends soon after they have been "relocated" from Vancouver to the interior of British Columbia—to, in their case, the ghost town of Slocan. It is a tale of a "long time ago" and of how, during a time of tribulations, an Indian brave set out to find "a good place with lots of good food—deer, fish, berries" (145–46). Then he leads his people to that refuge, even though "some [are] so weak they have to be carried. Took all of them together—how long? Months? A year? 'If you go slow,' he says, 'you can go. Slow can go. Slow can go.' Like a train chugging across the mountains" (146). Rough Lock Bill concludes: "We call it Slocan now. Real name is Slow-can-go. When my Granddad came, there was a whole tribe here. . . . But last I saw—one old guy up past the mine—be dead now probably" (146).

The story of how the place came to have its name is obviously intended to console those more recently and more reluctantly consigned to that place. Rough Lock Bill also told his story to dispute the construct of race: "'Never met a kid didn't like stories. Red skin, yellow skin, white skin, any skin.' He puts his brown leathery arm beside Kenji's pale one. 'Don't make sense, do it, all this fuss about skin?'" (145). In the context of this passage—the Japanese boy as paleskin, the brown white man—it doesn't, and, on one level, the story's merging of Native, Japanese, and white values (the conjunction of group cooperation with the self-determination of a little engine that could) seems to make the same point. Yet the narrative that tells of how the original inhabitants came to the great good place concludes with none of them in residence, and in Naomi's narrative as well the Japanese will be removed from the mountain site as completely as were the Natives (as Naomi finds when she comes back to Slocan in 1962): "The first ghosts were still there, the miners, people of the woods, their white bones deep beneath the pine-needle floor, their flesh turned to earth, turned to air. Their buildings—hotels, abandoned mines, log cabins, still stood marking their stay. But what of the second wave? What remains of our time there?" (117). Even the ghosts of Slocan are now all white. The story of first coming into possession of the good place is also the story of losing it; it is told to the victims of another prior displacement who will be displaced again, and these displacements reinscribe the "fuss about skin"—"red skin, yellow skin, white skin" that the story itself supposedly countered.

The missing Natives in the text also suggest other missing figures—Naomi's mother following the beginning of the war, her father with the end of the war, and neither absence, each attributable to the fuss about skin, is rescinded even when that fuss begins to be officially lamented:

> "It was a terrible business what we did to our Japanese," Mr. Barker says.
> Ah, here we go again. "Our Indians." "Our Japanese." "A terrible business." It's like being offered a pair of crutches while I'm striding down the street. (225)

What Naomi must learn is to dispute others' rights to that "our." She has to claim her family history, her loss and suffering as, finally, hers.

By the end of the novel she finally knows the significance of the opening August 7th annual visit. The atomic bombing of Nagasaki left the mother disfigured, unwilling and unable to return to Canada; its aftermath caused her premature death; she knows, too, that the details of the visit, particularly the stream flowing through the coulee and the wild roses growing in it, constituted appropriate grounds for a Japanese *Obon* ceremony to honor the dead and briefly be reunited with them. So "the silence that cannot speak" lamented in the opening epigraph of the novel has been countered all along by the presence of the mother in the flowers and the stream. Visiting the same site again at the end of the novel and after the death of her uncle, Naomi can mourn him too. " 'Umi no yo': he always said. 'It's like the sea' " (247).

As her last words echo his first ones, the novel comes full circle on its prairie setting. Past and present, life and death, tragedy and survival all seem to flow into one another. It is somehow appropriate that Uncle is buried beneath the sea of grass that recalls both the ocean off British Columbia where he fished in his prize boat and the other side of the same ocean where his ancestors also sailed.[48] It is also somehow appropriate that he is joined in death by the bones of the buffalo the Indians hunted, the bones of the Indians who hunted them. The "virgin land" (virgin still despite those who have commerced on it or entered into it) that was previously, with the slash of the coulee, the sign of Naomi's ongoing suffering and loss now symbolizes the novel's resolution: "I come to the bank. Above the trees the moon is a pure white stone. The reflection is rippling in the river—water and stone dancing. It is a quiet ballet, soundless as breath" (247). A Western novel about the new life in the new land is here crossed with a Japanese haiku poem on the transitory nature of all experience. The new life, entered into on this Alberta landscape, is to take the measure of the loss of the old one.

The use of the Native as a figure for loss and the merging of the ethnic novel and the Western novel is even more complex and idiosyncratic in Sky Lee's *Disappearing Moon Cafe* (1990), which, in Chinese boxes fashion, contains a lesbian coming-out account within a five-generation family saga within a story of immigrants establishing themselves in the new world within a Western. This novel, like *Obasan*, also portrays the working of racism and the consequences of that racism for the Asians (in this case Chinese) at which it was most directed, and it is concerned, too, with issues of cultural transmission and regeneration. But whereas a crisis of reproduction is visibly marked in *Obasan* by the death of Naomi's mother, by the childless state of both her aunts, and by Naomi's decades-long reluctance to hazard even dating, much less marriage and/or motherhood, childbirth figures prominently in the plot of *Disappearing Moon Cafe*. A good deal of the material in the novel is the family history related to Kae Ying Woo, the protagonist, by her mother following the birth of Kae's own first child. Matters of family, marriage, and generation are, however, hardly clear in that family history, which begins with the founding ancestor's affair with a half-Native girl whom he abandons for a proper bride from China and then traces the tangled interconnections between the products of both unions. The Wong family tree provided partly clarifies these matters even as it also indicates how complicated they are, with a clear case of incest (that is not admitted in the acknowledged family history) on one side and on the other a relationship that isn't incestuous and yet is seen as such in the novel.

Framed by incest that is and isn't, with miscegenation at the beginning (in the Chinese mode, not the white—one of the ironies of the text is the deployment of Chinese paradigms of race and gender as parallels to white ones) and with a lesbian relationship at the end, the textual/sexual ground occupied by the novel is complicated indeed, and I will not attempt to trace it here. Rather, I will briefly compare the opening episode, Wong Gwei Chang's venture into the interior of British Columbia and the realm of the Native, with the final one, his great-granddaughter's presumably permanent return to the East, in her case to Hong Kong. That his great-granddaughter is his descendant through his unacknowledged illegitimate "Indian" son and not, as all (except the two involved in the extramarital affair) assume, through the son born to Wong Gwei Chang and his proper Chinese wife, adds to the interplay, of stories of ancestors and descendants, of immigrants and Indians.

Appropriately enough, that interplay begins when Wong Gwei Chang is sent as a young man by the Chinese Benevolent Association of Vancouver "to search out the bones of those who have died on the iron road, so that they can be sent back home" to receive proper burial.[49] Lost in the forest, he is found by Kelora Chen, the daughter of a Native woman and a Chinese father. Under the tutelage of both daughter and father, Gwei Chang learns mixed lessons; to find the bones and honor the heroism they still expressed; to sympathize and share with the "uncles" left behind after the building of the railroad, to fend for themselves in rough mining and labor camps and little China Towns; "to talk tough and blunt, a chiselled edge to his words to express the backbreaking task of survival that all of them shared day after day" (13). But also, with Kelora, he learns to see the forest as "our grand-mothers"; "to love the same mother earth and to see her sloping curves in the mountains . . . he had [previously] thought of [only] as barriers"; to let "this beautiful mother [fill] his heart and soul" (14–15). Kelora, in short, as an odd amalgam of Chinese and Native, seems to embody, even before he makes it, Gwei Chang's crucial choice of primary allegiance. Will it be to a patriarchal order, the bones of the dead uncles and the traditions of a patriarchal Chinese past? Or to the possibilities of a new life in a new land and a different and more matriarchal way of living?

Wong Gwei Chang makes, by his own final admission, the wrong choice. The last episode of the novel is a "conversation" just before his own death with Kelora (who died forty-four years earlier). "Would it help my dying soul to tell you that I love you, Kelora?" he begins and goes on to confess how he "lost" not just Kelora, but their son too (235). He senses her waver-ing and momentary presence and, as he dies, she seems to answer even as, in the last words of the novel, he remembers them once making love: "Her cheeks beautiful, seductive, flushed. Her eyes still lewd; he wandered, help-less in their fiery depth. He closed his eyes, the heavy chant of the storyteller turning to mist in his head" (237). Against that background the storytell-ing of the novel still goes on, but it is the story of the great-granddaughter changing the telling of her family story to the living of a different story. Kae leaves her husband to join Hermia Chow in Hong Kong, to make the radical break that her ancestor could not make and that he regretted for almost half a century afterward, and to enact her own version of the Western plot by going, appropriately, further west to a new life in the East, now, for her, the West of promise, possibility, and difference. "The act of immigration," Aritha van Herk has observed, "enables the new immigrant to fashion her or his own fiction and to live it out." [50] Kae promises to be a better fictionalizer than was her great-grandfather.

As we have seen, there is no one unitary Canadian Western, but even in its decentered formlessness much of this fiction still portrays the Native as adjunctive to white purposes and designs. Not surprisingly, then, some of the most radical experiments in decentering come from the margin of the margin, from writers who are both Canadian and Native, and I can appropriately conclude this chapter by briefly considering one such work by Thomas King, a Cherokee/German-Greek American/Canadian author and critic. [51] Indeed, if the Canadian dream, as Kroetsch has claimed, is a dream of origins and the Canadian West is where that dream is ever made new again, then the "paradigmatic" Canadian Western well might be not Ross's *As For Me and My House,* but King's "One Good Story, That One" in which the one good story is an old "dream" of origins, the account in Genesis, here renewed and improved as it is recounted by a Native storyteller in a distinctly Coyote mode.

This narrator, beset by three visiting anthropologists after authentic Indian narratives, offers several possible tales, such as the one about "Billy Frank and the dead-river pig." The anthropologists, however, want older stories, more important stories, stories of "maybe how the world was put together." [52] They are put off and put on by just such a story:

> Okay, I says.
> Have some tea.
> Stay awake.
> Once upon a time.
> Those stories start like that, pretty much, those
> ones, start on time. (39)

What follows is a creation story featuring Ah-damn and Evening. The joke is on both the anthropologists who transcribe this "Native" account and on the account of Genesis from which it derives. Neither is the fairy-tale opening the least of the insults and injuries inflicted on that founding Judeo-Christian narrative. Western cosmology and Western values are pervasively travestied. God, Margaret Atwood observes in her apt analysis of this tale's subversive humor, is "selfish, loud-mouthed and violent. Adam is stupid, and Eve, who is generous, level-headed, peace-loving, and nurturing, comes out the hero of the story" because, not coincidentally, she is also "pointedly identified as an Indian woman" in contrast to Adam who is white.[53] As Atwood concludes, "the biblical fall of man has seldom been recounted with such insouciance," and white readers are here "forced to experience first hand how it must feel to have your own religious stories retold in a version that neither 'understands' nor particularly reverences them," an experience usually reserved for Natives.[54]

Adam/Ah-damn is particularly mocked—another subversion and reversal. While Evening is scouting around and finding food, her mate uselessly sets about "writing things down," just as the anthropologists are tape-recording the story they are being told. Such recording (the character's and, by implication, the auditors') strikes the narrator as "pretty boring" (41). It is, at least in Ah-damn's case, of dubious worth as well. He mistakes the blue-flower-berry for an animal and, "not so smart," doesn't notice as the animals pass by telling him their names that one of them is playing pranks on him. Coyote "come by maybe four, maybe eight times. Gets dressed up, fool around" (42).

That fooling is in and integral to this good story. Ah-damn is fooled in the framed Genesis narrative which, recast, gives creation itself a different starting point, neither androcentric nor Judeo-Christian. The anthropologists are fooled in the frame story. Native creation tales are not necessarily what they are presumed to be and, after this one, neither are white creation tales. Furthermore, when the anthropologists beat a hasty retreat as soon as the framed tale is ended, they leave the narrator with "my friend Napiao" ready for another pot of tea after—the last words of the story and the narrator still speaking—"I clean up all the coyote tracks on the floor" (43). Coyote is still fooling around, in the text and beyond it, a master at coming by again in yet another guise. So any story, including this one, can be differently retold, which is to say again that Coyote is the patron of the different retellings that make the Canadian Western different.

In King's "Good Story," the marginalized Native storyteller knows the master's narratives/master narratives well enough to retell them to a different end. Similarly, the Canadian Western writers in whom I am most interested are thoroughly conversant with the hegemonies implicit in the popular Western (who isn't?) but reject those narratives in favor of stories that are multiple, multivocal, hybrid, and antihegemonic. The best of these Canadian Western writers (and King ranks with the best) thereby succeed not just in challenging the ideology of the popular Western, but also in creating alternative models of the West. In place of a frontier rolling inexorably westward to produce America and Americans, they suggest a borderlands model of the West as a wavering and elusive site of hybridity, cross-fertilization, complication, and ideological contestation and transformation (as opposed to manifest certainty). Gloria Anzaldúa, in her influential *Borderlands/La Frontera,* has postulated such a border along the Rio Grande. The Western Canadian writers find it at the forty-ninth parallel as well.

Part II Canadian Westerns: New Forms

2 Untelling *Tay John*

Christian myth posits the coming of a Messiah. A Tsimshian myth, "The Dead Woman's Son," describes a bereaved husband who sleeps on his late wife's grave until winter, then returns in spring to find a little boy playing there. The child pines toward nothingness until a wise woman in the tribe realizes he craves full human life and gives him a shadow. Early in the nineteenth century a blond half-breed Iroquois trapper called Tête Jaune "discovers" a pass through the mountains and is murdered by the local Indians. Later, the pass is named for him, Yellowhead Pass, an English translation of his French nickname. An early twentieth-century Canadian anthropologist, Diamond Jenness, collects "The Dead Woman's Son" and other myths, legends, and accounts of Native life in his important work, *The Indians of Canada*. A young man from Alberta, Howard O'Hagan, goes to Montreal to earn his law degree, but returns to Alberta to knock around the Rockies, working as a packer, surveyor, reporter, and guide and collecting stories from the whites and Natives who inhabit the mountains. These sources, multiple and contradictory, merge with others as diverse as the Bible, Plato, and the fiction of Joseph Conrad to inspire *Tay John*. Published in 1939, this novel is Canada's first metafictional mythic Western and the prototype for subsequent postmodern fictions that will come to characterize the Canadian Western at its idiosyncratic best.

It is a remarkable book by any standard and extraordinary when viewed against conventional novels of the West being written in North America in the late thirties and early forties: Max Brand's *Gunman's Gold* (1939), Luke Short's *Hard Money* (1940), or Zane Grey's *Western Union* (1939). And even much more serious Westerns such as, in the United States, John Steinbeck's *The Grapes of Wrath* (1939) and Wallace Stegner's *On a Darkling*

Plain (1939, and set in Canada) or, in Canada, Bertram Brooker's *Think of the Earth* (1936), the first novel to win the Governor General's Award, and Sinclair Ross's *As For Me and My House* (1941) do not exhibit *Tay John's* radical experimentation with the nature of narrative itself. As Margery Fee observes of the latter: "Its self-consciousness about the fictive quality of *all* versions of reality, elicits the label 'post-modernist' despite its 1939 publication date," while "O'Hagan's replacement of divine authority in the making of myth, indeed his replacement of even a human author by a collective 'intertextuality' connects him to post-structuralism," just as his "definition of story in terms of material, historical, and ideological constraints rather than in terms of individual artistry can be connected to Marxist criticism."[1] Jack Robinson similarly points out that "the proliferation of stories, with several characters taking over the narrative briefly, embeds in the text the postmodernist assumption that all reality is fictive," and that the novel's mythic matter and metaphors of trace and division anticipate a "postmodernist view" of the self as "flickering" and "elusive."[2] A proto-postmodernist, poststructuralist, metafictional Canadian Western, *Tay John* was, indeed, a novel before its time.

The artistry whereby the narrative untells, more than it tells, the life of its eponymous blond Indian hero/antihero was particularly unprecedented in the thirties, when Western Canada was supposedly still finding its fictional voice, not its metafictional voicelessness. Now, however, we can more clearly see how and how much O'Hagan exemplifies the "process that Robert Kroetsch has argued is characteristic of recent Canadian fiction" and particularly Canadian Western fiction.[3] For Kroetsch, Canadian writers must "by the radical process of demythologizing" resist "the systems that threaten to define them" and, through that demythologizing, "uninvent the world."[4] Or, differently put, through a different mythologizing they differently invent it. Language itself, Claude Lévi-Strauss argues, embeds the "primary codes" structuring reality, whereas myth differently sets forth different "secondary codes" that are, like language, beyond "man's consciousness" but also beyond language as well.[5] How, then, can the "cooked" text set forth the "raw" subject, present the "raw" hero? O'Hagan's basic solution to this unsoluble problem is to turn, as much as possible, the text of the novel into its spoken analogues, ostensibly verbal narratives oddly conjoining myth (both Native and white) with Western tall tale, and then to have that different tale telling fall far short of the narration to which it aspires, "The Story of Tay John."

"He who represents his own discourse on myths as a myth," Trinh T. Minh-ha maintains, must be "acutely aware of the illusion of all reference to a subject as absolute center. The packaging of myths must somehow bear the form of that which it attempts to enclose."[6] But how (this assertion turning into a question) do you package the anonymity, multiplicity, and radical freedom of myth without destroying myth in the process? Or how, switching from Minh-ha to Kroetsch, do you invent uninventing? And, the same question in still a different guise, how do you tell the story of Tay John by not telling it? In my reading of this first major Canadian mythic Western, I aspire not to answer those same questions, but only to circumscribe them.

Starting even with the naming of the protagonist, the novel foretells more its own untelling than any final narrating of the protagonist's definitive story. "Tay John" is a mispronunciation of "Tête Jaune"—the French designation for the blond Indian as voiced by men who do not speak French. Yet the English name at one point given to the protagonist is also "Yellow Head," and, furthermore, his original Indian name, "Kumkleseem," partly meant "Yellow Head" as well. One name subsumes and replaces another by differently saying the same thing and thus attests to the arbitrary nature of names as well as to the transitory nature of identity, for the original Kumkleseem who first enters the white man's world is not synonymous with the final Tay John who at last takes himself out of it.[7] "Tay John" differs, too, from "Tête Jaune," and the change in spelling even more than any change in pronunciation serves to obscure the French origin of the name, to make it more a conventional cognomen than a descriptive one. Conjoining the comfortably familiar "John" with the vaguely esoteric "Tay," "Tay John" becomes basically another version of "Indian Joe" (not quite a regular Joe but hopefully on the right track) and as such voices more the program of those who employ the appellation than the being of him to whom it is applied. Naming, in short, is misnaming, and even the most seemingly obvious descriptive designation is strangely deflected as it travels from one tongue to another.

Narrative fares no better than naming. As the successive titles of the three sections of the novel ("Legend," "Hearsay," "Evidence—without a finding") suggest, mere hearsay succeeds and subverts the legend of the protagonist with which the book begins, while such evidence as is set forth in the last section—and throughout the entire work—conduces to no final finding. Narrative does not lead to any truths in or of the novel, but merely allows for the proliferation of other narration, as when Jack Denham, O'Hagan's primary narrator and an Irish-Canadian version of Joseph Conrad's Captain Marlow, would subsume legend, hearsay, and evidence into his "Tale," his "gospel" of Tay John.[8] He fails, of course, and hands the task of telling on to still another narrator.

The "gospel" note in Jackie's Tale portends still another failure, the failure of myth, too, to provide a definitive rendering of the world. As the numerous gospel references and religious parallels in the novel attest, Tay John's story is deliberately counterposed to the most widely accepted "legend" in the Western world, and a narration that takes us from a miraculous birth to an equally miraculous death necessarily invokes the Christian prototype for all such narrations. But O'Hagan's tale of a failed messiah who cannot save his people or the woman he loves or, finally, himself persistently counters the larger story with which it is framed. Biblical teleology and typology are regularly inverted or undermined. Biblical borrowings and echoes are deployed in passages that emphatically do not aspire to the anagogic. For example, in contrast to the Biblical "In the beginning was the Word," we have, in *Tay John,* three (incongruous trilogies pervade the novel) emblematic endings in silence—a "skull" with a "stone . . . still between its jaws"; a corpse, its lips sealed with frozen froth; a pregnant woman, dead, her open mouth "chock-full of snow."[9]

That first stone especially sets forth the silence and death out of which both the novel's protagonist and his consequent story originate. The stone also ends a story, a story that begins with a man whose "voice overtopped all . . . others" (15) and his conversion experience. Red Rorty, crude, drunk, and loud, down from the mountains to sell his furs and carouse away the proceeds in an 1880 Edmonton as elemental as the man himself, is on his way to the whorehouse when he is stopped by the sound of singing from a nearby church. Soon he is loudly proclaiming the tenets of this church— "That whosoever believeth on Him shall not perish but shall have everlasting life" (17)—and presently, as drunk on religion as he ever was on whiskey, he kills his horses, burns all of his other material possessions, and sets out, like Saul of Tarsus, for a different life. He will go among the Indians to preach the Word.

The Shuswap, whose myths tell of a "leader with yellow hair who [will] come to take them back over the mountains to a land full of game, fish . . . and berries" (23), take Rorty in but soon decide that he is a forerunner of their promised messiah and not the man himself. Rorty tells them, loudly, of another who will "come again one day to be a leader of mankind" (24), to save those who believe and to afflict those who do not. This differing as to deferred leaders lasts until Rorty briefly lapses into his old ways. He sees a young wife shredding cedar bark by rubbing it on her thigh, which, "bare, and oiled with the cedar, shone in the sunlight" (26). The temptation is more than he can resist. She apparently does not resist either. But even if she did consent, her people do not. Next day the other Indian women beat Rorty, drive him into the forest, seize him and tie him kneeling to a tree.

The children shoot arrows into his stomach. The parodic Paul who became a parodic John the Baptist here becomes a parodic Saint Sebastian and (tied to the tree) a parodic crucified Christ as well.[10] The women then set fire to his hair and to the tree. As both burn, the last words that he might have cried out are stopped by a stone jammed into his mouth. Later the young wife dies, and still later a baby is born from her grave. The baby is Tay John.

I have briefly summarized the chief legend in "Legend," the story of Red Rorty's end and Tay John's beginning, because that dual account especially exemplifies two dialectics implicit in this novel. The whole account of Rorty's failed missionary career illustrates a faltering opposition of sex and salvation on the one hand and sound and silence on the other. But not a total opposition; these different terms are intertwined as well as at cross purposes. Thus the roisterer of the mountains who for sheer delight "hurled his voice" until it "rolled . . . from one rock wall to another" (14) stands silent in the town, caught on his way to the whorehouse by the hymns emanating from a "new" and "different" church. Turning from his originally intended mission, Rorty soon sings the loudest in the choir, and after listening, in a setting vaguely homoerotic, to the whispered counsel of the unkempt minister, the "echoes" of Rorty's affirmation of belief "rolled in the emptied church louder than ever they had in the mountains" (16). Rorty then decides to return to the mountains to be, in a new and different way, a voice in the wilderness. His model here, as already noted, is "Saul of Tarsus, afterwards called Paul, who had left one path of life for another; who went out into the world, among strange people, and preached The Way, and became a great man whose words were remembered" (17–18). Forfeiting sex for salvation might prepare him, he imagines, to voice the living word, and that word, surviving the silence of death, might allow a kind of continuing existence even on earth—which is ostensibly also the purpose of sex.

His tenuous program hardly works out as planned even though the dialectic of his categories remains as confused as ever. Indeed, Rorty's sermon to the Indians—"the people said that no man had spoken with such a great voice before" (24)—is soon followed by his silent seizing of Hanni, the Shuswap woman.[11] And that act is followed by his demise and a consequent reevaluation of his earlier words. Three days after Rorty's apocalyptic death by fire, the Indian women return to the still smoldering scene to find that he has not risen again:

> They found [instead] the skull, fallen to the ground and caught in the black twisted roots of a tree. The stone was still between its jaws. Yaada took a stick and pointed.

"See!" she said, "he was a great liar, and the word has choked him." (28)

The word is the Word and the Word is stone.

Although itself compromised in the Indian setting, Christian myth still serves to undermine the Indian myth that, in this novel, comes after it, not before. To start with, there is the cross-cultural confusion embodied in Rorty's mission into the wilderness. As both prophet and precursor, just what does he promise to the Shuswap? Signifying, to them, the coming of their messiah, he speaks, to them, of the coming of his. So Rorty as a sign equally asserts two contradictory meanings, one firmly embedded in one mythology and one in the other, and either reading cancels the other out.

Unless, of course, the two different promised leaders turn out to be one and the same, a possibility that the Indians also early consider. But, whether either, neither, or both of Rorty's annunciations are valid, the result for Tay John is still the same. He is born bearing an impossible burden—a supplement of deferred hopes that deprive his life, from the very beginning, of human possibility by imparting to it a surplus of mythic meaning. Conjoining Christianity and Platonic thought, the Shuswap define their leader and their need:

> Their faith was the substance of things hoped for, the shadow of what they could not yet discern. They believed that the world was made of things they could not touch nor see, as they knew that behind the basket their hands made was the shape of the perfect basket which once made would endure for ever and beyond the time when its semblance was broken and worn thin by use. (29)

Kumkleseem cannot be merely Kumkleseem; he must also be the perfect man behind his name, not just the particular individual who bears it. No wonder sustained ceremonies of rebirth and renaming are required to keep him in the world at all.

That the paradigms for the father will be somewhat different for the son is early indicated by the way in which the boy, born from the grave, "walked in the sunlight as other children, but alone with no shadow to follow him and protect him" (41). He is a presence marked by an absence and still marked even when that telling absence is undone. Although the child is united with his shadow through the agency of a wise old woman, the union is not secure. The first faint shadow flees when it is early stepped on, so the reforged bond is never tested. "The people were careful not to tread upon his shadow nor to touch it, fearful that it would leave him" (42), and he them. Consequently, only "when the sun was gone and his shadow had left him for the night . . . could [Kumkleseem] come close to his people" (43). The quotidian division of day and night, of light and dark, modulates the different (preternatural) division between this prospective leader and his people who await his future mission.

That division is magnified by the vision journey whereby Kumkleseem would determine "the shape and the colour of the life before him and . . . the spirit that would guide him" (45). This same ordeal should prove, too, Kumkleseem's readiness to become the promised leader whom the Shuswap have long anticipated, and so parallels Christ's trial in the wilderness. Yet there is, from the first, a shadow over the venture. Kumkleseem travels into a dark valley dangerous to man. The danger is of supernatural separation from others and loss of human status: "Men feared that one night . . . [the spirit of that valley] would come down upon them in their sleep and leave them with a coyote's howl for voice and only a coyote's claws for hands, and each man would be for ever a stranger to his neighbour" (46). For Kumkleseem, already markedly apart from others, the darkness of this valley especially threatens to undo that other more natural darkness only in which he and his people can draw close together. Coyote, moreover, as a figure of loss and iso-lation, stands in contrast to Christ as a figure of transcendence and so also suggests how tricky the interplay of Native and Christian contexts can be in this novel, as when Tay John later heeds the biblical injunction to cut off an offending hand and ends up wearing a hook, a version of Coyote's claw.

Kumkleseem returns from his vision quest with two signs of what his journey might signify, his account of the animals he encountered and a sample of the dark gold-bearing sand he found at the head of the dark river. The Indians read only the first sign and emphasize the implication, for them, of the last animal that watched over the youth's watch, a grizzly bear. "The bear-spirit will be your guardian spirit. His strength will be your strength, and his cunning yours. . . . He will pull back the cape from his face so that you may see him, and he will talk to you with a man's voice" (49–50). That reading promises them the possibility of a great leader. But a better reading might be based on the second sign, for the *gold* from the *head* of the river names the protagonist and grounds that name (all of his names, in fact) in absence and separation, which soon follow with the arrival of other whites on the scene. Three prospectors (the wise men from the East?) can immediately discern at least one paramount meaning in the glittering sand Kumkleseem discovered and promise him a modest reward if he will lead them to it. He thereby acquires a rifle, powder and bullets, a new red coat, a new name that no one can properly pronounce, and a growing taste for white ways. "His rifle was his own, and no man could touch it" (56). With such new ownership, as opposed to the old communal ways of the Shuswap, Tay John can now hunt more for furs to be privately traded than for food to be communally shared.

Kumkleseem becomes Tay John. An anticipated mission as messianic Native leader gives way to a paradigm of presence/absence, which is mostly the sound/silence of Tay John's "prophet" father translated into another medium. The Indians await their future (chronologically elsewhere) leader in the person of Tay John, who is now mostly geographically elsewhere, and hope thereby to be rejoined to their past (another chronological and geographic elsewhere). Elsewhere, Tay John is learning the white man's ways, which are more and more copied by other Indians too. "Days came when the young men, following Tay John, failed to hunt meat and hides for the village," but sought, instead, furs to trade for rifles and "red scarves and sashes" (56–57). Successful hunting in this new fashion soon reduces them all to general starvation and a crisis of expectancy as they wait "for a sign from Kumkleseem" to "go whither his finger pointed" (57). Unfortunately, they are already well on their way. Their leader is conducting them into their future which, in the white man's world, not the Indians', will be an increasing placelessness.

The final severance of Tay John from the Indians is precipitated, however, by the other dichotomy of sex versus salvation, which also passes in somewhat altered form from father to son. The latter does at last briefly take on the role of leader but even then he refuses to be the leader whom the Indians expected: "The woman of Tay John is the people. He is a leader of the people and is married to their sorrows" (67). Tay John would subvert this mission and "marriage" by seizing a woman already promised to another man of the tribe. The resultant crisis is resolved not (as with Red Rorty) by execution, but by exile, after which the Indians tell each other tales of the missing man being away on a particularly arduous hunt and perpetually anticipate his imminent return. With the advent of winter, for example, they make him "a new house," and "each day they brought fresh boughs, laid them there for his bed, and made a fire against his coming" (68–69). But only occasionally at night can they sometimes believe they hear him near, "and in the morning no one would speak of what had happened during the night" (70).

"All that winter smoke rose from the new house built for Tay John. At night an owl perched by it and hooted" (70). Ending thus, "Legend" attests that the end of legend, for the Indians, is an enduring absence made bearable by the most tenuous hints of presence and by the hope, sustained through holding fast his story, that their leader might come again. Legend is, here, the perpetual deferral of things hoped for as marked by the telling of that hope. It is an Indian and oral version of the Western's long-sustained enterprise of trying to write into being the right West.

Since the paradigms are the same, neither Tay John nor legend will fare any better in the white world than in the Native. Deferral and disappearance and parodic substitution, carried over from the Indian context to the white, continue to govern the text of the novel and to undermine the larger text on which it is modeled. Consider, for example, the crucifixion of Father Rorty who played at imitating Christ to find only the imitation real. Catholic, slight, timorous, an obvious inversion of his missing older brother whom he came west to find, this priest finds only another version of his brother's death. In love with Ardith Aeriola, the third woman in Tay John's adult life, Father Rorty decides, when he finds a crotched pine tree shaped roughly like a cross growing on the edge of the cliff high above the setting of his recent "temptation," to take the burden of his desires and doubts on his naked shoulders by mounting this cross. He has, not coincidentally, just been reading *The Imitation of Christ.* At first the charade redemption proceeds exactly as intended. "Stars shone for a time. The Big Dipper wheeled above him. Then clouds came and with them the rain. It touched his brow, cool and fresh as salvation" (220). Yet the saving waters soon shrink the rope; the rain changes to snow and the cold numbs his hands; the early September storm lasts three (of course) days, during which time the priest dies naked on his cross with the "froth" of his last sobbing frozen in his mouth. A parodic apocalypse of fire is balanced by one of ice, and in both cases the word is silence.

The silence here, however, reverberates with hints of mythic meaning immanent in the evocative description of the discovery of the dead priest: "The arms upon that tree were still outspread, waiting to embrace the world, and the naked feet hung yearning for the soil. A hawk circled overhead" (221). What, especially, might that circling hawk signify?[12] The mystery seems not to be the possible meaning of the parodic crucifixion that Father Rorty, like his brother, has undergone, but the subsequent mythic intermingling of life and death. In the circle of the flying hawk, Father Rorty's outstretched arms do "embrace the world" but not, as he anticipated, either Ardith or Christ. Dead, he is included in that larger circle of the hawk's flight, just as, earlier, his brother's skull was found "fallen to the ground and caught in the black twisted roots of a tree" (28). Denham, with fine irony, similarly wonders if, in his last "delirium" before "dying," the priest saw "the shape of the cross . . . or the face of the woman—pale, round, close and real as the moon that stared him down? Or," a third possibility, "up there, so high above the earth, was there only the sound of wind blowing, and far away the sound of running water where men who thirst may drink?" (222).

Such controverting of Christian story with its promise of teleological finality beyond life and death on this earth continues through to the end of *Tay John*. Thus Christ, who in a transcendent sense walked out of death to save all men, is countered by Tay John, who—just as transcendently— once out, walks back in again and does so to save no one. Furthermore, this protagonist's passing and the end of the novel—"He had just walked down, the toboggan behind him, under the snow and into the ground" (264)—is conjoined with the burden he takes with him, and Ardith Aeriola, pregnant and dead, tied to the toboggan, her open mouth "chock-full of snow" (262), embodies the third and final parody of the promised last word frozen in time. From beginning to end, then, *Tay John* denies transcendence; translates "In the beginning was the Word" into the opposing dictum "In the end was silence"; and then translates that ending into a new beginning.

The narrative mode of "Legend" is an ironically aloof omniscience so distanced from the action it describes that it can give us a bird's-eye view of the Rocky Mountain setting of the novel and of man set in the peaks and valleys of his whole history—recorded and unrecorded. "The time of this in its beginning, in men's time, is 1880 in the summer, and its place is the Athabaska valley, near its head in the mountains, and along the other waters falling into it, and beyond them a bit, over the Yellowhead Pass to the westward, where the Fraser, rising in a lake, flows through wilderness and canyon down to the Pacific" (11). In this beginning there are two parallel double perspectives. The opening panorama portraying the "place" of the novel is set in a still larger panorama of "wilderness and canyon" beyond, and beyond that the broad Pacific; and so too is "men's time" set in the larger perspective of what we might term "Legend's" time and beyond that timelessness.

Yet the two times of the novel—chronological, historical, on the one hand; and, on the other, timeless legend verging toward timelessness—also stand in opposition to one another. For example, the metaphoric "Word," the Bible as the book transcending time, is subverted and silenced in the here and now of 1880 Alberta by a single stone, and with that stone, Red Rorty's mission to eternity ends in stasis and parodic death. Nor does Indian legend, Indian theology, fare any better in the present human time in which that legend unfolds. The Indians await their promised leader who will guide them to an earthly heaven but they await him in a land already transgressed by fur traders and prospectors and soon to be penetrated by the railroads too. In a very real sense, the whites, in history, seeking their lost Eden in the New World, are busily destroying all possibilities of paradise through the very rigor of their search. There will be no other place left, for them or for the Indians. Tay John, then, is deprived of his mission before it can be begun. Not kingdom but exile must be his fate, and exile into a world of other exiles seeking (like Red Rorty or Jack Denham or Alf Dobble) some kingdom in the mountains.

Just as legend's time with its attendant timeless hope is undone, for the Indians, by the intrusion of white history, so, too, is it undone by the intrusion of Indian history, which is now white history writ small. When the Indians, in the exigencies of an exploited present, still pin their "faith" and "hopes" on Tay John, they wait for him to "speak with a great voice" (57) and to resolve thereby their suffering and their doubt. Yet "a great voice," it must be remembered, has previously spoken, so the promise of the mythic future is already the fact of the actual past, and that fact calls the anticipated future not into being but into question. The Shuswap have already had their leader and he failed them, or, at best, he presaged the subsequent leader who will also fail them. The Indians drop from sight; Tay John falls from transcendent destiny into bare survival; the story declines from legend to hearsay.

That final declination might, at first, seem to represent a narrative gain. Because omniscience and timelessness are both beyond human experience, perhaps the only authentic speaking possible in the novel is the human voice with all its limitations. And "Hearsay," combining (by meaning) "rumor" and (by etymology) "repetition," insists on both the humanity and the limitations of the voices whereby the rest of the text is rendered. Again, however, the novel is built around structuring polarities which are themselves structured to collapse.

To start with, the paramount speaking voice in "Hearsay" regularly aspires to transcendence. The text denies truth. Nevertheless, Jack Denham, the capable narrator of the middle section, implicitly insists on the higher truth of all that he says and does so by positing the "magic" of naming.[13]

> For a country where no man has stepped before is new in the real sense of the word, as though it had just been made, and when you turn your back upon it you feel that it may drop back again into the dusk that

gave it being. It is only your vision that holds it in the known and created world. . . . A name is the magic to keep it within the horizons. Put
a name to it, put it on a map, and you've got it. (80)

The world called into being by the ordering word constitutes his great image
of authority.

The authority that Denham naturally claims for his own naming, his own
tales, is, however, denied to those of others: "For your backwoodsman is a
thorough gossip. . . . He pays for a meal, for a night's lodging, with a tale.
His social function is to hand on what he has heard, with the twist his fancy
has been able to add. . . . What he has not seen he deduces, and what he
cannot understand he explains" (114). And those others, and the novel, in
turn, deny Denham the authority that he denies them: "He might meet a
friend at the street corner and follow him to his destination, talking, *stretching his story the length of Edmonton.* It became known as 'Jackie's Tale.' It was
a faith—a gospel to be spread, that tale, and he was its only apostle" (77,
emphasis added). Faith and gospel do not fare well in the novel. Nor are
we reassured as to the absolute truth of his "stretched" tale when we also
notice, in one offhand comment, that it is all told in a bar.[14]

Denham's extended defense for the higher truth of naming is, in fact,
refuted by the very occasion that prompted it, his excursion into "country
where no man has stepped before" (80). This excursion first brings Denham
into the presence of Tay John—on the other side of the river that Denham
was exploring to its source and over which Denham himself had earlier
crossed. The narrator is not therefore envisioning the naming of his own
new world, but the renaming of Tay John's old one; he is not an Adam taking
his first green inventory of Eden, but a latter-day Columbus still deaf to the
Indians' words and blind to the Indians' map, the Indians' claims on the
country. He will name the land; he will name Yellow Head too; such naming is also an unnaming and a dispossessing. Even more to the point, by
Denham's own logic, the true first name that endows possession precedes
any voicing of later and necessarily inauthentic names. With authenticating origins deferred ever further into the past, does not any story become
dubious repetition, mostly rumor, mere hearsay?

Denham's practice of naming, as opposed to his logic, is portrayed in the
novel, which is to say that the processes and program prompting "Jackie's
Tale" are themselves embedded in his narrative. That embedding is especially
seen in his account of his first crucial encounter with Tay John just across
the raging mountain stream and of Tay John's immediately subsequent encounter with the bear. For Denham had "dreamed of—of [he haltingly early

admits] meeting a bear one day close up, hand to hand so to speak, and doing it in. An epic battle: man against the wilderness. And now I saw the battle taking form," he continues, "but another man was in *my* place" (85–86, emphasis added). His anticipated Western tale of adventure and conquest becomes, instead, the story of his dispossession, a recounting of how "only the width of a mountain stream kept him from the adventure of his life" (77). So, deferring from the first the critical question of just whose adventure, whose text, it really was, he slowly works out—"It took me a time to find the words" (90)—his narration of Tay John's victory over the bear. That account of how a man armed only with a knife killed a huge grizzly concludes by emphasizing the symbolic rebirth of the victor from the beast just killed: "Then the mass quivered. It heaved. A man's head appeared beside it, bloody, muddied, as though he were just being born, as though he were climbing out of the ground. Certainly man had been created anew before my eyes. Like birth itself it was a struggle against the powers of darkness, and Man had won" (87–88). That last general "Man," however, gives Denham's game away. The rebirth here imaged is not just Tay John's, for the Indian soon "vanished, as though he were leaving one form of existence for another" (89). The protagonist can exit from the scene because the narrator has entered more fully into it, reborn into his own tale by envisioning a recreated image of himself. "He [Tay John] had won. *We* [he and I] had won" (88, emphasis in the original). Denham will participate in Tay John's triumph by his telling of it; by telling of it he will reclaim his adventure, his victory. His sustained enterprise of recounting is thus more an exercise in pretended becoming than in authentic being, and even he at one point admits that his dealings with Tay John were at least in part "frantic efforts at evasion" (84).

Yet the paradigms of sound/silence and presence/absence come into play for the narrator too, particularly since Denham, we are told just before the voice of omniscience hands the novel over to this narrator, has his own personal story yet declines to recount it: "His name was Jack Denham, but he was known generally as Jackie—a man whose pride was in his past, of which he seldom spoke, but over which loomed the shadow of a great white house in the north of Ireland. . . . From that past, and because of it, he received four times a year a remittance" (75–76). The remittance man was usually present in the New World because he had become a family embarrassment in the Old and was being paid to stay far away. Denham is clearly marked by the absence of his former place, his former higher station.[15] Not to sound that absence, he substitutes one story for another, and the hero of a New World narration replaces the failure of an Old World one.

The replacement, however, more and more proves the failure. Although Denham can share in the victory over the bear through the narrative subterfuge of casting himself as Tay John or Tay John as a version of himself, that doubling is undone by another doubling. Balancing, contrasting to, and canceling out Denham's first episode in his celebration of Tay John's exploits is the final episode, the account of Tay John's victory over Dobble and all his men and of the victor's subsequent flight into the mountains with Ardith Aeriola. Denham, who is himself clearly drawn to the woman, must once more tell of another who is in his place, but now there is no reward in vicariously sharing that other's triumph. The story he tells thus takes on the same contours as the one he does not tell, as in each he ends up a marginal man. Out of place in his first story, he is displaced from the second one too and, in consequence, increasingly disassociates himself from its telling. As we near the end of *Tay John,* Denham first interposes Inspector Wiggins and Sergeant Flaherty between himself and his account. Then he abdicates entirely. At its conclusion the narration is no longer "Jackie's Tale" but has been handed over to Blackie.[16] Repetition circling back upon itself must sooner or later circumscribe its own emptiness, and Denham, capable narrator that he is, is left finally fictionally bankrupt, without even a tale to tell.

The title of Part III, "Evidence—without a finding," turning as it does on a legal trope, gives rise to the pertinent questions of just who or what is on trial and on what grounds is judgment deferred. The most likely candidate for sentencing is, of course, Tay John. After all, he gives his name to the novel, and throughout that novel he regularly both invites and evades some final summation that might deem him a hero (in the Indian context or the white) or a sham (again in the Indian context or the white). Yet what we might term the transcript of this protagonist's extended but inconclusive trial could itself constitute evidence for another's transgression. As previously noted, the substance of Tay John's life is confiscated to become "Jackie's Tale," which might well lay Denham open to charges of narrative theft. Furthermore, in the final section of the novel, the faith of Father Rorty, the enterprise of Alf Dobble, and the virtue of Ardith Aeriola are all at issue and in doubt.

The issues and the doubts are further confused by the way in which they mix and merge as one inconclusive trial verges into another throughout the novel. Part II, in fact, ends with Tay John's one official encounter with the law, his quasi-summons—"request, only request mind you, that he come down here" (150)—to answer an imputed charge of rape. That encounter, however, lurches toward inconclusion instead of proceeding to any official finding and then is followed by Part III, still more "Evidence—without a finding." In effect, then, the clearest inconclusive trial comes before the longest and concluding section of the novel that is ostensibly grounded (or at least named) in just such a trial. That trial merits attention, first, because it embodies in miniature the narrative strategy of the whole novel—a promise of at last getting at the truth but a promise that is denied in the practice of attempting to do so. The trial is also noteworthy because it constitutes a test of Tay John's response to an immediately previous and more tenuous test of authenticity, his answer to the proto-existential question that Julia Alderson, the young American wife of an older Englishman, poses on the last night of the Aldersons' hunting expedition into the Rockies: " 'Suppose,' she said, lifting her head of auburn hair, 'suppose that for each of us, to-night was his last night but one, and that to-morrow you could do anything you wanted to do, be anywhere you liked, what company you desired, what food, anything yours for the asking—for that one day, your last—what would you do?' " (133).

The simplistic and hedonistic responses of the cook and the wrangler (they would, they claim, settle for a good meal, a good binge) are in contrast to their subverbal responses, the slow blush of the one, the "hard" stare of the other that "bored" into Julia. For each man, that second response also voices the obvious bad faith of what each first affirmed. But Tay John's answer, when he is pressed to give it, is all of one piece:

> Tay John . . . looked across the fire towards her, seeming not to look at her so much as to include her in a general survey of his surroundings. . . .
>
> Then he looked more closely at Julia. He considered. His glance passed on, over her into the tree tops, into the great wide heavens of the northern night.
>
> "I guess, I go hunting," he said.
>
> "You would only do what you are doing now?" Julia was unbelieving.
>
> "Of course . . ." (136–37, final ellipsis in the original)

Michael Ondaatje has emphasized that "Tay John himself says hardly more than two sentences in the whole book," and thus "his life, in the midst of all the words, is wordless."[17] That largely wordless life lends substantial weight to the rare pronouncements that this protagonist does voice. As Denham, a man of many words, at one point aptly observes: "Those with few words must know how to use them" (91). We can note here, too, the clear existential implications of Tay John's curt response.[18] But it must also be noted that the next day Tay John does not go hunting; he goes guiding instead, and that is not quite the same thing. He is in service when Julia poses her question, which is why it can be put to him. And his answer is his fiction that he is not; thus the "of course" trailing off into ellipsis and the ellipsis into absence, as Tay John leaves the campfire but not the camp.

The precise manner of Tay John's being or not being in service is also partly the issue of the aborted inquiry that follows the last day of the Aldersons' mountain excursion which was itself the "to-morrow" of Julia's question, a question she might well have asked of herself. Arthur Alderson turns his ankle and returns early to camp, leaving Tay John with Julia to complete the final hunt. By nightfall the two have not returned. The next morning Tay John's permanent departure (he has taken his horses and his bedroll) can be read in the newly fallen snow. As the other men are preparing to follow that trail, Julia rides into camp to proclaim to her husband, but loudly, for all to hear, "Arthur, Arthur, don't you understand?—Are you blind?—he—he—imposed himself upon me" (145).[19] Yet the indirect terms with which she asserts the alleged assault and her inconsistencies in bearing and behavior, along with the contradictory metaphors of concealment and exposure through which the whole scene is described all compromise her original accusation, and neither can Mrs. Alderson bring herself to say at all during the official hearing what she earlier said for all to hear in the camp. So the charge, which was never officially laid, is just as unofficially dropped, and Tay John, in not so much a departure but another characteristic disappearing, again withdraws from the scene and the novel.

The question of what might have happened between Julia and Tay John on the mountain that night is never resolved. She will not testify as an official witness, and neither will he. Such irresolution invites the complicity of the reader just as it elicits the suppositions of the other characters:

> "I figured she was sore and maybe frightened at being left alone while Tay John went for the horses. Or maybe she just wanted to impress her husband. I don't know nothing about it—but that's the way I figured it out." "Maybe," he suggested on a more private occasion, "she wanted it all along—still then why would she talk about it? And why would Tay John pull out the way he did?" (146)

"Charlie's opinion" is symptomatic. He and almost all the other characters in the novel contrive a fiction of Tay John and Julia alone on the mountain which is necessarily their own fiction. Thus, Charlie the horse wrangler's assessment was "perhaps based upon bitter personal experience" (146). Furthermore, not only do such peripheral fictions as Charlie's stand in for the missing facts (facts that, by definition in this novel, are forever beyond human reach), they also stand in for the missing more central fictions. Neither Tay John's nor Julia's version of what happened is given. Indeed, every aspect of the legal proceeding is undone into unconvincing fiction. For example, Porter, the young Mountie fresh from England, who is sent to bring in the culprit, sets out in terms of one story—"like . . . in *Chums*, chasing a half-breed hunter through the mountains" (150)—and comes back in terms of another just as dubious. Tay John is now the finest fellow he has ever met and has changed Porter's life "entirely." The tenderfoot has been taught to decipher the mountains; "the hidden was now revealed" (151). But what is here mostly revealed is how this character reads only his own self-gratifying fiction, reads it contradictorily, yet takes his reading for a full rendering of what is going on around him.

In the light of such pervasive fictions, any trial must be exactly that, a trying, a provisional telling; it might conclude with a judgment (a rendering of decision) but never with a verdict (a voicing of truth). On the largest level, then, the contradiction of the trial carries over to the contradiction of Part III and to the contradiction of the entire novel. The split is in the word, the story; the word as Word and the word as word; the story as truth and the story as tale. More specifically, the point to the legal trope of the title of Part III is the continuing disjunction in "Evidence—without a finding" between the first promising term and the missing final one. On the one hand, we have legend as evidence, hearsay as evidence, trace as evidence, provisional verbal construct as evidence. On the other, we are denied gospel, authority, transcendence, the final enduring word.

So speech, in this novel, never reaches the status it aspires to, and such speech, transmuted into text, perpetually questions its own voice and validity. The result is a novel forged mostly out of silence and ever on the verge of slipping back into silence, a novel that presents the life and legend of Tay John in order to explore the much larger absence that surrounds its protagonist's brief and sporadic presence in his story. In this sense, the most representative sign of Tay John is the last one he leaves, the one that Blackie, deciphering the disappearing trace of Tay John's disappearance, reads not on any page but in the blank snow-covered landscape itself: "Blackie stared at the tracks in front of him, very faint now, a slight trough in the snow, no more. Always deeper and deeper into the snow" (263–64).

Yet that last text written in the snow, the sign of the protagonist's return to the ground from which he came, might not be the last word of the novel after all. First of all, it only seems to Blackie—"he had the feeling, he said, looking down at the tracks"—that Tay John has "just walked down . . . into the ground" (264). Moreover, Tay John's descent into the earth to join in death a pregnant woman (his mistress/his mother) too obviously returns us to the novel's beginning and the possibility of having it all to do and re-count all over again.[20] The reader might also note the calculated similarities between Jackie and Blackie—in name and in function. The one perpetually repeats his "gospel" of Tay John's life. The other is left to mull over and to tell over (with obvious religious implications too, for Blackie is twice equated with a prophet) the mystery of Tay John's disappearance into absence and silence.

The contradiction at the heart of the story is not resolved; it is instead endlessly extended. The word sounds only as it emerges from silence; silence is known only by the word that names it and/or intrudes upon it; the text that sounds its own limitations must break off into silence and must do so over and over again.[21] This pervasive resonance is best summed up in the novel by Denham's parable of men and mountains, names and story and silence:

> Every story—the rough-edged chronicle of a personal destiny—having its source in a past we cannot see, and its reverberations in a future still unlived—man, the child of darkness, walking for a few short moments in unaccustomed sight—every story only waits, like a mountain in an untravelled land, for someone to come close, to gaze upon its contours, lay a name upon it, and relate it to the known world. Indeed, to tell a story is to leave most of it untold. You mine it, as you take ore from the mountain, . . . and when you have finished, the story remains, some-thing beyond your touch, resistant to your siege; unfathomable, like the heart of the mountain. You have the feeling that you have not reached the story itself, but have merely assaulted the surrounding solitude. (166–67)

Mountains here are paradigmatic and so is Tay John as a kind of ultimate mountain man. Not even Tay John can escape his names and his story. Not even those names and that story can hold him in the world. Yet the story remains to be recognized, finally, as one of the major mythic novels of the Canadian West. It looms large in the country's literary landscape precisely because O'Hagan wisely—he knew his mountains—left most of it untold. What is untold, the story of Tay John—both Native and white; neither Native nor white; present and absent in the narrative that bears his name—is, moreover, a trickster discourse that plays the form, ethos, and voice of the Western off against a countering indeterminacy, evasion, and silence—these last as monumental as they are metaphysical.

As Gerald Vizenor notes in his "Postmodernist Introduction" to *Narrative*

Chance: Postmodernist Discourse on Native American Literatures: "The trick-ster is agonistic imagination and aggressive liberation, a 'doing'" in narrative points of view and outside the imposed structures. . . . The trickster is an encounter in narrative voices, a communal sign and creative encounter in a discourse."[22] *Tay John* is such a doing and such a discourse. Native myths and oral story telling mediate and undermine the limited models of rationality and the linear paradigms of progress (Manifest Destiny) that con-stitute the epistemology of expansionism basic to the Western as, finally, a tale of conquest (the suppression of Others and the incorporation of wilder-ness into America). By calling into question the nature of the Western's self-evident "truths," O'Hagan conjectures suppressed but no less powerful versions of its story. He thus issues both an indictment and an invitation—an indictment against the narrow and linear ways of framing Western truth and progress; an invitation to heed precisely those narratives suppressed in conventional renderings of the West. "The story remains, something beyond your touch, resistant to your siege." *Your:* the implied audience here is the Western/Western reader, who is here counseled to read differently.

3 Coyote at Dog Creek

Sheila Watson's *The Double Hook,* published twenty years after *Tay John,* also deploys trickster discourse but more obviously ties that discourse to the figure of Coyote, who is both a major character in the novel and its imputed narrator. Watson insists, too, as even her title implies, on the duality of Canadian fictions of the West. Such fictions cannot aspire to universality, to claims of providing the one definitive account. As much as Howard O'Hagan, Watson knows that a different Native story and name occupies the same ground as does the white story of coming to claim and name that ground. Even suppressed and mostly silenced, Native stories are still there to contradict the social and natural order white narratives would recount into place. But whereas O'Hagan achieves the duality of both telling and untelling white and Native tales mainly by having white narrators attempt to render Tay John's at least half-Native story, Watson employs the reverse procedure of framing a substantially white narrative (or at least one with pervasive white literary echoes and analogues) "under Coyote's eye" and then recounting it partly in the words of that traditional Native American trickster as well.[1]

The extensive borrowings in both texts—from the Bible to Joseph Conrad in *Tay John,* from the Bible to T. S. Eliot and particularly *The Waste Land* in *The Double Hook*—similarly serve still another shared duality. Each novel is both obviously in a mainstream Eurocentric literary tradition and eddying on its edge. That marginal and double movement—on the side, going with and against the flow—suggests the Canadian provenance of both texts and suggests, too, that the "colonial cringe" literary position often enforced by perceived marginality (the supposition that nothing of worth exists here and so we must write about somewhere else) has been superseded by a more upright stance (the recognition that especially on the margin there is much to write about precisely because it does not fully fit the established paradigms). Are crucifixions in British Columbia, for example, the same as those in Palestine? Does a British Columbia *Waste Land* resonate the same as Eliot's vaguely Old World one, especially if the main voice in that New World "Waste Land" is the laughing bark of Coyote and not the rolling dictates of the Sanskrit thunder?

Even more than O'Hagan, Watson pervasively insists that the paradigms of the popular American Western do not fit the Canadian West. Tay John can resolutely refuse to be cast as the traditional hero even as he half plays that same role. Thus, although he is clearly the best man among the Shuswap, he does not become, as they had anticipated, the one leader who can save them. Killing the grizzly bear in single-handed combat, his most heroic exploit from Denham's white perspective (and think what a wonderful movie episode it could be), is also a major failure in the context of Tay John's Native heritage, for the bear should have been his guardian spirit, not his enemy, and it was protecting its cub, as he was not protecting his people. But Watson's male protagonist, James Potter, departs far more radically from any prescribed pattern of Western heroism when his conflict is with his mother whom he kills to flee from that crime and from Lenchen Wagner, the young woman he has left pregnant. And he can't even successfully run away but, somehow, has to come back to reestablish the domesticity he had seemingly so decisively destroyed. Were a movie made, the role of James Potter hardly cries out for a John Wayne.

Yet *The Double Hook,* again like *Tay John,* explicitly invokes the conventional American Western that it also countermands. The central matricide is, after all, a grotesque literalizing of the condition of many Western heroes, men who have, in a figurative sense, murdered their mothers to achieve a radical freedom from all claims of dependence and domesticity. Suffice to say, it hardly works out that way when the figurative killing becomes literal but somehow still remains as normal, as natural as the figurative one. Both novels, in fact, parody the traditional Western right up to their final episodes. Tay John opts for the wilderness, a standard heroic ploy, but he takes Ardith with him and that ruins the whole effect of man alone against nature. James flees, first in the wrong direction, to the town, not to the wilderness, and then, even worse, he runs back again to Lenchen and the coming baby. The two novelists thereby undo that central tautology of the classic Western whereby the lone hero proves his manhood which validates his independence which reaffirms his aloneness.

Watson, however (and unlike O'Hagan), also plays female narrative off against male, usually to the detriment of the latter. The historical and fictional presence of women, she insists, like the presence of the Native, counters the conventional Western's claims to univocal universality. White men will not have the last words either as whites or as men. "This is my day. You'll not fish today" (19) James says to his mother as he pushes her to her death on the stairs in the family cabin, and he is wrong on both counts. She still has her day and her fishing. She remains, despite the fact of her death, an uncanny presence in the novel. He never had a worse day in his life. O'Hagan, as Marjorie Fee aptly notes, keeps "a firm narrative focus on [the] cleavages" of his women characters and even when he sends Ardith into the mountains with Tay John she "is 'freed' only to become part of another male myth, where she does the cooking, and depends on Tay John for survival."[2] Watson eschews such sexism. Even Coyote is never specified as (a common Native designation) Old Man Coyote. Maybe she is Old Woman Coyote.

Despite *The Double Hook*'s immense critical success (it has been deemed the work that "made modern Canadian writing possible")[3] and despite her long career as a professor of English at the University of Alberta, Watson herself has been reticent about her achievement as an author. In one of her few public statements as a practicing artist, provocatively titled "What I'm Going To Do" and first delivered as a preface to a reading from *The Double Hook,* she does indicate something of the book's coming into being. As she makes clear, it is a process that starts when, in 1934 and at the height of the Depression, she accepted the one teaching position she was offered and, with "no idea where it was," set off for the small isolated Indian village of Dog Creek in the interior of British Columbia.[4] Dog Creek is then played off against Toronto as another setting for the novel's genesis. Later, "right in the middle of Bloor Street," Watson decides to attempt the novel "in answer to a challenge that you could not write about particular places in Canada: that what you'd end up with was a regional novel of some kind."[5] The figurative and literal distance between those two places sets Watson her task of writing of a different place without falling into the trap of the merely "regional."[6]

That challenge was a product of Canadian literary history as well as of Canadian social geography. As Stephen Scobie notes: "The argument against 'regional' writing was a late vestige of Canadian colonial insecurity. It was not so much that a novel could not be regional as that the region could not be Canadian."[7] Watson anticipated as much and in another part of the passage previously quoted slyly enlists colonial insecurity in solving the same problem that it partly caused:

It was at the time, I suppose, when people were thinking that if you wrote a novel it had to be, in some mysterious way, international. It had to be about what I would call something *else*. And so, I thought, I don't see why: how do you . . . how are you international if you're not international? if you're very provincial, very local, and very much a part of your own milieu.[8]

The mystery of the international novel lies in it being "about . . . something *else*," and that "else," ever elsewhere, forces a different reading of centers and margins. If Bloor Street is seen as the center that defines Dog Creek as marginal, there are still other centers—London, Paris, New York—from which Bloor Street is going to look rather like Dog Creek. From Dog Creek, however, they are all equally distant and very much the same. The claimed center is marginalized, and the ostensible margin is made central to and inseparable from the lives of the characters who inhabit it. Toronto can hardly be the center that defines Coyote.

Watson goes on to note that she also "wanted to do something too about the West, which wasn't a Western; and about Indians which wasn't about . . . Indians," and she does so by erasing, on a more immediate level, another ostensible distinction between the central (i.e., white) and the marginal (i.e., Native).[9] We simply are not told whether the characters portrayed are Native, white, or of mixed ancestry, and they have been, in different readings of the novel, differently consigned to each of those categories. On one edge of the setting there is an Indian Reserve; on another edge there is a seemingly white town. The characters and the action of the novel occupy some indefinite ground somewhere between these edges, and thus there is no way to read the novel in terms of racialist or antiracialist biases for or against either race. The murder on which the plot turns can be read as an allegory of white alienation in the most isolated reaches of the country and, simultaneously, as a parable of Native self-hatred and violence, the inevitable consequence of colonial rule. Coyote would no doubt laugh at both readings, a laugh that might also warn us of the ways we typically encode actions according to racial stereotypes.

Coyote figures prominently in the way Watson worked out what she wanted to do and how she might do it. Coyote, right from the first, from before the story even begins, also plays a large role in the novel itself, for *The Double Hook's* oblique, self-generated, poetic epigraph shows Coyote doubly at work, in the text and on it:

He doesn't know
you can't catch
the glory on a hook
and hold on to it.
That when you
fish for the glory
you catch the
darkness too.
That if you hook
twice the glory
you hook
twice the fear. (15)

This is an elusive passage. Just who are "he" and "you"? What does he know? What can you catch? Does catching "the darkness too" mean that you can, after all, catch the glory that earlier you could not? Furthermore, how do you hook, even conditionally ("if"), both "twice the glory" and "twice the fear"? From no catch to a catch to a dubiously doubled catch and all in the same brief passage, which is beginning to sound rather like a tale told by a fisherman—full of sound signifying exaggeration. Somehow metaphor has merged into mysticism or hyperbole but without ever making clear its terms, its tenor, and its transformation, all of which "he doesn't know." Perhaps Coyote does. After all, the entire novel, as earlier noted, unfolds "under Coyote's eye" (19). But at the outset Coyote is not talking, and could we believe that traditional trickster if he did? Coyote, after all, "is a master of lies."[10]

The problems posed by the epigraph, Douglas Barbour argues, can be largely answered by noting that its very existence "was the result of an editorial decision which McClelland & Stewart made without consulting Mrs. Watson. Because Professor Salter's Preface did not quite fill all the pages set aside for it . . . , Kip's statement . . . was inserted as a prefatory quotation." That prominent placing, unsanctioned by the author, has made the passage, Barbour contends, "appear far more important to critics of the novel than might have been the case had it existed only as the thoughts of a single character at a certain point in the narrative."[11] Consequently, for Barbour, the intrusive epigraph can only misdirect the too-attentive critic or reader. But does not the epigraph unauthorized fit the novel far better than it ever could authorized? A promised preface a little too short along with the exigencies of publishing give us a separate page and a "prefatory quotation." This is contingency, accident, and misdirection at work, or, in a word, Coyote. The narration that unfolds "under Coyote's eye" is, seemingly, transmitted into text under his supervision as well.

The novel unfolds under the watchful eye of Coyote, and, up to a certain point, it just as much unfolds under the watchful eye of Kip, who is early designated by Coyote as "my servant Kip" (35). As a servant, however, Kip also has a program of his own that explains his attempt to be a one-man panopticon even as he plays Pandarus too. More specifically, he keeps close tabs on the unfolding affair between James Potter and Lenchen Wagner not just for his vicarious and voyeuristic pleasure, but because he also plans to take James's part. Thus the lovers, even at their most secret meeting, could not elude his keen vigilance, and that attention casts, as intended, a certain shadow over their lovemaking, a shadow under which James's personal crisis grows marvelously to include even matricide. James, in effect, is being pushed into acting as Kip's servant—and as Coyote's. Through the agency of James, Coyote can have the old woman, James's mother, and carry her away, as Kip sees or foresees, "like a rabbit in his mouth" (57), and, also through the agency of James, Kip well might end up with the young one. That at least is his plan, and as he watches it unfolding and finds it good, we encounter the passage that appropriately—it sits in the middle of the mischief of the text—provides the epigraph:

> Kip's mind was on James. James's strength. James's weakness. James's old mother. James and Greta [James's sister]. James and the girl Wagner. The messages he'd taken for James.
> He's like his old lady, Kip thought. There's a thing he doesn't know. He doesn't know you can't catch the glory on a hook and hold onto it. That when you fish for the glory you catch the darkness too. That if you hook twice the glory you hook twice the fear. That Coyote plotting to catch the glory for himself is fooled and every day fools others. He doesn't know, Kip thought, how much mischief Coyote can make. (61)

Some of the earlier questions implicit in the epigraph can now be resolved. "He" is, to start with, James. The "glory" and the "darkness" reflect those dualities in which James, his baby about to be born and his mother recently killed, is at this point inextricably entangled: family (either one) as refuge and trap; love as gain and loss; life as birth and death. In short, James, as fisher and as fished for, is himself doubly and thoroughly caught. Yet what Kip says about James is, we soon see, just as true of Kip. He has been fishing too, and it is he who especially catches the darkness when he is literally blinded in the text by a blow from James's whip precisely because of what he did not see even as he prided himself—"these eyes seen plenty" (56)—on missing nothing. Kip didn't "know" either the "mischief" Coyote could "make" for his own servant as much as for anyone else.

Blinded, Kip does begin to see better. He can, for example, finally admit just what he was trying to do and recognize the justice of the consequences: "I keep thinking about James, Kip said. I kept at him like a dog till he beat around the way a porcupine beats with his tail" (133). But is James exonerated for the blinding when Kip takes the blame on himself? Still more to the point, can matricide also be attributed mostly to Kip as a would-be Coyote making mischief badly; can it be exonerated as a kind of innocent "porcupine" reaction to Kip's (or Coyote's) badgering? Those are questions that the novel neither specifically answers nor, for that matter, ever even poses. Indeed, one of the more idiosyncratic features of this idiosyncratic text is the resolute indirection with which it never faces the crucial killing on which so much of the action turns. Do we have grounds for a charge of murder or of manslaughter? Or was the death mostly an unfortunate accident, a misplaced push on the stairway that got out of hand? When James much later "asked himself now for the first time what he'd really intended to do when he'd defied his mother at the head of the stairs" (98), he does not himself have an answer and declines to accept the one (intentional self-destruction) that Coyote at once conveniently provides. Was there even any "death" at all or do we have merely a transformation from one continuation to another, for the murdered mother gone fishing grimly endures her death in much the same manner that she apparently endured her life.

There is something coy in the presentation of the killing from the very start. Corresponding to the epigraph is another passage set apart from the text to follow. The novel proper begins with a poetically cast listing of the characters, who "*lived*" (emphasis added) "in the folds of the hills/under Coyote's eye" (19). Heading the list is "the old lady, mother of William/of James and of Greta." It would seem that this *dramatis personae* has been provided only to be at once rendered inaccurate. We can notice, too, how it trails off into an appended qualifying and textually isolated phrase—"until one morning in July"—that serves to call the information just presented into question, whereupon, with another break in the text but no break in punctuation, the action of the novel commences:

> Greta was at the stove. Turning hotcakes. Reaching for the coffee beans. Grinding away James's voice.
>
> James was at the top of the stairs. His hand half-raised. His voice in the rafters.

James walking away. The old lady falling. There under the jaw of the roof. In the vault of the bed loft. Into the shadow of death. Pushed by James's will. By James's hand. By James's words: This is my day. You'll not fish today. (19)

Baking hotcakes, making coffee, and killing mother: those actions make an odd mixture with which to begin the morning and the novel. The dead-pan conjunction of the three evokes the grim humor of the theatre of the absurd. Even the phrasing introducing the mundane ("Greta was at . . .") and the matricide ("James was at . . .") equates the two and thereby suggests that murdering mother and preparing breakfast are either equally meaningless or (much the same thing) equally meaningful.[12] The double hook is already being set. The crime is also curiously disclaimed even as it is enacted, for that enactment is not described but only its immediate aftermath—"James walking away," leaving responsibility elsewhere, to "James's will," "James's hand," "James's word." With this trio of unlikely suspects, James's action is not at all broken down into constituent parts to provide a human calculus whereby that action can be reconstituted and explained.

Explanation is itself mocked in the text from the very beginning by being comically embodied in James's prolix elder brother. As the authorial voice early observes, even before this character is encountered, "William would try to explain, but he couldn't. He only felt, but he always felt he knew. He could give half a dozen reasons for anything" (20–21). The test case is "a spool of thread" William was asked, as postman, to fetch "from the town below" for a woman on his route. "He'd explain that thread has a hundred uses. When it comes down to it, he'd say, there's no telling what thread is for" (21). Excess of explanations cancels explanation out, and William's perpetual bemusement regularly yields mostly anecdote: "I knew a woman once, he'd say, who used it to sew up her man after he was throwed on a barbed-wire fence" (21). The narration explains William even as it calls explanation into question and then cagily verifies its own explanation with the anecdote into which his devolves. That same "anecdote" also explains on a larger level. William characteristically fails to notice how close to home his story of a fractured family rethreaded together comes. What the text takes away with one hand, it gives with the other.

It gives, however, no reason or justification for the crucial killing, so a number of critics have labored to remedy that lack. One easy explanation is to blame the victim, and there has been a good deal of Ma-bashing, starting with early reviewers who described Mrs. Potter as the "sinister force which has held [James and Greta] since childhood in a net of fear and sterility";

as James's "tyrannous, possessive mother"; as "the old lady whose tyranny had held [James] and his sister in thrall."[13] And subsequently Mrs. Potter has been generally cast as a woman "whose concentrated ferocity brought fear, darkness and death" to the community, as a mother who has "given life only to strangle it."[14] Even if she does not obviously deserve to die, it is still somehow right, a recent critic argues, that she does: "James had to kill the old woman, to descend into the 'valley of adversity,' to confront his fear, before he can be redeemed."[15]

In its more modest form that last quotation especially illustrates the agenda of this whole explanatory enterprise. It is James whose fate matters, whose actions must somehow be redeemed. Such concern constitutes what could well be termed a cowboy reading of the text—casting the son as hero, having him finally claim his home on the range. This privileging of the male protagonist, however, strangely domesticates him at the cost of whatever radical innocence may have inhered in his original action as portrayed in the novel. A fable that problematizes the constructs of good and evil, that may be in the Nietzschean sense beyond them, is mythologized in the most mundane Barthesian sense into the simplistic virtue and vice of the conventional Western, as if James wore a white hat and was never the first to draw, while Ma twirled her black moustache and cheated at poker.

What the mother might have been before her death is not described in the novel. What is portrayed is her enduring afterward, and so the problem of interpretation that centers in Mrs. Potter would seem to be not what she, living, might have done, but what she, although dead, continues doing:

> Still the old lady fished. If the reeds had dried up and the banks folded and crumbled down she would have fished still. If God had come into the valley, come holding out the long finger of salvation, moaning in the darkness, thundering down the gap at the lake head, skimming across the water, drying up the blue signature like blotting-paper, asking where, asking why, defying an answer, she would have thrown her line against the rebuke; she would have caught a piece of mud and looked it over; she would have drawn a line with the barb when the fire of righteousness baked the bottom. (20)

Action beyond apocalypse; the dead woman's design defying God's; this is still fishing with a vengeance, all of which poses the question of just what does she fish for with such implacable determination. Is it the very salvation that in this same passage concerns her so little?

One is tempted to conflate the numerous Biblical references in the text, including the possible Christian implications of Mrs. Potter's postmortem fishing ("the fish is, of course, a conventional symbol of Christ")[16] and the way in which she apparently at last finds peace, "just standing [by a 'pool'] like a tree with its roots reaching out to water" (118). Put them all together and they do seem to spell out a Christian parable of life lost in life to be found after death, a parable that is all the more tempting when also applied to the other (living) characters who are thereby seen as finally working out a more earthly model of redemption as they too make their way through a sterile wasteland world to the symbolic waters of rebirth and regeneration.

Like the cowboy reading of James's innocence, this Christian reading of the text's morality has been widely argued. "The message of *The Double Hook*," one critic insists, "is religious. It is a story about redemption written from a Christian vantage point."[17] Another maintains that through "the process of identifying the biblical associations one makes in reading *The Double Hook*," even "Coyote's identity is revealed," and he turns out to have "his prototype in the Jehovah-figure of the Old Testament."[18] Thus Mrs. Potter, carried off by Coyote, "is 'redeemed' like the other characters," and the whole novel becomes "a re-telling of the universal, supra-regional, and timeless story of God's love for mankind."[19]

The problem here, however, is that Mrs. Potter's proclaimed salvation after death, like her proposed sinful life, is a postulation largely extraneous to the text. "By the process of association," Beverley Mitchell argues, "Mrs. Potter appears to have her prototype in those figures of the Old Testament whose actions brought suffering to others."[20] But the critic has provided the associations that "define" the character. "Like the cunning and crafty men described in Job, Mrs. Potter is one of those who 'meet with darkness in the daytime, and at noonday . . . grope as though it were night' (Jb. 5:14)."[21] Why these fumblers from the Book of Job? Why not a female Diogenes with her lantern looking for an honest man or even an honest son?[22]

Coyote especially problematizes any Christian reading. Consider, for example, the frequent Biblical cast of her speech. By borrowing the diction of the Christian God, does she become a stand-in, even an agent for that God, or a mock, a parody? Does the double demonstrate identity or difference, and, even more to the point, what does identity or difference itself prove? Thus Mitchell equates Coyote with God to see Coyote as a version of God, but why could not the same equation just as validly render God a version of Coyote? Similarly, Steven Putzel argues that "Coyote's biblical echoes transform the dry rocks of British Columbia into a Palestine, a holy land" and never considers the possibility that the echoes might reverberate quite the other way to translate even a Palestine, a holy land, into more dry rocks and just another British Columbia.[23] Neither is difference necessarily definitive. Disputing Mitchell's reading of Coyote as God, Scobie insists that the Biblical "parallels do not establish an identification." Rather, they establish the fraudulent nature of Coyote's "claim," which, for Scobie, is "presumptuous parody, seen at its most blasphemous when [Coyote] welcomes Greta's pitiful suicide with the words of the Song of Solomon."[24] Yet the very privileging of God implicit in positing blasphemy is hardly sanctioned in a text in which Coyote has the best lines (not always Biblical) and the last word too. Moreover, functioning as both God (ubiquitous, controlling, beyond human ken) and not-God (contingency, accident, a trickster often tricked himself), Coyote, like the text, calls the very possibility of definitive difference into question. Indeed, from the Coyote point-of-view, God is just another Coyote who comically but quite characteristically overstates his claims.

So for what, metaphorically speaking, might the old woman have gone fishing? One possibility is for Coyote himself. With his sign—tracks, voice, spittle in the form of prickly pear—everywhere and he himself nowhere, Coyote, like the dead Mrs. Potter, is uncannily both present and missing in the text. And appropriately so. Coyote as an Indian trickster god enigmatically given to Christian claims and phrasings is a supernatural figure partly in one cosmos and partly in another, with each calling the other into question. Coyote is thus roughly analogous to the little community of the novel situated, as earlier noted, indefinitely between the residual world of the surviving Indians and the larger world of white civilization with its local outpost of the town. Presided over by Coyote, there is a conjunction between the broken present (the state of the town) and the broken past (the state of the Reserve) enacted in and on the broken landscape—"as if it had been dropped carelessly wrinkled on the bare floor of the world" (22)—in which the novel is appropriately grounded. Caught in that conjunction are all of the characters. Mrs. Potter, "fishing upstream to the source" (21), could be searching for Coyote and thereby attempting to resolve after her death one of the ambiguities of her life. But if she seeks to at last ground her being in its Indian source, that source itself well may be in the process of disappearing or at least becoming something else as indicated by Coyote's propensity (protective disguise?) to pass herself off as the Christian God. Or perhaps Mrs. Potter fishes to evade Coyote. Or maybe she wants merely to continue after death as before, to just go fishing. It is an eternity any fisherwoman would understand. In short, the obvious consideration that Mrs. Potter is a wounded (unto death) Fisher Queen does not tell us how her wound or her fishing signify in the "Waste Land" context of *The Double Hook*.

The fate of the dead mother never becomes clear, and neither do we fare much better with the surviving son who, late in the novel, claims for himself a new freedom (freedom from freedom) and then attempts, with the full complicity of the text, to put that limiting freedom into definitive practice. It is a freedom founded, first, on the almost preordained failure of his attempt to flee from both the death of his mother and the affair with Lenchen, but a freedom also founded on his own and the text's duplicity in claiming it and, as such, cannot be taken at its own paradoxical and oxymoronic face value.

Arriving in the town knowing nothing as to how he might proceed farther—"He had no idea what a railway ticket would cost. He'd no idea where to buy a ticket to. He knew nothing about the train except that it went to the packing house, no way of boarding it except through the loading-pens" (99)—James withdraws from the town bank all his family's money, flaunts it, and consequently soon loses it. He is taken in hand, taken to the bar, taken to the whorehouse, and then simply taken. After he had already paid for food and company but enjoyed neither, one of the girls follows him out into the night. Pretending a special attraction, she lifts his wallet with all his remaining cash and then abandons him to rejoin Traff, the "friend" who had been showing James the town. Peering in through the whorehouse window, James sees Traff counting the money, knows he has been robbed, and accedes to that fact with the realization that carries him through to the end of the novel: "The flick of a girl's hand had freed James from freedom. He'd kissed away escape in the mud by the river. He thought now of Lenchen and the child who would wear his face. Alone on the edge of the town where men clung together for protection, he saw clearly for a moment his simple hope" (121).

We might notice, first, that the paradox of James's being freed "from freedom" by a fortunate theft highlights a problematics of freedom characteristically ignored in conventional Westerns. The freedom to abjure the constraints of civilization and, in Huck Finn's terms, light out for the territories is a freedom not so much of radical possibility, but of evasive action. It is a freedom rigorously patterned into the very form of the standard Western and consists of little more than the hero's perpetual potentiality for dislocations in space and action (particularly romantic action). In other words, the Western hero's requisite refusal to be bound in one place, to be claimed by domicile and domesticity, leaves him bound by movement, bound in and for many places instead of one. Thus, in old-fashioned Westerns, the hero at most kissed the girl and rode away. In modern versions he might sleep with her first, but he still must move on. To wait almost nine months and then to ride frantically away a day or so before the baby arrives spoils the whole effect. The call to further adventure ("a man's gotta do what a man's gotta do") begins to look suspiciously like a callow shirking of responsibility. Yet what fundamental difference does a few months make? So James's belated flight compromises departures more judiciously timed. Neither does the end of that flight—to be willingly robbed by a prostitute—counterbalance the support he was not prepared to provide for Lenchen.

James claims to be saved by his fortuitous fleecing; by accident and hazard; by, if one will, Coyote, all of which glosses over his own complicity in his victimization. The text, however, foregrounds and exposes this glossing but not the similar glossing of the murder of the mother. For example, James's first purchase in town, is, suggestively, a wallet for which he pays cash because, he suggestively asserts, then "you've got ownership rights on it and can smash it up if you so choose" (95–96). In his fashion he so chooses and soon loses both the wallet and his remaining cash to the comically noxious Traff (note the reversed word that gives him his name). Even the parrot in the bar, conveniently trained to proclaim "drinks all round" and "drinks on you" (100), was plucking the young man clean, which is one of the reasons Traff hustles James away. As he observes, "it might as well be me as someone else" (102), especially a parrot. Even after Traff has the cash, the town knows that he is a thief, so any kind of outcry could have brought action, and James well might have recovered most of his money. James, in effect, desires and promotes the resolution he achieves, but he also wants it to seem as if that resolution is quite out of his own hands. The forced nonfreedom (contingency) that frees him from the false freedom of evasive escape is itself a fraud and is shown as such.

The novel, too, participates in the protagonist's strategy of both claiming and disclaiming a desired punishment. Consider, for example, how James at one point acknowledges his unconvincing rationale for being "drawn to Traff," by his "cap of hair, straight and thick and yellow as Lenchen's" (106). The author and the character here contrive a redeeming victimization that somehow reverses James's previous mistreatment of Lenchen. This time he will be the one seduced and abandoned and by a Lenchen at that. In much the same fashion, "the slanted edge of the bank" (107) and "her hands pressed against his chest" (108) as his wallet is taken evoke the stairway and his killing of his mother. Again he suffers a parodic diminuendo of what he has already done, and the text writes his coming restitution every bit as duplicitously as he is seeking it through his complicity in his own victimization.

The text labors in another way, too, to return the reader and the protagonist to the impending resolution. As Margaret Morriss early observed, the "nature [of the town] is basically that of the wilderness," and "in effect,

James has merely escaped to another wasteland." The two are "parallel" to such a degree that the second can even give James versions of what is concomitantly happening in the first. Thus "the brothel smells of 'bodies and kerosene burning away'" evoke "Greta's self-destruction of which James is unaware."[25] Other connections can also be noted. Lenchen is briefly replaced in James's fumbling and ambivalent embrace by Lilly: "Go away, he said. His arm pulled her close" (108). Felicia, the keeper of the brothel, is, of course, the feminine form of Felix, the one admirable man in the village, and Felicia offers, like Felix, food and other comforts (admittedly for a price) to those who come to her door.

The smallest and most dubious of communities, the prostitutes and their patrons, mirrors, especially in its imperfections, the very mess from which James fled, and thus the limit of his escape, the farthest that he can go (experientially, psychologically, financially), returns him to his origins and the reasons for his flight. The woman who will soon rob him, moreover, tells him as much. "We all mean all right, Lilly said. It's just there's no future in it. Drinking and crying, and everything being washed up the next day" (106). It is precisely that "no future" that the novel arranges for James in the town which allows him a future back in the folds of the hills, a future different from the forced and lonely freedom the standard Western has long demanded of its heroes.

The Double Hook forces itself into plot and pattern, into regionalism and psychological realism in order to force a resolution. With that resolution coming, the novel too can come home again, can return to the mythic play of its first parts, a turn which comes at the very conclusion of part four:

> The life which Traff and Lilly led behind Felicia's dull glass belonged under Felicia's narrow roof. In the distance across the flats James could see the lights of the station and across from them the lights of the hotel where the parrot who lived between two worlds was probably asleep now, stupid with beer and age.
>
> James stood for a moment in the moonlight among the clumps of stiff sage which shoved through the seams and pockets of the earth. (109)

Opposed to life as narrowly constrained, as dull and stupid, we have the potentiality of the man in the moonlight with life burgeoning around him even through the cracked and broken earth. Whatever the message or meaning that might be abstracted from these moon-illumined clumps of sage thrusting through a desert landscape, it is qualitatively different from that of the drunk parrot at last silently asleep.

The same suggestive scene of contemplating the finally indeterminant poetry of things which ends part four is then repeated in a distinctly different key as the first sentence of the final section of the novel. "William stood looking into the charred roots of the honeysuckle" (113). How does one read those burned roots, the smoke that "rose from the charred logs," the "bones [that might] come together bone to bone" for one to "prophesy upon" (113–14)? William's answers are, characteristically, different, diffuse, and contradictory: "A hammer never hits once, he said. It gets the habit of striking" and "Ma was hard on her [Greta], he said. She thought grief was what a woman was born to sooner or later" (113). Ara's answer is a vision of welling water and leaping fish. Coyote's is a bark from a dry rock ledge: "Happy are the dead/ for their eyes see no more" (115). The rock is definitely there whereas the water is not; nevertheless, Coyote's response cannot be the final one either. Life goes on, as marked by the birth of the baby. So, too, does death, as indicated by the continuing passing of Mrs. Potter whose active dying has been an issue from the start. The end of that process— the end of her fishing—seems in sight when she is last seen "standing by [Felix's] brown pool . . . . Just standing like a tree with its roots reaching out to water" (117–18).

The young lovers together again, the baby born, the house of Potter to be rebuilt—this conclusion does tempt us to see the novel as finally affirmative. It is a temptation easily acceded to. As George Bowering notes, "all readers of the text agree that we have a more-or-less happy ending, a kind of transformation or resurrection, a new testament. A revelation (I, Coyote, saw this) under the seer's eye." But Bowering also rightly warns against going "too far" in positing "James as redeemer and renewer," for he did kill his mother, blind Kip, and abandon Lenchen.[26] We can remember what he has previously done and have also seen how much his return is premised on his continued misreading of who and what he is. Ara, near the conclusion, maintains that James "never in all his life had strength enough to set himself against things" (123), an observation that seems as true at the end as at the beginning. James let himself be carried away and he let himself be carried back.[27] Any proclaimed final regeneration of this character is therefore doubly suspect in that it is both unprecedented and untested.

If anything, the conclusion of the novel attests to how little James has changed. Particularly germane is his first reaction to the "seared and smouldering earth, the bare hot cinder" of what had previously been his home. "He felt as he stood with his eyes closed on the destruction of what his heart had wished destroyed that by some generous gesture he had been turned once more into the first pasture of things" (131). The gesture points to only his own still self-deceived desire. At the end of the disastrous process he dreams origins again and, despite the different evidence all around him, posits some green Eden in which, by definition, there would be no trace of what he has already done. But there would be, of course, every possibility of him doing it all over again.

The same point is even more implicit in James's immediate promise to rebuild the family house. His decision to locate the new dwelling "further down the creek" can well represent a wise move from the previous disastrous site, but his decision to build "all on one floor" (131) is definitely suspect. No stairway, no shove, no death. The equation need not hold even in a one-story house of Potter and definitely doesn't hold in the world of the novel. Coyote, in the last words of the text, sets the feet of James's and Lenchen's baby "on soft ground; / . . . on the sloping shoulders / of the world" (134). As has been amply demonstrated, those same shoulders slope for parents too.

With this concluding conjunction of set feet and soft ground, set feet and the sloping shoulders of the world, the novel demonstrates again its ability to unsay what it says even in the act of saying it. In other words—and this book both perpetually demands and precludes "other words"—the reader is caught on the double hooks of the text (living/dying, articulation/silence, God/Coyote, meaning/meaninglessness, even, if one wishes, construction/ deconstruction) as firmly at the end as at the beginning. Or as the epigraph in retrospect suggests, you can't catch the glory of this text on the hook of a final definitive interpretation, for when you fish for story you catch the darkness too, especially if your fishing partners are a dead Fisher Queen who still waits for the right questions and Coyote who happily provides all the wrong answers.

4 The Archaeology of *Badlands*

In a 1980 essay, "On Being an Alberta Writer: Or, I Wanted to Tell Our Story," Robert Kroetsch retrospectively grounds his career as one of Canada's most versatile postmodernist authors in a story from his premodernist childhood. On his father's farm, a large farm worked by horses, was "a ring of stones in the prairie grass," which was "strangely, plowed around" instead of being plowed under. He asked his mother once about this unusual feature of the local landscape, and, because "she had, then, never heard of a tipi ring; she said the stones were magical. I suspect now," Kroetsch continues, "that her notion of magical went back two or three generations to the forests of southern Germany, surviving that long transcription through Wisconsin and Minnesota to the District and then the Province of Alberta. The connection between the name and the named—the importance and the failure of that connection—is one of my obsessions." And even more to the point, "I was that day on my way to embracing the model of archaeology, against that of history. The authorized history, the given definition of history, was betraying us on those prairies."[1]

The betrayal works the other way too. A few years later his father allowed workers building a dam to remove the stones, after which the sod where they had been was broken by the plow. But one evening at supper, "out of nowhere," the father admitted that "he'd made a mistake. . . . For reasons he couldn't understand, he felt guilty." There are lessons for the future writer here also: "Where I had learned the idea of absence, I was beginning to learn the idea of trace. There is always something left behind. . . . Even abandonment gives us memory."[2] The interconnections between artifact and absence, between betrayal and history can be complex indeed.

Kroetsch concludes this same essay by suggesting a mode of entrance into that complexity and interplay. "Archaeology allows for the fragmentary nature of the story, against the coerced unity of traditional history. Archaeology allows for discontinuity. It allows for layering. It allows for imaginative speculation."[3] As he elsewhere observes, the "archaeological model [also] allows us to . . . keep . . . systems very tentative. Instead of a sense of failure at not being able to pull it all together, what excites us is that very incompleteness. Systems are open to adjustment, to change, to game, to our elaboration."[4] In short, "it's like the man looking for Troy—he's always finding one more city beneath the city."[5]

The foregoing quotations conjoin archaeology as practiced by Michel Foucault with archaeology as practiced by Heinrich Schliemann. Kroetsch, moreover, admits as much. "On Being an Alberta Writer" concludes:

> I am aware that it is the great French historian, Michel Foucault, who has formalized our understanding of the appropriateness of the archaeological method. But the prairie writer understands that appropriateness in terms of the particulars of place: newspaper files, place names, shoe boxes full of old photographs, tall tales, diaries, journals, tipi rings, weather reports, business ledgers, voting records—even the wrong-headed histories written by eastern historians become, rather than narratives of the past, archaeological deposits.[6]

All items up to the final one in this Kroetschian catalog give us archaeology as an uncovering of the hitherto buried site (Schliemann); conjoined with the last they give us archaeology as a remapping of previous discursive practice (Foucault).

Like Rudy Wiebe, Kroetsch obviously distrusts the official history (and, indeed, any and all master narratives). "Unlike Wiebe, however, Kroetsch," Linda Hutcheon has recently argued, "embodies this view most materially— almost literally—*not* in his fiction, but in his poetry" and particularly in such works as the "1977 edition of his *Seed Catalogue* [which] takes an original 1917 catalogue" that he found in the Glenbow Museum in Calgary "and prints the first poems of the book on faint reproductions of its pages."[7] Hutcheon sees such a conjoining of literature and history as "a poetic form of [what she has aptly termed] historiographic metafiction."[8] *Seed Catalogue* is certainly that, but it is something more too. The retrieval of the 1917 catalog and the interplay between the 1917 text and the 1977 text, part of which repeats part of the 1917 text onto and against which it is set, can also be seen as a poetic form of what might be designated archaeologiographic (in the modes of both Schliemann and Foucault) metafiction. Nor is the poetry, viewed from this perspective, that different from the fiction, which is also written out of and onto earlier texts. "In a very real sense," Kroetsch observes, "we make books out of books."[9]

Kroetsch also observes that, considering his interest in archaeology, "it's no accident that [he] wrote *Badlands*."[10] Certainly, this novel, recounting a daughter's search, after her father's death, for that dinosaur-hunting antecedent, most thematizes archaeology, just as, of all of Kroetsch's novels, it is most obviously structured through archaeological metaphors and consequently most demands an archaeological reading:

> As a *river* voyage that *descends* into *unknown territory* through stratified *layers* of rock back to *source* the *journey* [in *Badlands*] takes on a host of metaphoric connotations: it is a symbolic *Homeric* voyage, a descent into the *underworld*, another *heart of darkness* excursion into *hidden realms of consciousness*, a plunge into the *grave*, the *dig*, the *site*, into *chaos, legend, trace, text.* The packed, bone-filled landscape is indeed fertile.[11]

Robert Lecker's packed exegesis also effectively illustrates just how much *Badlands* is a composite narrative, a text forged out of references to other texts such as, for obvious example, the novel's near namesake, T. S. Eliot's *The Waste Land* (1922). Furthermore, and as in that poem, literary references are also calculated reading directives and part of a structure of meaning. Thus the singular *Waste Land* can be subsumed in the plural *Badlands* that provide a singular physical site for fictional journeys themselves mirrored by the metaphysical quest enacted by and in the poem. In each work, moreover, quest is itself largely rendered through references to other quests, which sets up an interplay between the context of the present narration and the other texts that partly comprise that context. For example, the modern master narrative for the ordering quest, for shoring fragments against ruins, *The Waste Land* is itself countermanded by *Badlands*'s exploding of quest, by the novel's refusal to shore anything or be shored anywhere. As Mark Simpson points out, *Badlands* "aims to remain aimless, to offer, in insistently playful fashion, oscillating and palimpsestic narrative possibilities."[12] But those possibilities are still grounded in the text, in the texts within the text, and consequently a literary dig is again in order.

Most immediately (and especially from a Canadian perspective), *Badlands* clearly has a *Surfacing* (1973) stratum. Through "a journey into the wilderness" and a "process of uninventing," Kroetsch early observed of Margaret

Atwood's novel, the protagonist "give[s] birth to her true identity."[13] The same could well be said of Kroetsch's protagonist, Anna Dawe (with the cavil that "true identity" is a composite of fictive possibilities). In fact, both women start out on a search for the father but repudiate that search with its attendant patriarchal implications for the more pressing matter of discovering their missing selves—selves substantially missing because of those same "missing" fathers. Moreover, as the father sinks in significance (each sinking marked, not coincidentally, by the fact of his literal drowning), the mother rises. The protagonist in *Surfacing* recovers her mother through a sustained revision of who that mother was, while Anna Dawe recognizes Anna Yellowbird as her real figurative mother, a role the other woman accepts. In Jeanette Seim's apt summary: "Anna Dawe's naming (of the mother) and unnaming (of the father) marks the culmination of a liberating process of legitimization: the legitimization of Anna Dawe as daughter, as woman, and as narrator/artist."[14] These are the same legitimizations to which the protagonist of *Surfacing* aspires.

There is also a *Double Hook* horizon even though Kroetsch has claimed that he does not "think" this novel figures "in the strata" of any of his own "to any great extent."[15] Coyote, after all, does appear doubly in *Badlands,* prominently (as I will discuss later) in one of the two epigraphs and fleetingly in the text. Much of the novel, moreover, is doubled and duplicitously doubled at that—two quests, two Annas, two birds (a Dawe and a Yellowbird), two bears even. There are also, I would suggest, certain inversions of *The Double Hook* (reflecting it by turning it around). Watson's novel begins with an act to abrogate the mother; Kroetsch's ends with an act abrogating the father. James obviously fails in his attempt to leave his past behind; Anna seemingly succeeds. Furthermore, *The Double Hook,* as Kroetsch has noted, provides the "paradigmatic" place of Canadian fiction—"a house, an isolated community, a small town." In place of that place, *Badlands* features a river, a raft, characters settled only into their journeys and not very settled at that. Inversions do, indeed, again in Kroetsch's phrasing, "assert themselves, on this double hook."[16]

A more obvious layer, however (and one which takes us beyond Canada), is the novel's Faulknerian stratum. An early reviewer observed that *Badlands* "reads like a deliberate and sustained parody of Faulkner" and deemed that feature of the novel "unnecessary"; another praised the book's "Faulknerian tones of grandeur and wonder."[17] Faulkner's language is much in evidence and so too are some of his standard fictional ploys. Consider, for example, an early passage in *Badlands* describing how Anna Yellowbird, a fifteen-year-old Native widow, is first found huddled in a grave:

William Dawe, hunchbacked, small, made smaller by a broad-
brimmed black hat, moved stiffly off the open prairie and into the stand
of poplars. If he saw the scattering of graves, of roofs, he did not let
on; and yet he saved his shins from their grass-hid corners, marched
in abrupt irritation through Web's strawberry patch and stopped at the
base of the mound itself, stood combing his black beard with his fingers, watching while Web put out a hand in preparation to grasp and
then lift up the apparition that he, Web, could not quite believe in.

Dawe, watching, deciding.

And the woman also, the girl, watching, staring with luminous eye at
the tall man who bent over her, the hunchbacked man at his side; and
they, not she, might have been the apparitions, spirits at or even from
the surrounding graves that were themselves fading back into prairie
and bush.[18]

Dawe here comes onto the scene and into the novel in the same me-
chanical mode that characterizes Popeye in *Sanctuary* (1931) or any one of
the Snopeses (other than perhaps Flem). The second sentence then runs on
through action piled on action with interjected qualification marking the
participants' unwilling half-suspension of belief in that same ongoing action,
all of which leads to a participial suspension of grammar and action and a
balanced suspension at that—Dawe, watching, deciding; the girl, watching,
staring. With each side unreal to the other, a further balance, any possible
center for the scene is lost in a mirroring of apparitions. Reflection reflects
reflection and is thereby frozen by suddenly being framed through a much
vaster time scheme in which the graves themselves are seen dissolving back
into the landscape. The passage, in short, is a virtual compendium on how
to write Faulkner.

Faulkner is also conspicuously present through obvious *Absalom, Absalom!* (1936) parallels. As Ann Mandel has observed, Kroetsch "makes of
Dawe a kind of shrunken Sutpen who fails to found the dynasty and fame
he wants because he lives with an obsession that ignores human passions,
human error."[19] Dawe, again like Sutpen, is also specifically at war with
time, yet, thanks to a prefatory chronology, in both *Badlands* and *Absalom,
Absalom!* this assault on time is itself hopelessly grounded in time. Moreover, Dawe's assault on the past to defeat the future is also all couched
in a desperate rhetoric of "nothing is lost" that serves mostly to obscure
the fact that he is losing everything—wife, daughter, substitute sons, even
his beloved *Daweosaurus* (that was not found by Dawe)—just as Sutpen,
despite his furious enterprise, loses everything too, including his epony-

mous Sutpen's Hundred (that was not worked by Sutpen). So both *Daweo-saurus* and Sutpen's Hundred increasingly mock claims of success instead of proving them.

The son denied by the father in *Absalom, Absalom!* returns as the daughter denied in *Badlands*. In effect, the racial crisis of the one novel is transposed into the problematics of gender of the other, and in each case the point and etiology is the same. The father's design reflects the values of the society, values contravened by the disastrous effects of the design on his own family. Each father is also, as a father, a disaster. Sutpen aims Henry at Bon, which leaves one son literally dead and the other figuratively dead for years afterward. Dawe repudiates Anna to leave her figuratively dead for years and leaves Tune, the substitute son he half adopts in her place, literally dead when he consigns to Tune, a fifteen-year-old with only two weeks experience as a miner, the task of excavating a dinosaur with dynamite. It might also be noted that Sutpen's daughters fare somewhat better than his sons, resisting him and surviving him, which means that Anna has partial analogues in Judith and Clytemnestra as well as in Bon.

Underlying Faulkner are, obviously, James Joyce and Joseph Conrad. Perhaps Joyce and Conrad underwrite virtually every subsequent modernist or postmodernist author. But there are Joyce and Conrad horizons in *Badlands* that are something more than a ubiquitous concern for art. For example, just as Joyce's *Ulysses* (1922) is a resonant repetition of Homer's *Odyssey* in a different context, Kroetsch's *Badlands* is, in part, an inverted parody of that already parodic inversion. More specifically, Kroetsch turns the figurative son's search for a figurative father into the real daughter's search for the real father and then turns that into a search to shed the father, just as he also turns Joyce's encyclopedic documentation of his 1904 Dublin into an unwriting of an Alberta past that culminates in the literal destruction of the record, the photographs that Anna Yellowbird has previously saved and the field notes that Anna Dawe has. And of course Kroetsch's portrait of the artist as a middle-aged woman is itself a parodic double inversion of still another Joyce novel.

Conrad, too, is both echoed and reversed. The voyage in "Heart of Darkness" (1902) is up the river and then down, a course that Anna inverts. More to the point, the voyage in "Heart of Darkness" is also, for Marlow, a journey to a crushing awareness of his complicity in contemporary history (imperialism) and a recognition that a savage darkness characterizes Europe far more than it does Africa. In contrast, Anna Dawe's journey to the river's source ends in a carnivalesque liberation from the weight of her personal father-dominated past. Or perhaps it only seems to, for another possible item in the Conrad strata might be the artifact of the concluding lie. Marlow is at least partly compromised by his last action, the lie he tells to Kurtz's Intended. So, too, Robert Lecker argues, is Anna compromised by her final claim that "we did not once look back, not once, ever" (270), for her whole narrative is a subsequent retrospective account of how she at last reached that point of not looking back.[20]

Two other Conrad items might also be noted. Dawe, who "shook himself free of any need to share even his sufferings with another human being" (139), is a version of Kurtz in "Heart of Darkness" who had also kicked himself free of common life, which, incidentally, casts Anna as a latter-day Marlow in search of this terminally missing man. The Chinese cook in *Badlands* also has a Conradian provenance. Grizzly, who regularly triumphs over the other men on the voyage, is an avatar of Wang, the Chinese servant in Conrad's *Victory* (1915), who also triumphs because he was not limited by the Western views (and the contradictions in those views) of the man who was only ostensibly—that is, according to the Western view—his master.

Other possible strata can be more briefly noted. Rafting down a river is rather closer to *The Adventures of Huckleberry Finn* (1885) than to "Heart of Darkness," just as the odd characters and doings encountered along the way derive more from Twain than from Conrad. The fugitive gambler in *Badlands* who has his hand pinned to the deck with a miner's pickaxe or Sinnott as the trickster photographer or the elusive woman that Web cannot bed, the Drumheller prostitute named, significantly, America, all suggest a *Huckleberry Finn* horizon. A *Moby-Dick* (1851) horizon might also be indicated by the raft journey, which was in search of the remains of a huge creature, and, furthermore, *Daweosaurus* is discovered in a "single preposterous unnatural white butte" (209), a Moby Dick of a hill. Furthermore, the friendship of Ishmael and Queequeg, a relationship transcending race, is partly reenacted in the bond between the two Annas but not in the cross-racial relationships of any of the men in *Badlands*.

In a somewhat different fashion, Dawe's descent in the ABC mine suggests a Dantean horizon, as does, too, the hell of World War I which provides the background to Dawe's quest for dinosaurs, which is itself an attempt to understand the scope and scale and working of all creation—paleontology as the multifoliate rose. The descent to the underworld in a time of war can also be evidence of an *Aeneid* horizon, just as the search for the father indicates an *Odyssey* horizon underlying the previously noted *Ulysses* one. The *Odyssey* is also in evidence with Anna's early observation that "women are not supposed to have stories. We are supposed to sit at home, Penelopes to their wars and their sex. As my mother did. As I was doing" (3), which clearly embeds in the text the early embedding of women in Western literature as basically homebodies. Moreover, Ulysses's return to home and wife becomes Dawe's virtual farce of regular annual returnings, his custom of coming back for only two days and two nights which he continues for twenty-seven years and varies only once when he stays three nights and his daughter is conceived. Finally, the very quests, both daughter's and father's, out of which the novel is structured give us, perhaps, a base horizon, the *Gilgamesh* one. The oldest—so far as we know (archaeology ever open to revision)—surviving work of literature, this ancient Sumerian epic portrays a paradigmatic quest. Gilgamesh, it will be remembered, attempts, as does Dawe, to defeat time, death. However, when the snake that steals the flower of everlasting life, leaving Gilgamesh to return empty-handed to his city, reappears at the end of Dawe's quest, it hangs dead in his hands, just another loser.

No immortality for the animal through the suggestive fact that it can shed its skin and renew itself. Dawe, as Simpson notes, prefers his reptiles extinct.[21] No dynasty for Dawe either; not even a photograph to commemorate this final "triumph," the killing of the snake, for Sinnott, the photographer, briefly present again at the end of Dawe's voyage, has already departed, taking Anna Yellowbird with him. Nevertheless, Dawe's desire for that memorial token demonstrates the vanity at the heart of all of his endeavor, and as the end of Gilgamesh's quest conjoins with the end of Dawe's, the whole enterprise of questing seems to close into a futile circle of vanity and conceit already largely summed up early in the novel in the self-contradiction of Dawe's own particular quest for "the rib or femur or skull that would insinuate to him, however grotesquely, the whole truth; the one gigantic and perfect skeleton of his dreams that would cast man out of everlasting vanity and conceit" (8). From anticipated particular bone to postulated "whole truth" and dreamed of "perfect skeleton," with the consequent—and contradictory—expulsion of man from his "everlasting vanity and conceit," the layering of Dawe's imagined archaeology renders him not master but captive or even contaminator of the site. For there is an archaeology of archaeology too, and, as Kroetsch has observed in another context, all those early digs in the Alberta Badlands now need to be massively and with almost impossible difficulty redone in that, after only big bones, the earlier excavators missed almost everything else.[22]

The search for significant layers (big bones?) that I have just conducted cannot be translated (no more than can Dawe's search) into an account of genesis and origin, into some basis for recounting a master narrative of narrative—or dinosaurs—coming into being. The novel mirrors its own problematics of interpretation. More specifically, any critic's quest for meaning, for mastery of the text, necessarily reenacts Dawe's 1916 expedition into the Alberta Badlands and the beginning of his lifelong desire to "get back to the source itself, the root moment when the glory of reptiles, destined to dominate the world magnificently for one hundred million years, was focussed in one bony creature, one Adam-seed burrowing in the green slime" (139) just as it also reenacts his daughter's reenactment of his quest, her attempt, fifty-six years later, accompanied by the same woman who accompanied him and after whom she was named, to retrace the course of his journey down the Red Deer River to get back thereby to the source of her own life. The father's "endless search for the origin" (the phrasing is Foucault's)[23] is mocked throughout *Badlands,* and the daughter's briefer version is wisely, radically renounced. Yet Dawe's example and Anna's counterexample—the quest and the quest questioned—both presented through a layering of other quest narratives, do justify or at least exemplify Kroetsch's deployment of archaeology in that double Schliemannesque/Foucauldian sense. "The book," Foucault observes, "indicates itself, constructs itself, only on the basis of a complex field of discourse."[24] The Schliemannesque dig reveals the Foucauldian discourse.

Kroetsch's excavation of the myths of Western civilization is more than a clever parody of informing myth. Rather, it is a critique of the coercive power of any attempt to posit "origins." A discourse of origins is always a discourse of sameness, of inheritance and genealogy. Whether the early archaeologist's quest for the biggest bones or the structuralist's maneuver of reducing experience to certain elemental and universal oppositions, any attempt to find one mythic primogenitor necessarily obscures the national and local inflections of myth (from *Gilgamesh* to *The Virginian* (1902) to *Surfacing*). In contrast, Kroetsch's textual program is clearly poststructuralist. He suggests that critical interpretation which seizes on the most elemental or totalized narrative (structuralist universalisms) likely slights the more intriguing features of a text—those not accounted for by conventional generalizations, those generated outside the usual hegemonies of origin. A *Canadian* Western? That, of course, is an anomaly only if one allows the traditional—which is to say the American—"Western" to obfuscate and obviate any variations on its margins.

Kroetsch, with this sly archaeology, suggests that the Western has too readily served to universalize highly ambiguous and even morally reprehensible local events—conquest, imperialism, Manifest Destiny, destruction of the environment, patriarchy, racism, and other exercises in domination and control which are, after all, different names for or perspectives on "heroism" writ large. Manifest Destiny is not, however, so manifest to the Apache or the Sioux, to the Cree or the French Canadian. Kroetsch's archaeology— the tipi ring abandoned to the homesteaders and later confiscated for a dam—reverses the "destiny" of disappearance and questions the positing and empowering of centers.

This writer, too, resists being centered, totalized. As Hutcheon observes, "Kroetsch, the master of double-talking paradox, drives his critics into paradoxical formulation."[25] And reformulations: "Robert Kroetsch and his writing have become a 'cottage industry' in western Canada," Margaret E. Turner suggests, largely because Kroetsch demands "recognition of the complex relationship between himself and his texts" as well as "recognition of the self-reflexive nature of his work."[26] Simpson somewhat similarly maintains that "any interpretation of . . . *Badlands* meets with failure from the start . . . because [the text] invites the sorts of readings it intends to undercut."[27] In effect, the novel elicits repeated reassessment through its self-reflexive self-parody, through persistently refusing to abide by any assessment's terms.

A text that resists being reduced to "meaning" is not, however, thereby rendered a meaningless text. Archaeology's unfolding layers may contradict attempts at totalized narrative, at some full and official history, but that in no way denies significance to those successive layers, a significance partly determined by the very succession of the layers. More particularly and more to the point, almost all of the allusive horizons previously considered, from *Gilgamesh* to *Absalom, Absalom!*, archetypalize the male quest, even as that patriarchal enterprise is being, in *Badlands,* reinscribed as Dawe's search and deinscribed as his daughter's. In short, by giving the narrative voice of the novel to the daughter and by playing that voice against the regularly invoked male voice of the quest narrative, *Badlands* doubly questions the sexual politics of the traditional quest and, it should be added, the traditional Western. If Penelope, for example, not only recounted her husband's adventures but retraced his journey the better to relate it, his ostensibly singular prowess would be substantially compromised, which is why, as Jane Tompkins has recently pointed out at some length, the cowboy plot promises a cast of mostly cows and boys.[28] No cowgirls need apply.

The foregrounding of considerations of gender invites a gendered criticism. It is tempting, for example, to see Kroetsch's variations on the quest and the Western as a feminist interrogation of those masculine forms. Connie Harvey has even argued that the novel exhibits an "essential duality" whereby it dramatizes "the difference between masculine and feminine perceptions" and finally privileges the latter.[29] Harvey, in a sustained symbolic reading of the novel as a symbolic voyage, concludes by postulating that "the two Annas . . . complete [both for themselves and the men] the men's movement towards self-realization and a transcendent vision" and thereby realize that the way to this transcendence was partly through "their refusal to resign [themselves] to the male vision."[30] Anna Dawe, in this reading, especially frees herself from both her father's scant regard and from his commitment to language; thus freed, she need not even tell herself what her real story might be. For Harvey, the text, like its enveloping silence, finally speaks the primacy of female voice, of female vision.

In contrast and in the masculine mode, Robert Lecker questions Harvey's "conventional approach to the novel [that] sees Anna freed at the end as she hurls away her father's notes and redefines her individual, and female, identity."[31] For this critic, the silence which sounds most meaningfully in the text is Dawe's, not Anna's: "And while Anna is struggling (as Kroetsch does) to give form to formlessness, Kroetsch will contemplate those heroes he truly envies: not Anna, who falls prey to narrative in the worst way, but Dawe, who lives out a magnificent antistory, inhabiting the narrative but defying language at every turn."[32] Consequently, Anna's story must be compromised at every turn lest it be taken at face value and thereby mask over that more important "antistory" that it does not tell. To this end, we are advised to see the surfeit of narrative echoes, parodies, and ploys that the novel exhibits as confused signs of Anna's past "voracious reading," of her present inexperience as an author, and of the duplicity of her drive to authorship. But we can best learn "to 'read' Anna," Lecker maintains, through her final lie, that retrospective denial of retrospect, and once we have done so, "her narrative tricks become more and more obvious. To get the 'true' story we have to invert everything she says." For example, "when she claims that the men of Dawe's expedition 'were trying to tell each other' a 'western yarn,' we read: the men told each other nothing, but from that void Anna would contrive a 'western yarn.' "[33]

Lecker reinverts Harvey's inversion, her claim that "the women are superior to the men."[34] Yet his enterprise is rather more suspect than hers, for a narrator totally reliable in her unreliability turns out to be a device whereby the narrative can be transformed into whatever one wants on the basis of the particular statements selected for scrutiny and inversion. For example, we can change Badlands back into that thoroughly conventional "western yarn" Lecker disallowed simply by noting and thereby "countering" Anna's obvious desire to "belittle" her father by portraying him as the hunchback and ineffectual head of a ragtag expedition. Was he really heroic, capable, ramrod straight, and tall—a Gary Cooper figure of a man? Or was there no search for dinosaur bones at all because Anna says that there was? Similarly and by the same logic, was there no father either, which would turn Dawe's "antistory" into Anna's anti-antistory. In short, the breakthrough to antistory and its attendant freedom that Lecker praises in the novel proves to be mostly another version of the same old story. "Now that storytelling is aligned with Woman, Man is free to live in the silence of antistory," which is to say that the only story worth not telling, the "antistory" of *Badlands,* is, not surprisingly, still man's.[35]

The larger point here, however, is that to align the text exclusively with the perspective (and the sexual politics) of *either* Anna Dawe or William Dawe is to reduce a complex, multivocal, and willfully contradictory novel to a simple and schematized tract. Moreover, it means reducing both daughter and father to little more than representatives of their gender—as if gender were monolithic, and every human being, as well as every reading, had to be sternly sexed.[36] It seems fairer and certainly more fun to see *Badlands* as an attempt to unwrite the tired scripting of gender in the very quest epics which the novel pays tribute to—and parodies.

Contradictory and parallel as their interpretations are, Harvey and Lecker do suggest one seeming truth of the fiction, Anna's early claim that "there are no truths, only correspondences" (45). The novel is, indeed, replete with correspondences, so much so that, again, a kind of archaeological excavation is in order. And again that task is not so much a search for the final truth of the novel's correspondences, but an investigation of the provisional narrative of this narrative that can be constructed on the basis of how correspondence itself foregrounds difference to disclaim "truth." For example, one of the most obvious correspondences, the structuring device of two Alberta journeys—his and hers, so to speak—readily invites a reading that privileges, depending on the proclivities of the reader (witness Harvey and Lecker), one of these journeys over the other. Yet the other remains, a compromising double thwarting any definitive gendering of quest and text. Similarly, the difference between the men's journey and the women's is itself rendered in terms of other correspondences when the Rocky Mountains into which the two Annas travel at the end of the novel are described as "the Badlands upside down" (265). Either is the perfect setting for a Western adventure; each is rendered imperfect by the missing corresponding other.

To see more clearly the work of such correspondences in the text, we can note how Dawe's record of his search for source down the river ends up in the source of that river, the mountain lake. Anna Dawe, moreover, can at last cast away her father's field notes because Anna Yellowbird has just shown her how by throwing the photographs she has previously kept for over half a century into that same lake—one fling eliciting another. And the photographs here discarded themselves connect back to earlier photographs, such as Sinnott's "See the Monsters Returning to Life," which, as a picture of the boat about to land and unload, conjoins the men with the fossils they have found. Or Sinnott's title for his final portrait of Dawe, "Champion Bone Hunter of the Wild West. Hero of a Thousand Close Calls. The Winner," (246), as Rosemary Sullivan observes, is a "monstrous mythification" of Dawe's propensity to mythify himself.[37]

The photographs taken correspond, too, to those not taken, and one of the early photographs, "The Charlatan Being Himself" (128), well could have been the title for the picture Dawe wanted as a commemoration of his killing the snake. The creature finally killed is also one of the living descendants of the long dead reptiles whose remains Dawe would recover, so his search for dead bones is partially compromised by those living fossils (birds and sturgeon are also named to this role in the novel) who still embody what he is after. The dead animals will "live" again (at least in the museum dioramas) and the living one dies, both as proof of Dawe's prowess as a leader, which gives, of course, another correspondence with the snake's demise, Tune's. Dawe would claim one killing but not the other. As his crossed out entries in his field notes attest, he wants somehow to erase Tune's death. The consequence of allowing that fifteen-year-old to play with dynamite is devastating proof of Dawe's incompetence as a leader even as it serves up another set of correspondences, the skeleton of the dead dinosaur uncovered at the cost of the living boy being buried alive.

The carried dead snake also partly corresponds to the grizzly bear carried aloft "to be born into a new life" (268). Suspended (like the dead snake) from a yellow helicopter (another yellow bird?), the bear is being borne "away from garbage cans" to a new beginning "on the high avalanche slopes" (268) and so also corresponds to the two women who are making a similar new beginning on those same slopes. Yet the bear, "his prick and testicles [hanging] over [the women] like a handful of dead-ripe berries" (269), also constitutes a comic picture of male sexuality. "He was running in the air, straight overhead, so comically human and male that Anna [Yellowbird] fell backwards, laughing, off the fallen tree" (268) and immediately Anna Dawe is laughing too, which is itself another crucial correspondence in that earlier she was only "ready to laugh. Not the pained and uneasy and nervous laughter of a lifetime of wondering, of trying to recover and then reshape and then relive a life that wasn't quite a life. I was ready for real laughter" (263–

64). It is in that carnivalesque laughter, when it comes, that she can at last throw away the notes of her father who, grim and harried and desperate, never laughed.

This liberating comic view of male sexuality corresponds (and contrasts) to the twisted view of female sexuality implicit in Dawe's dream of his wife, the lover, and, yet again, the snake. Dawe's interweaving of snake, sex, sin, and death invokes, moreover, the Biblical interweaving of those same ingredients in Genesis (another correspondence for the snake). Neither does Dawe find release and escape in sex with Anna Yellowbird, and she retrospectively remembers mostly him "crying out, 'Mammal,' in the middle of it all" as opposed to the "old man with the pigtail" who "never talked about it. . . . Just did it" (263–64). The old man is, appropriately, Grizzly, another correspondence for the bear at the end who also reembodies, running through the air, Web's various runs through the course of the novel.[38] The fact that Old Man is also the traditional Blackfoot trickster whom Kroetsch has used often in his poetry, and thus a version of Coyote, further emphasizes the interplay of correspondences—human/animal, cultural/natural, textual/sexual—through which *Badlands* concludes. Again Kroetsch sets up one mythology of origins (the Judeo-Christian) only to counter it with another, the Indian figure who evokes a different cosmos and a different version of the Western.

The novel begins, too, much as it concludes, with competing mythologies. The two epigraphs, one from a Nez Percé Coyote tale and one from bp Nichol's *The Martyrology,* set forth different views of time and process, and both differ, as I have more fully argued elsewhere, from the straightforward chronology that follows.[39] Furthermore, the shadowland where Coyote, in the first, seeks his dead wife corresponds to the Alberta Badlands, where Anna Yellowbird seeks her dead husband, but where Dawe, fleeing his living wife to seek fossils, inverts Coyote's priorities and enterprise. Similarly, in the brief excerpt from Nichol, the "desert" corresponds to the Badlands, but it is not the river, but the desert that "flows," that becomes itself the all embracing Heraclitian river of flux (corresponding to the Red Deer River running back through time and even becoming a river of time as, in its onward course, it cuts through to older and older geological formations). In that desert, this second epigraph concludes, "death &/breath makes us wary." Death & breath are here grammatically conjoined as a single entity, and in the novel too they conflate together, as in Anna *Kilbourne* Dawe, whose middle name faces equally in those two same and different directions.

Anna's middle name also situates her in terms of two crucially corresponding figures, William Dawe as limiting father and Anna Yellowbird as enabling mother. The daughter must symbolically kill the one in order to be born into a new life through the agency of the other. The older Anna is finally named as mother and accepts that role as Dawe never accepted his role as father, denying his daughter the single time she called him Dad even as he was on his way to the lake to drown himself. On the way to a different lake and on quite a different mission, the older Anna mothers the younger one, sings her a Blackfoot lullaby when she falls into a crying jag, and is named as the "mother." The belated daughter has to learn even to swear from this mother, not the father, and her first fumbling attempt at profanity is here paradigmatic in that it stands in for still other forms of freedom only the "mother" allowed: "and then I dared it too, tried those words on my mouth: and glanced at her face and saw she was letting me try in the same way that my father had stopped me—" (259).

In the popular Western a young and often Eastern tyro is regularly taught the requisite forms of frontier male freedom—swearing, whoring, drinking, gambling, fighting—by an older father figure expert at such manly activities. The two Annas obviously embody an odd version of just this relationship and so correspond to more conventional renderings of family romance and patriarchal filiation. The imperative, "Go West, young man!" is reordered into "Go West, middle-aged woman!" and the consequence of that going is itself another inversion, not the discovery of the rule of a new father in the guise of the Western hero (another white male), but the discovery of the license of a new mother in the guise of the Native woman.

The rule of Dawe as father is also compromised by the multiplicitous interplay of corresponding/conflicting roles required from those whom he would cast as his family. For example, he early makes Anna Yellowbird both a substitute wife and a substitute daughter. As a substitute daughter, she corresponds both to Tune, a substitute son who is also fifteen, and to the biological daughter born later but given Anna Yellowbird's first name (a substitute substitute daughter?). Dawe, still later, would make that daughter even more a counterpart of the earlier Anna and, by extension, his wife, when, as the chronology tells us, he varies "his annual fall pilgrimage to his wife's bed" and "goes home to visit not his dying wife but his daughter" (1). As the adult daughter later reports, he came into her room and lay down beside her in bed and kissed her and cried "and then, in the midst of his maudlin crying he told me; 'You were named for that Anna, and she was fifteen, then, too; your mother dying then, too, always dying—'; and he kissed my neck, my shoulders, my young breasts" (262). That almost (it is apparently unconsummated) incest casts the three women here referred to into a dizzying whirl—the daughter as mistress as wife as mistress as daughter. . . . No wonder Anna Dawe is, years later, still trying to figure out just who she is.

Dawe persistently denies the real daughter in favor of the substitute son, Tune, who thereby becomes, for Anna, "in some lost way, . . . the brother [she] never had" (232). The "lost way" is in being lost, in losing his life in the service of Dawe, just as she also has largely done. Tune, however, is not the only substitute son. Web also is, but his relationship with Dawe is more obviously oedipal. Having totally repudiated his own biological father (as Anna will later do), Web, with Dawe, can have another father and fight him too. It is also possible that Dawe has one biological son about whom he does not know. At least his daughter considers the possibility and asks the other Anna first if she had any children and then, more explicitly, "Any relations of mine, mother?" (262). Moreover, just as Dawe named his daughter after Anna Yellowbird, she more than returns the favor when she names each of her four or five (she is a little vague on just how many she had) sons Billy Crowchild. They are all, in fact, doubly named after William Dawe, whose last name means crow. Such naming comically overinscribes Dawe as a father and mocks his own aspirations to just that status. Patriarchal filiation, the father-son imperative of the standard Western, is also undercut by the consideration that it is the daughter who, with her own quest reenacting his, proves to be the best son.

One can begin with virtually any detail in *Badlands* and trace out a web of suggestive correspondences. For example and to return to some of the correspondences previously considered, behind Sinnott's photographs is Sinnott himself with his regularly repeated claim that "everything is vanishing" (114) in pointed contrast to Dawe's counterclaim that "nothing vanishes. Everything goes on" (117), which are basically two different ways of saying the same thing, depending on where the emphasis falls. Indeed, Sinnott's first appearance, with his "huge head, as white-bearded as Dawe's was black" (113) constitutes a sly clue to the world of early black and white still photography that each differently inhabits, neither dreaming of video cameras or technicolor. As Sinnott, not Dawe, sees, the two "are both peddlers" (118), and each is trying to sell his own view of life, a not very accurate view at that, so the two also "are both charlatans" (119), as is, perhaps, anyone (even the novelist?) pushing a particular vision or perspective. Sinnott also observes that the bones Dawe seeks are, after all, "only mineral replacements of what the living bones were" (128) and so correspond to Sinnott's photographs in that both represent some different reality but do not at all embody it. Fossils and photographs, as re-presentations, correspond, moreover, to the novel itself and its metafictional representation of representation. As

Peter Thomas observes, the dubious photographs "match Dawe's 'fake' field notes" just as their parodic captions correspond to Kroetsch's "droll, if not 'camped'" chapter headings.[40]

Other correspondences also give *Badlands* a distinctly metafictional cast. For the story of quests in this novel is also the quest for story. Dawe has his narrative, and Anna has hers. Each partially stands in for the author's telling of those tellings, which is to say that the archaeological metaphors of the text invoke the writer's plumbing of his material as much as the critics' plumbing it. Or in a somewhat different vein, Web as "a true bull-shitter" (137) tells his tall tales in antic imitation of the tall-tale telling of the text itself. Or the distinctly male subject matter of much of the novel corresponds to Anna's different telling and her insistence that women have stories too. Her pattern for this claim is Penelope: "Why it was left to me to mediate the story I don't know: women are not supposed to have stories. We are supposed to sit at home, Penelopes to their wars and their sex. As my mother did. As I was doing" (3). Penelope, however, did more than sit. She was, not coincidentally, an artist and maintained her sitting by the weaving she did by day and the unweaving by night. As the figure for the female art-ist, Penelope can indeed be Anna's pattern for an unweaving and untelling (an un-Webbing even) of the story the men expect, which corresponds to Dawe's different duplicity of writing when he records in his journal such entries as "*I despise words*" (34, and a statement that deconstructs marvel-ously even before we see him contemplating it and finding it good) or I "have come to the end of words" (269), the precise point to which one has not come when one is still saying so or attempting to leave a written record of that coming.

Finally, to return to those horizons considered in the first part of this chapter, we can notice how much they themselves are counterparts and metafictional correspondences. The texts embedded in this text give us numerous paradigms of problematic parenthood. Taken together, they con-stitute a virtual plot of family plots, a textual undoing of any one provisional genealogy through the invoking of other possibilities. Thus, if *Surfacing* resurrects the mother, *The Double Hook,* in turn, immediately dispatches her once more. Or just as *Absalom, Absalom!* writes the father into defeat and death, *Ulysses* (both Joyce's novel and Homer's protagonist) writes him out again. As these various plays and postulations work mostly to cancel one another out, the text sets forth a family plot for both protagonist and author.

The correspondences between author and protagonist can be seen, too, in the analogous way each resolves what we might term an anxiety of in-fluence crisis. Anna, written into limited being by her father's proscriptions and limitations, goes searching for the origin of Dawe's cramped writing and then unwrites that origin first by duplicating it and then by reversing it. As the father's own attempt at an authenticating quest is both doubled and inverted, his claims to textual primacy and originating word are all deconstructed and his notes go, finally, the same way he has gone, into the lake. Anna will write her own story, thank you. But to write that writing, unwriting, and rewriting, Kroetsch, as we have noted, regularly rewrites other writers, which is to say that they also write him. So his problem is a version of hers. And so is his solution. The artist can uninvent himself into freedom through an excess of fictional fathers and mothers, just as Anna frees herself from her quest for her father by overdramatizing (doubling and quadrupling—reenacting, then reversing and writing about) his quest.

That freedom for the author suggests one final correspondence. It is an antic freedom not a magisterial one and stands in contrast to more austere visions of authorial independence and integrity such as Joyce's portrait of the artist, like God, totally inhabiting the work, everywhere present but aloof, indifferent, paring his fingernails. The artist as God or the artist as Coyote? Kroetsch's own view is set forth in his claim that "the artist him/ her self: in the long run, given the choice of being God or Coyote, will, most mornings, choose to be Coyote."[41] In *Badlands* his definite choice is to be Coyote, to be a trickster figure at play in the text instead of an omnipotence informing it. But perhaps the truth of this last correspondence is that the two views of the artist might not be so different after all. As *The Double Hook* amply attests, Coyote's claims and God's can sound quite similar, especially when voiced by Coyote.

Much, and much more than the foregoing, can be done with the correspondences at play in this text. But the text is not thereby tied down, interpreted, by a string, a web, of correspondences. In effect, a dig for internal structuring as much as a dig for possible sources leaves the excavator with an embarrassment of riches, fragmentary riches, and "tons of fragments," we are told in the novel, well might yield "nothing" of "worth" (49). Unless fragmentation itself is the locus of value. Then the point of both the play of intertextuality and the intratextual play would be to remind us that there are always other stories. An excess of signification precludes privileging any particular textual detail or narrative line, just as the very number of literary strata (sources? analogues?) means that none of them can be cast as the originating text—the Ur-story—of *Badlands*.

It is a typically Kroetschean paradox that the "nothing of worth" in the very excess of intertextual/intratextual significations is precisely where the value of the text lies. First, by the way it both demands and resists interpretation the novel expands the field of critical discourse in which it situates itself. Second, it insists on the need (but not the validity, for that is ever in question) of a feminine discourse to counter the more conventional male discourse of most narration. "Total and absurd male that he was," Anna says once of Web, "he assumed, like a male author, an omniscience that was not ever his, a scheme that was not ever there. Holding the past in contempt, he dared foretell for himself not so much a future as an orgasm. But we women take our time" (76). Different times, different desires, different discourses. The presence of those differences in *Badlands,* as Kroetsch has observed in commenting on the novel, allows it to counter "the whole notion that a story speaks in what [he calls] the *male* story. The knight out (the night out!) questing or hunting. The knight, leaving his love in the castle, going out to kill or be killed, and in the process generating desire."[42] As this quote suggests, the Western has a long traditional genealogy, and one of Kroetsch's major archaeological accomplishment in *Badlands* is to go beyond that genealogy and history, to "undercut the whole notion of male quest and male story."[43]

Western quest and Western story are undercut too, and particularly by the first epigraph:

> But suddenly a joyous impulsion seized him; the joy of having his wife again overwhelmed him. He jumped to his feet and rushed over to embrace her. His wife cried out, "Stop! Stop! Coyote! Do not touch me. Stop!" Her warning had no effect. Coyote rushed over to his wife and just as he touched her body she vanished. She disappeared—returned to the shadowland.—"Coyote and the Shadow People," *Nez Percé Texts* (n.p.)

The epigraph, like the novel, has other texts embedded within it, most obviously the similar myth of Orpheus and Eurydice. "The Greek myth of Orpheus and Eurydice, and hundreds of analogous tales throughout the world suggest," Joseph Campbell points out in *The Hero with a Thousand Faces,* "that in spite of the failure recorded, a possibility exists of a return of the lover with his lost love from beyond the terrible threshold." But, he continues, "always some little fault, some slight yet critical symptom of human frailty . . . make impossible the open interrelationship between the worlds," and we can almost "believe . . . that if the small marring accident could be avoided, all would be well."[44] But Kroetsch makes the Greek myth analogous to the Nez Percé one and tells us, with the account of the "small, marring accident," part of a story most readers won't know, not part of a story that they will know. That displacement especially calls into question the supremacy of the West's epic genealogy of bygone quests and questors. Furthermore, Coyote himself is a figure of "open interrelationship" between radically different "worlds" and so mediates the failure over which he presides in quite a different fashion than does Orpheus, as Coyote's own free and frequent passage between the world of the living and the world of the dead (even in his cartoon Wile E. Coyote manifestation) should also suggest. By placing Coyote, not Orpheus, as the epigraphic questor, Kroetsch early and on the largest level signals the ways in which *Badlands* is both a revisioning of history and genealogy (archaeology in the fashion of Schliemann) and (in the Foucauldian mode) a reordering of the discourse of the Western, of the panoply of Western discourse.

Part III Feminist Revisions

5 "Smile When You Call Me That," She Said Cuttingly

A feminist Western might well seem, at first, a contradiction in terms. As Jane Tompkins has recently observed, Westerns "are generally written by men," and "the main character is always a full-grown adult male, and almost all of the other characters are men."[1] The action of the Western, she continues, takes place outdoors or, if enclosed, in characteristically male spaces such as the jail or the saloon, and not in the domestic space of kitchens or parlors. Not in bedrooms either; the protagonist's main romantic relationship (when there is one) is usually a covert homoerotic tie to a comrade or adversary rather than a sexual relationship with a woman. The main action, moreover, is action, male physical action (like the death-defying duel) that leaves little room for female concerns with emotions or relationships. Admittedly, women are regularly present on the margins of this action and often serve as a justification for it, but that very function, in Tompkins's apt analysis, de-authorizes them. Even as women provide "the motive for male activity" by requiring rescue or revenge, "what women stand for—love and forgiveness in place of vengeance—is precisely what that [same male] activity denies. . . . Indeed, the viewpoint women represent is introduced in order to be swept aside, crushed, or dramatically invalidated."[2]

Tompkins does not, at this late date, simply detail the male bias of the Western. That could go without saying. Rather, she argues that this bias can be seen as a "point for point" repudiation of the domestic fiction especially popular in America throughout the second half of the nineteenth century. "The discourse of Christian domesticity—of Jesus, the Bible, salvation, the heart, the home—[as] spread from horizon to horizon in the decades preceding the Western's rise to fame" precipitated a countering discourse:

> And so, just as the women's novels that captured the literary market-
> place at midcentury had privileged the female realm of spiritual power,
> inward struggle, homosociality, and sacramental household ritual,
> Westerns, in a reaction that looks very much like literary gender war,
> privilege the male realm of public power, physical ordeal, homosoci-
> ality, and the rituals of the duel.[3]

"The Western," Tompkins thereby concludes, "doesn't have anything to do
with the West as such. It isn't about the encounter between civilization and
the frontier. It is about men's fear of losing their mastery, and hence their
identity, both of which the Western tirelessly reinvents."[4]

This critic writes, of course, about the American Western. In Canada,
there is a different history, a different course of literary development, a
different sexual deployment of literary labor. As numerous scholars have
noted, Canadian fiction in the nineteenth and early twentieth century was
still not a firmly established form, and the Canadian publishing "industry" was fledgling at best. There were no mid-nineteenth-century Canadian
equivalents of Harriet Beecher Stowe's Uncle Tom's Cabin (1852) or Susan B.
Warner's The Wide, Wide World (1850), "women's novels" that sold hundreds
of thousands of copies. There was no occasion for the male revolt against
domesticity that shaped, according to Tompkins, the American Western.
There were no ready-made grounds on which to stage such a revolt either.
Most of the male-centered markers of the American frontier as traditionally
conceived—cattle drives, cavalry and Indian encounters, the high-noon
shoot-out, the vigilantes hunting down and hanging the horse rustlers—
had, as earlier noted, no substantial Canadian counterparts. There was, consequently, little impetus for male writers to claim a certain fictional form
and ground as quintessentially male.

This is not to say that some claims were not advanced. Thus Frederick
Philip Grove can see a solitary ploughman "outlined . . . against a tilted
and spoked sunset in the western sky" as "look[ing] like a giant."[5] Laurence
Ricou invokes the same figurative deployment of man against landscape
when he titles his study of Western Canadian fiction Vertical Man/Horizontal
World. But as Aritha van Herk points out, although the "phallic protuber-
ance" of such assertions can be seen as gendering the presentation of the
landscape, the prairie itself, "lying there innocent under its buffalo beans,
its own endlessness," remains "indifferent" and is therefore a receptive place
for the woman writer who does not attempt to define the "indifference" of
the West as masculine.[6] Canadian women, moreover, early found opportunity to write about the West and were not discounted because they did.

Nellie McClung, for example, could follow up the bestseller success of her first novel, *Sowing Seeds in Danny* (1908), a sentimental portrait of life in a small Western town, by becoming a major advocate for women's suffrage and then an important political leader and spokeswoman for the whole country, serving as a Canadian delegate to the League of Nations.

The literary gender war that Tompkins describes had no particular relevance for Canadians and was, like the Civil War and the Indian wars, an American luxury that nineteenth-century Canada could hardly afford. Nor was there any reason to import the masculine form of the Western that emerged victorious in the United States. As earlier noted, it was not particularly relevant to Canadian experience. To appropriate and deploy the inapplicable iconography of the American Western would serve mostly to reinscribe what I have elsewhere termed Canada's paracolonial (not exactly colonial and certainly not postcolonial) status. Canada, after all, stands to the United States in the world of global politics as "woman" stands to "man" in the plots of the conventional Western—on the sidelines, occasionally counseling restraint or offering advice and moral support, but definitely not packing the big guns.

The literary equation, "Western" equals "American" equals "male," is not going to appeal to Canadian authors, male or female, and they will with some regularity subvert that definition by parodying or reversing its final governing term. Robert Kroetsch's deployment, in *Badlands,* of William Dawe as failed Western quester and Anna Dawe as female Western quester has already been noted, as has George Bowering's camp casting, in *Caprice,* of a female Francophone poet as the avenger of her brother's death. But the most striking reversals of the classic American Western come, as would be expected, in works by Canadian women writers, a few of whom challenge, even to the point of figurative and literal castration, the primal thrust of their American primogenitors. In a Nietzschean transvaluation of values, these authors dispute the myth of man's Manifest Destiny inherent in the American Western. In place of the adult male hero, they put a woman or even a girl, and then they show her establishing a new and different order and subsuming men into it.

Martha Ostenso's *Wild Geese* (1925), for example, gives a definite feminist twist to its portrayal of harsh life on the prairies. Caleb Gare, by threatening to expose the illegitimacy of his wife's first son, for a time holds his family in thrall. But that illegitimacy itself calls the rule of this "father" into question. His wife could have a child without him, and his predecessor, the novel makes clear, was the better man. His daughter, Judith, soon even more decisively stages her own rebellion when she embarks, without benefit of matrimony or her father's blessing, on her own affair. Both Gares, as Dick Harrison observes, are figures of the land, but whereas "Judith represents communion with the land, Caleb represents power over it."[7] But that power is disputed by the land just as it was by the daughter. Judith, at one point, strips and embraces the earth, practically making love to it; later, with her lover, she conceives upon it; Caleb, in contrast, rushing to save his beloved field of flax from a bush fire, sinks and drowns in the muskeg. "The overstrong embrace of the earth . . . closing ice-cold, tight, tight, about his body" carries him to his death and thus further frees the daughter to embrace whom she pleases, to live her own life.[8]

With an even more idiosyncratic gender reversal, Margaret Laurence's *The Stone Angel* (1964) portrays an old woman, not a young man, who is searching for a Western escape from the limitations that circumscribe her life. Moreover, this search takes, in part, the odd form of lighting out from the retirement home, not for the frontier. In her first novel set in Manawaka (her name for the part of Manitoba that she fictionally creates—roughly analogous to William Faulkner's Yoknapatawpha County), Laurence graphically inverts the phallic-thrust teleology of the American Western, the celebration of the conquering of a new land as the simultaneous claiming of a future of boundless possibility. Hagar Shipley, Laurence's protagonist, has most of her life behind her. But she still has to come home to that life, to admit what it has been, to come to terms with it, to reinvent herself as the product of a particular Canadian West (instead of inventing the West as an expression of the id's unbridled desire—male desire, of course). Furthermore, Hagar's discovery of herself as a woman and her return from a long enforced exile from self strangely depends on a chance encounter with a man who "mothers" her as she could not, when a child, mother her dying brother.[9]

Similarly, in Sharon Riis's *The True Story of Ida Johnson* (1976) the female protagonist's declaration of independence is rather more graphic than getting herself illegitimately pregnant. She does that, too, at fourteen, but, to no one's surprise, that only gets her married. For over ten years no "local girl" has wed "for reasons less well defined."[10] Another baby later and still in her teens, Ida makes her break. In the middle of the night and with the meat cleaver she kills her husband: "A clean clean perfect clean slice down through the throat past the throat through the neck not quite through. Clean. And his blood so red and thick I didn't know. I kissed him" (60). She does the babies too: "Clean quick slice slice like a butcher. I'm a butcher. Everything red and clear as a bell" (60). Whereupon she turns on the gas, showers, sets her hair, manicures her nails, dons a "clean nightgown white and crisp and cool" and her husband's coat with "matches and a pack of Players in the pocket," and "outside . . . lit a smoke and threw it in through the door. The sky was red and clear as a bell" (60). She gets away with it too: "For months and months I just did what I wanted. Yeah I still remember that. I still remember how fantastic it was" (61). She even confesses to her father, on a two-week fishing trip, that she "kill[ed] them," and his only comment is "I thought that" (71). Much of the novel is her confessing again to a young man she meets in the cafe where she works and who offers to pay her for the true story of her life. But Luke turns out to be Lucy, Ida's childhood Native friend, and this "little known but extraordinary novel" ends with the two of them together again.[11] The novel also ends with Lucy asking, "Was all that stuff back there true?" and Ida answering, with a laugh, and with questions of her own, "What's the matter sweetheart? You miss the point or something?" To emphasize further the trickster quality of the whole narration (it is dedicated "to the careful reader"), "a coyote [at the end] calls out across the prairie" (111).[12]

The patriarchy that prevails at the beginning of these three novels does not reign triumphant with their conclusions. But I turn now to the two first novels of Aritha van Herk, *Judith* (1978) and *The Tent Peg* (1981), to consider more fully just how and with what implications the Canadian women's Western posits fictive possibilities beyond the realm of the fathers and the rule of their law. It is in this larger context that such loaded episodes as the climactic castration scene in *Judith* must be read: "She castrated them all. Swift and cruel she pierced them, slicing so fast there was hardly time for blood to flow, flicking their testicles onto the floor of the chorehouse like offending parasites."[13] Although those raining parts suggest a symbolic reordering of male and female potency, they do not exactly tell us what the new order will be, although the consideration that the shorn testicles come from pigs is itself significant.

Even the novel's two epigraphs foreground the figurative role swine will play in *Judith*. The first of these, from Lewis Carroll's "The Walrus and the Carpenter," is the brief catalog of the "many things" which the walrus deems worthy of current conversation ending with, "And whether pigs have wings" (n.p.). The walrus's talk, however, is mostly self-serving verbiage directing attention away from the ongoing consumption of oysters; it is thus of little symbolic import—unless those oysters are "mountain oysters" (i.e., the fried testicles from castrated farm animals). But the second epigraph, taken from an old English folk song, more clearly deploys flying pigs to raise covert questions about a symbolic order and so conjoins the possible "addition" of wings with the possible "subtraction" of testicles:

> There is a herb in father's garden,
> Some calls it maidens' rue:
> When pigs they do fly like swallows in the sky,
> Then the young men they'll prove true. (n.p.)

Until then, however, men need not do so, which is to say that the phallic herb in father's garden, like the walrus's gift for gab, serves him very nicely. No wonder he cultivates his garden, ordered around that ordering herb, and calls it nature. "Nature" should surely preclude any possibility of something most unnatural, such as some maiden cutting down the offending stalk instead of being ruled and "rued" by it. Thus the flying pigs in the second epigraph, more than in the first one, serve to suggest that some major changes might be in the air.[14]

In the novel itself, pigs are the vehicle and sign of change. As *Judith* begins, Judith, the twenty-three-year-old protagonist, is back on a pig farm but not the one on which she grew up. She had fled that father-dominated upbringing (he wanted her to take over from him and to become an extension of him) for work in the city. Soon she is having an affair with her employer, who, as a stand-in for her father, is also determined to impose his values on her and her life. To escape this man who is himself a bit of a pig, she returns to the country and the real swine. She might thereby also atone to her father for earlier refusing to come back to take over his farm, which had then been sold. So a stand-in pig farm can cancel out the male chauvinist boss as a stand-in father and reaffirm her relationship to her real (but male chauvinist) father, an affirmation that she even more requires in that both of her parents have been killed in a recent automobile accident. Her complex, contradictory, and pig-beset motivation and circumstances are incorporated into both the content and the structure of the novel. It begins with Judith on her second farm, but regularly shifts back and forth between the ongoing action of that present and the two different pasts that brought her there—her earlier country life with her father and her city job with the concomitant affair.[15]

Both men have left her fractured and self-divided, an internal state of affairs also appropriately reflected in the discontinuous structure of the novel. First, the father has raised her as both his petted and protected daughter and as the unsatisfactory substitute for the son he did not have. In the one parental mode, he can comfort and console her when she is frightened during a thunderstorm: "It's only noise, Judy, it's only noise. I'll take care of you. Listen to the rain singing" (56). In the other, he criticizes her for the work she could not quite do, leaving her "crying with rage at his demands, his blindness to her inability to lift and carry, to swing like a muscular boy" (67). Her boss subsequently imposes another version of this double bind of indulgence and critique. As the employee with whom he is having an affair, she is sometimes his pet reclamation project (a raw farm girl greatly in need of the polish he can provide) and sometimes his most prized possession (almost the woman he loves). Small wonder she is having considerable trouble figuring out just who she is.

That "trouble" derives from and foregrounds a myth much disputed in the text, the myth of male domination and control around which pigs also signify—even metafictionally. "It's ridiculous," Judith at one point observes, "pigs and pigs and pigs. Shoveling shit and carrying feed and water and bloody births and castrating pigs and pigs and pigs" (171). The circularity of that statement, from "pigs and pigs and pigs" to more "pigs and pigs and pigs," along with the centrality of "shoveling shit" applies equally to Judith here assessing the possible course of the "rest of [her] life" (171); to the natural processes, the procreation of pigs, to which she has apparently devoted that life; and to the novel itself which also begins and ends with pigs, pigs both literal and figurative. From pigs to pigs to pigs also gives us the circular plot of the novel, Judith's return to the realm of the father as an attempt to escape from another father figure into whose realm she fled to escape the original rule of her biological father.[16]

A circulation of—and through—pigs also underlies the novel's narrative structure. The juxtaposition of two different pasts, country and city, against an ongoing country present, allows for almost any minor detail from that present to key a memory of or a time flip into (the novel does not specify which) one of those pasts or the other or both. The three different times thereby effectively merge, and both men can continue to control the protagonist's life even though her father is dead (which does not stop her from carrying on his life with the pigs), even though her former lover gives no sign of wanting to renew their relationship (which does not stop her from making almost daily trips to town hoping for a letter from him that will tell her he is finally coming to save her from all those pigs that are saving her from him). Much this same point is also made by one of the more idiosyncratic features of this unusual text, the regular reporting of her animals' reactions to everything about her, from a new haircut to what she is feeling at some particular moment to the fact that she has just had sex. In their almost omniscient responsiveness, the literal pigs show an attentive concern never exhibited by the more figurative ones.

Both symbols for and counters to the unsatisfactory men in Judith's life, the admittedly mythologized pigs also demythologize the standard man-animal economy of the Western. Pig herding? A pig round-up? Driving the pigs to market? It just does not wash and even less so with pigs whose consciousness, so to speak, has been raised. For the very sensitivity of these animals subverts another pervasive Western dichotomy, the division between animals viewed only as commodity and those allowed other functions—one of which is often to serve, in clear contradistinction to woman, as man's best friend. Judith's concern for creatures she is raising to sell questions the conventional ethos of literary animal husbandry, the constructs whereby the cowboy can care for his horse in a distinctly different sense than he cares for his cows. Or perhaps she merely differently deploys her emotional investment in her animals and, as a woman, feels a certain sisterly affection for the sows. As the novel soon makes clear, she has no problem at all castrating the boars.

With that castration, the pigs (male, of course) especially stand in for the men in her life and so serve, despite their better qualities, to designate those men as pigs (particularly the father for the way he has tried to force his way of life onto Judith and the father-figure employer for the way he forced his attentions). That the "fathers" as representatives of the "law" hitherto governing Judith's life are pigs (police) in the sixties slang sense is also suggested in the novel by a series of brief scenes that equate the rule of the two men and, in the process, conjoin love and power, concern and rape.

These interconnections begin, appropriately, with an action that seems innocent enough. Judith awakens one morning to see the first snow blanketing her new farm, and that sight triggers two other snow scenes. The first of these also initially seems innocuously innocent. As a small child she once awoke to find the ground newly covered and slipped outside to make angels in the freshly fallen snow before coming back in to be tucked in bed by her father. In the second, at work but watching the snow fall, she is summoned by the boss to accompany him on a brief "business" excursion that turns out to be a drive to a city park and an hour walk in the snow, after which he solicitously dried her face, gently kissed her, and then took her back to the then deserted office where, high above the lights of the city, he half forced her into intercourse. At night instead of in the morning, on the floor instead of on the fresh covered ground, and hardly making angels, this second scene crudely inverts the first. But just as the first one, even with its physical details—"feeling the dampness creeping through the seat of her pants to her skin" (62)—looks ahead to the second, so too does the second look back on the first, and much of the novel details the way in which the not quite "rape" followed by the subsequent affair with her boss recapitulates the long extended not quite "seduction" (in that it was apparently never physically consummated) conducted by her father. As Judith herself finally admits: "It all pivoted back to her father, guilt and desire; thick and bent as he was, it was really him she wanted" (117).

Judith clearly subverts certain features of the classic Western. It is a woman, not a man, at home on the range. The range is a pig barn, not a cattle ranch. Instead of shrinking from the violence of "men's work," Judith has a happy knack for castrating swine. Such castration, seen symbolically, is the culmination of the largest reversal enacted in the novel, Judith's return to the realm of the father to dispute his rule. "Western" movement is characteristically male, is from the law of the mother as represented by the constraints of "civilization" to the frontier as the place where one can become one's own man. But how do you become your own woman in a symbolic order that is totally patriarchal and after the father has already seduced you into desiring him, into desiring to be just like him (anatomy as destined disappointment)? That question brings in Sigmund Freud and, even more, Jacques Lacan—two figures not usually invoked by the usual Western.[17]

The father/daughter psychosexuality on which *Judith* turns is cogently analyzed in Jane Gallop's *The Daughter's Seduction,* so much so that this critical study could almost serve as a gloss for the novel. Particularly pertinent is Gallop's assessment of the inequalities of the Lacanian Law of the Father as it applies to the daughter:

> In Lacan's writing, the Name-of-the-Father is the Law. The legal assignation of a Father's Name to a child is meant to call a halt to uncertainty about the identity of the father. If the mother's femininity (both her sexuality and her untrustworthiness) were affirmed, the Name-of-the-Father would always be in doubt, always be subject to the question of the mother's morality. Thus the Name-of-the-Father must be arbitrarily and absolutely imposed, thereby instituting the reign of patriarchal law.[18]

Subject to this unequal distribution of social and sexual power, the daughter sees in the father the arbiter of value and, to quote Gallop again, her "desire for her father is desperate" in that, "[i]f the phallus is the standard of value, then the Father, possessed of the phallus, must desire the daughter in order to give her value."[19] He, on the other hand, "must protect himself from his desire for the daughter" which "threatens his narcissistic overvaluation of his penis" and so seduces her more to his law than to his bed.[20] Because "the only way to seduce the father, to avoid scaring him away, is to please him, and to please him one must submit to his law which proscribes any sexual relation," the daughter is caught in a "vicious circle."[21]

This same vicious circle spins the father-dominated circular plot of *Judith* as well as the protagonist's plan to return to the country and begin with another pig farm as "expiation" (167) for the one she would not earlier take over from her father. Her plan is itself a kind of Lacanian family romance, a fantasized life with father in which she stands partly in his place, partly in her mother's place. She had held off telling him what she intended because she "wanted to present it to him whole and ready to carry out, to be able to say to him, her father, 'Look, I'll do it. I'll begin like you did and we'll start over. I will, I will'" (168). In that "like you" we see her attempt to be him in order to be with him, and when she goes on to insist, confronting the news of her parents' death, that she had "meant to redeem them all, the two of them together again, forever and irrevocably joined" (168), we notice the complete suppression of the mother.[22] The envisioned reunited family is only the father and the daughter as an avatar of the father "forever . . . joined." She had "hugged [this plan] to herself" (168) as a substitute for the father and after the accident she still carried it out because "whether he was alive or dead, she had to show him that she would hold herself for him, her father" (169).

The earlier quoted excerpt from Gallop highlights the markedly different prerogatives allowed, under the Name-of-the-Father as Law, to the capital-ized Father and the effaced and subjected mother. That difference depends on a much more problematic one, the difference between the penis and the phallus: "The father's penis is reminiscent of the extra-legal beginnings of the child. The Father's Name is, by law, unique; the father's penis is but one of many organs involved in the production of the child. If the Name-of-the-Father is phallo-centric law, then the father's prick is the derision of his Name."[23] Although Lacan and his supporters read this second difference one way, Gallop (and numerous feminist critics of Lacanian theory) read it another way. As Gallop observes, "Lacanians think feminist claims are based on a confusion of penis and phallus," two "notions" which should remain "separate" in that "neither sex can be or have the phallus," and "thus women have no reason to rail against the phallus's privilege." But, she continues, even though "the signifier 'phallus' functions in distinction from 'penis' . . . it must also always refer to 'penis.'"[24] So instead of attempting the dubious task of completely severing the two terms, why not look at the ways in which they covertly merge into or stand for one another? More specifically and more pointedly, does the father's penis, for example, really measure up to his phallus? To answer that question requires measurement, of the extent of both his rule and his endowment. It is in this sense that "the father's prick" (note the term's diminutive and bubble-bursting implications) embodies "the derision of his name."

Judith comes to her version of this recognition through castrating the pigs and seeing thereby male sexuality more in the animal concrete than in the Lacanian abstract. Again Gallop provides a pertinent perspective: "According to Lacan, the phallus 'can play its role only when veiled.' To clear all this up is to reveal/unveil the Father's 'Phallus' as a mere 'penis', as one signifier among others, prey to the contingencies of the letter [not to mention the knife], of the materiality of signification, alienated from the referent."[25] Castration is, of course, the ultimate unveiling. Moreover, by leaving the penis but a penis substantially shorn of any engendering (signifying?) status, castration strongly suggests that the claims of the phallus did attach to a penis—a penis attached to functioning testicles.

The novel works its way to its anti-Lacanian resolution through means drawn from the traditional Western. First, the castration scene is anticipated by an earlier barroom confrontation in which we see that the hero will not be bullied (just as later she will not be bested). Jim, a young man from a neighboring farm, coerces Judith into spending a night on the town, and they end up in the local bar where she ends up facing a pack of locals braying over their beer about lady pig farmers. "I don't want to get in a fight here," Jim had insisted, to which she had answered, "*I* do" (134, emphasis in the original), dismissing his suggestion that because he might feel called upon to act on her behalf he can consequently speak on her behalf too. As much as the other men in the bar, he would consign her to her place in a male-ordered scheme of things, but she declines to be "protected" (the traditional place for women in the Western) and, instead, claims the male prerogative of entering the fray.

This saloon standoff looks forward to the conclusion of the novel, which is another incursion into the masculine and another scene derived from but radically reversing the iconography of the Western. Indeed, the climactic action of the novel well might be designated "the cut-out at the O.K. Corral." One element of animal husbandry that Judith did not learn from her father was how to geld pigs. "Even when she was eighteen [he refused] to let her near the barn while they were castrating" (167), lest the sight of castration become the site of castration. Prompted by much the same considerations, Jim volunteers to do the cutting. He also twice suggests one of his brothers serve as his assistant, but Judith insists that they are her pigs and that she will help. When he awkwardly botches his first operation and hesitates over his second (protecting her from castration does not protect him), she further insists that they trade places. He now holds while she cuts, and with a "slice, quick and clean" (166) she shows him how it should be done. It is work that comes naturally to her hand, so much so that after she has gelded all the pigs "[s]he could almost have asked him to lie down on that bale" (167) to provide one final proof of her mastery.

This figurative depotentizing of one man extends outward to others in the text. Framing the castrating scene are references to the two dominant men in her past that deprive each of them of much of the power they have previously exercised over her. Even as she begins to cut she sees that action as an "atonement for the acts of barbarity she had committed on herself" at the instigation of her lover and can for the first time consciously resent "his careful honing of her" (166) and rue her complicity in that process. Now she is shaping things male according to her desire. She also realizes that her father, in keeping her from the sight/site of castration, had also kept her— and him—"from her discovery of his own sexuality" and, consequently, "from her discovery of his common humanity," which was why "she could immortalize him" and also "ache to have him take her, father and daughter in their complicity, their mutual preservation of the lie" (167). The lie is the lie of his own perfection, of his embodiment of the Law of the Father to be, in her terms, "father/god perfect always, unfailing, showing her only birth and death and never the sordid in-between, the soiled and rumpled edges of what the others were so eager, so pleased, to show her" (167). In short, the symbolic order of the phallus that he represented to her is here refuted by her realization that all along all he had was a penis very like others that have been thrust upon her. There is, she now sees, nothing particularly heroic in the fact of that possession. Anatomy might well be destiny but it is not necessarily election. Anatomy, moreover, can be modified, which is to say that the symbolic order of the phallus falls under the symbolic order of the knife.

The novel does not conclude with the climactic implications of the castration scene. Jim returns to admit the fear that previously sent him running away. He and Judith presently make love. That act partly expresses her earlier desire for her father who, not coincidentally, was also named Jim. In other ways, too, the present man in her life sounds suspiciously like his namesake predecessor: "Judy, shhh, listen, little girl, don't be so afraid all the time, you're safe now, my little Judy, shhh" (175). Partly repudiating her earlier desire even as she reenacts it, she immediately counters his "Daddy's girl" tone and language—"I'm not little. I'm twenty-three years old. And if you dare to call me Judy, you'll pay" (175)—and then leads the way to the subsequent lovemaking, which she finds "very good," but more in terms of what she has just done than what they are jointly doing: "There was something about denying her childishness that made it better than it had ever been" (175).

An act of intercourse signifies somewhat ambiguously in Jim's case as well. Symbolic cutting is not the real thing? A certain degree of castration anxiety improves performance? When it comes to having sex with a woman, a physical penis takes precedence over a symbolic phallus? Such questions are not resolved in the novel because his pleasure, his meanings, his significations, are all subsidiary to hers. Yet the reader cannot help noticing how the "drawnout wail" that marks her climax comes from beneath "his still and beating body" (175). They have made love in the position that traditionally marks woman's subservience.

This ambiguous rebalancing of male and female sexuality is itself further qualified. A penultimate scene of human sexuality is juxtaposed against a final scene of pig sexuality (rebreeding one of the sows whose litter has just been weaned) which Judith and Mina, Jim's mother, oversee and read (pigs still signifying) symbolically. The two women first wonder at the act itself: "It's crazy, the positions we let them put us in. Having just got rid of eleven babies, that sow is going to let him put his forelegs up on her and stick that thing in her cunt, and god knows whether she will get any joy out of it" (177). Then they notice what short shrift the sow gives the boar once she is done: "'You tell him, Marie Antoinette [the name they have given this sow],' cried Mina. 'You tell him.' And together they laughed, those insane women, laughed at everything they could and as hard as they could as they danced about in the melting snow" (178). That laughter is a little less cutting than the castrating knife but, directed first at the boar and then "at everything" male-ordered, its point is much the same.

The writing of castration constitutes, in *Judith,* a different metafictive text that especially serves to redress the subservience of the woman in the traditional American Western. Furthermore, by placing a female protagonist within the very mythic structures that would exclude her, the novel comically undercuts those same structures. A duel with a woman? A castrating contest to determine who is the better man? Such ironizing of the elements of the Western is emphasized by the women's final laughter. But there is another note, too, to that laughter and one that comes partly from undermining the forms of the predominant Western, partly from superseding them. Significantly, the duel gives way to the dance. The distinctions, the individualization, the resolution of the Western all dissolve into a shared female mirth that most conveys the feminist implications of van Herk's novel. Hélène Cixous has argued that the woman author "writes of not-writing, not-happening" and that, "finally, this open and bewildering prospect goes hand in hand with a certain kind of laughter" that is women's "greatest strength" in that it "sees man much further away than he has ever been seen."[26] Even more than the threat of the knife, the women's concluding laughter puts man in a different place and claims a Western space for woman.

A penchant for using the forms of the Western to alter its function is equally obvious in van Herk's second novel, *The Tent Peg*. But the Lacanian implications of curtailing the Law of the Father (i.e., changing the nature of the pig) traced out in *Judith* give way, early and obviously in *The Tent Peg*, to hints more traditionally Freudian. Starting with the title and even more with the dedication, in part, to "all my women friends who carry tent pegs of their own," we are more on the level of the penis than in the realm of the phallus.[27] Or perhaps a little above that level. No Freudian penis envy here: on the contrary, the novel suggests that in a contest between a penis and a tent peg, the smart money will be on the tent peg every time.

Both novels are obviously fictions of female empowerment and both are similar in a number of other ways as well. Each, for example, playfully dismantles its quest plot into disparate sections the reader must fit together. In *The Tent Peg*, however, these separate sections are, with a few exceptions, organized chronologically and are clearly labeled as to their source, each one representing a snippet of observation or experience provided by one of the various characters who first prepare for and then conduct a Yukon geological expedition. As Reingard Nischik observes, in *The Tent Peg* "the reader is called upon to integrate the different points of view applied as elements in a mosaic rather than [the] different time levels" used in *Judith*.[28]

The central figure in that mosaic is female, which means that *The Tent Peg*, again like *Judith*, imposes a woman's story on the usually androcentric Western. In fact, much of the second story recapitulates much of the first one. We see J.L., the protagonist in the later work, looking for an escape from a city life not going anywhere. To leave civilization and its sexist discontents behind, she signs on as a cook for the wilderness expedition. But the wilderness provides no refuge; she still must stand up to the men around her and finally defeats her worst tormentor by figuratively castrating him, whereupon she performs a concluding dance of triumph that echoes Judith's final repudiating laughter. The two protagonists are also conjoined by occasional hints of special powers such as each woman's almost preternatural identification with female animals.

Furthermore, in each novel the protagonist and her one woman friend have a complex relationship distinctly tinged with homoeroticism but not explicitly lesbian. J.L. even observes that she "loved" Deborah and at one point "wanted to abandon men forever." But, she continues, "of course I didn't. One doesn't easily give up a centuries-old habit. And she wouldn't let me. She had men herself, and needed them as I did" (111–12). The subsequent portrayal of Deborah's difficulties with the few men in her life suggests that she needs them, as a seventies feminist slogan would have it, like a fish needs a bicycle, and J.L. throughout the novel pointedly does not need any of the nine men who constitute the other members of the expedition. Thus the protagonist's brief explanation of why she and her friend did not become lovers is compromised by the novel that calls the "of course" of heterosexual "habits" into question. Similarly, when Judith, talking with Mina, decides she will use their names for the last two sows as yet unnamed, the two women embrace, "and when they broke apart their faces were no longer laughing, but still and frightened, as if they had seen too much of something" (*Judith*, 160). One suspects that, but for "of course" and "habit," Judith well might have preferred the mother to the son. One also suspects that in both novels van Herk is deliberately inverting the standard Western's flirtation with male homoeroticism to provide a gynocentric counter to that unexamined phallocentrism.

Finally, the Biblical naming of the two protagonists early underscores the feminist politics of each novel and, contrary to the claims of the popular Western, gives the female hero a long heritage (if only in resistance). But the implications of such naming are more clearly worked out in *The Tent Peg*. The Biblical reference in the protagonist's name is itself pointedly referred to early in the text when the leader of the crew who has just signed J.L. on as the cook asks what her initials "stand for." She answers that they are, in a way, her name: "I was really named after a person in the Bible. J, A, dash, E, L. People used to string it together so it sounded like 'Jail.' I didn't like that, so I decided I would go by my initials, J.L." (14). Her employer, who has not "looked into a Bible for twenty years" (14), makes little of this explanation. Should the reader be similarly unversed and not remember who the original Ja-el was, the second reference, near the end of the novel, is unmistakable. One of Deborah's poems celebrates her friend's name and namesake: "Ja-el,/the wife of Heber the Kenite,/of tent-dwelling women most blessed" put one "hand to the tent peg," the other "to the workmen's mallet;/[and] struck Sisera a blow,/[that] crushed his head,/[that] shattered and pierced his temple" (223).

At the conclusion of *The Tent Peg* and after she has just crushed her chief male opponent, J.L.'s initials represent an explicit Biblical labeling of the female hero as hero. At the beginning, however, they constitute more an exercise in cross-naming and a consequent assessment of the prerogatives of gender: "I knew that if I put down my name, J.L., and left the sex, F for female, box unchecked, they would assume I was a man. Only one gender has initials, the rest of us are misses and mistresses with neither the dignity of anonymity nor the prestige of assumption. All men are equal".(23). Cross-named and cross-dressed too, in boots, blue jeans, and an old fedora, she is taken for a he, signed on by the leader of the expedition, and even shares his Yellowknife hotel room as he makes his final preparations for the journey into the wilderness. Such cross-dressing, as Cathy N. Davidson has shown, is, in new world fiction, a venerable convention whereby a female character claims freedoms that would otherwise be denied her.[29] In a few of the first novels published in America, a woman transvestite hits the open road and in one early American best-seller, *The History of Constantius and Pulchera* (1794), the cross-dressed heroine swashbuckles her way through a whole host of unlikely adventures. J.L. has, then, fictional foremothers other than her Biblical namesake. In *The Tent Peg,* however, van Herk presents not so much a cross-dressed woman protagonist (J.L. early gives up her attempt to pass as male), but a cross-dressed Western plot.

Even more obviously than *Judith,* with its barroom stand-off and its pig-cutting duel, *The Tent Peg* borrows from the conventional Western and, more specifically, from "the Kid and the Villain" plot. We all know the story. When the Kid signs on for, say, his first cattle drive, one of the older cowboys loses no opportunity to bully the inexperienced new hand. The boss, a basically decent man, tries to head off this hazing and on a few early occasions does step in to end an incident but knows that he cannot do so too obviously or too often. A man must take care of himself. The Kid has to learn that. And the Kid does learn. In a few late minor encounters he bests his tormentor. But that only serves to raise the stakes of the game, to push the opponent further than he might otherwise have gone, and in the final forced confrontation the Kid claims his manhood by being, not surprisingly—the reader remembers those earlier hints of capability that the bully, determined to assert his own superiority, unfortunately overlooked—the better man.

Much of *The Tent Peg* is the novel just summarized. J.L. is even called, at the beginning and before confessing that she is female, the "kid." Jerome is out to get her all along, insisting that she be fired before the expedition is under way because "women just don't belong out there" (29) and early criticizing, quite unfairly, the quality of her work. There are even the requisite hints of things to come, the most obvious of these being, appropriately, an impromptu shooting match. Because of the possibility of a bear attack, everyone on the expedition must know how to use a rifle. When J.L.'s first practice shot leaves her "sprawled flat on her back" (73), Jerome leads the laughter and then shows her how to do it, just missing the bull's eye. J.L.'s response is her second try, "perfect . . . dead . . . center" (75). So we are not totally surprised when she later thwarts his rape attempt by outgunning him and with his own gun at that.

The two main differences between the demands of this conventional plot and the details of van Herk's rendering of it both center in the hero. First, he's a she and, second, she's a cook. How can a woman be the better man? And, by the same logic, cooking being women's work even when done by men, how can a cook? The conventional Western hero comes in many guises, hiding his now regretted outlaw history or his ostensibly renounced lawman past under almost every conceivable cover. But seldom is it the cook who will rise up to save the ranch, to defeat the outlaws, to make sure that the herd gets to market.

The author calculatingly plays on this conventional deprivileging of cooks. One of the more effective scenes in the novel is the first minor victory J.L. scores over Jerome when he criticizes her work, which is, of course, her cooking. " 'Lack of experience,' she says airily. 'You have to develop a taste for these things.' And she smiles at him like he's a little boy who simply won't eat carrots" (32). When he then tries to answer her back, only Mackenzie, the expedition leader, notices what Jerome, true to the demands of his role, overlooks:

> But I'm watching J.L. and that's when I see the snake in her undulate, just a shade. Jerome doesn't see it, or surely he'd have the sense to let her alone. She faces his scarlet fury with a look like lucid ice. "Jerome," she says, laying her knife and fork correctly, so precisely across her plate. "I can cook dishes that you don't even know how to pronounce." (33)

Such a confrontation, although part of the "Kid and Villain" plot, seems comically incongruous in a kitchen, almost like the Dalton gang or the James boys having a pillow fight.

The cross-dressing seems incongruous too. Why, one might well wonder, must J.L. dress as a male in order to obtain work traditionally regarded as female labor? The reason given in the text, that "most outfits don't like to hire women" (24), and the reason for this reason, "common theory is it's bad for camp morale" (24), does not answer the question but only defer it. Furthermore, and a second puzzling matter, why does J.L. give up her pretense of being male yet retain her ungendered initial name and her male guise? What are we to make of a disguise acknowledged but not discarded? The point, I think, is that a failed cross-dressing (the garb seen through but not removed) poses a greater challenge to essentialist paradigms of gender than does a successful one. Furthermore, when the revealed cross-dresser is a woman, we also see the traditional double standard in operation even on the threshold of gender transgressions, for sexual boundaries, doing social work, are hardly created equal. Thus the woman must assume male dress to claim male prerogatives, to light out for the freedom of the frontier, whereas a man can simply sign on as a cook to enjoy a woman's exemption from the imperatives of "real manhood." Moreover, if she is discovered she should be put back in her proper category, whereas he need not be. This odd asymmetry itself interrogates the ostensible "naturalness" of the gender boundary.[30]

A female cross-dresser challenges that boundary by, first, demonstrating that it can be transgressed and, second, that, contrary to "nature" again, a woman can desire to do so. Yet the challenge implicit in the successful cross-dresser's "male" exploits is often muted by a final reskirting of the very matter addressed in the text. For example, in the previously noted *History of Constantius and Pulchera,* Pulchera, despite her numerous adventures under the name and dress of Valorus (note how overinscribed each designation is), ends up married to Constantius who, a bit of a cross-dresser himself, patiently waited her return. As, finally, Mrs. Constantius and safely ensconced in "the suburbs of Philadelphia," she embodies no substantial threat to the patriarchal institutions of her society.[31]

J.L. would also pose no particular threat to a patriarchy if, in her original disguise, she simply fulfilled her original intentions—"to head for nowhere and look at everything in my narrow world from a detached distance" (23)— and then returned to that narrow world to become again a female graduate student in sociology. Reshaping her escape as a failure (reassuming the burden of being a woman) even as she successfully accomplishes it (achieving that detached perspective) changes the focus of the cross-dresser's attack on gender essentialism. Of course, the completely successful female cross-dresser actually challenges nothing. She is simply taken for a man, and naturally "men" act like that. If the reader is in on the disguise, as in literary renderings the reader necessarily is, then definite questions are raised when

a woman claims, covertly and by snatches, some of the prerogatives of the
male sex, but such questions are still posed in terms of aberration and mas-
querade. But if the cross-dressing comes out, so to speak, in the fiction yet is
still retained, then it becomes an ongoing crisis for everyone and especially
for characters—and readers—who previously had no doubts about which
sex was which, with what each one was endowed, just who belonged where,
and to what end all of this division worked. The confusions of those mostly
male certainties are all dramatized in *The Tent Peg*.

Just as J.L.'s "tent is situated right in the middle of the camp," so, too,
Nischik points out, is "the development of the relationship between each of
the men and J.L. . . . at the centre of the novel."[32] That centering is, for all
of these men, decentering. Subscribing to different—and contradictory—
views of just exactly what a woman is, they must confront J.L. as both a
"woman" and a "man" to discover that there is more to her than they dreamt
of in their philosophy of woman as convenient Other. Consider, for example, the simplest case, that of Cap, the camp factotum, who views woman
only as a site for possible sexual activity. Consigned, like J.L., mostly to the
base camp, he regularly informs her that she is "responsible" for him being
"horny" (105), and she just as regularly turns him down until one day, when
she is showering, he decides to force matters to a crisis by stripping and
pulling aside the camp shower tarp to join her. Instead of screaming and/
or fleeing, she invites him in, embraces him, comforts him when he finds
himself crying, then dries herself and him and gets dressed, leaving him
oddly, for him, embarrassed:

> I can't look at her. After all that, walking into her shower and then
> just holding her and crying, not even remembering sex, not even getting
> a hard-on. Bawling like some baby.
> And then she does the funniest thing. I'm bent over, ashamed, pick-
> ing up my pants, and she lays her hand on my head, like a blessing.
> I remember the priest doing that when I was little. She just rests her
> hand on my head and says nothing, looks at me so warm and gentle
> I'm suddenly calm, washed clean, complete. That's all. (193)

That "all," the closest thing to a mystical experience he is likely to have, is
all he will have: "I know if I want to, I can go and hold her and she'll let
me, she'll rub my back with that circular motion and murmur softly, but I'll
never make love to her. It's like that. Hard to believe" (193).

The others also come to her with their different desires: to read one's
poetry; to pose for another's photographs; to be simply the object of some-

one else's sustained gaze; to commiserate with a youth missing his native England; to help one member of the expedition decide if he should get married; to help another (Mackenzie, the expedition leader) discover how and why his marriage failed, questions that he has been worrying for a full ten years. "They're coming to me one by one," J.L. writes to her friend, Deborah, "pouring their pestilence into my ears, trying to rid themselves of the poison." She goes on to acknowledge some sympathy for these men with their "heavier" burdens, heavier "because they cannot admit that they're carrying any" (172). But when all their burdens would be transferred to her, she decides that some relief is in order: "It's time we laid our hands on the workman's mallet and put the tent pegs to the sleeping temples, if ever we are going to get any rest" (173).

The climax of the novel gives J.L. a perfect opportunity to peg away. Her very survival, in fact, demands it. Prompted partly by his view of women (the site not of sex but of subjugation) and partly by his need to punish someone for his own setbacks (a failed attempt to supplant Mackenzie has just left him hopelessly compromised in the eyes of the visiting company officer), Jerome would rape J.L. to reaffirm thereby his own often proclaimed potency: "The little bitch needs to be taught a lesson and I guess I'm the only one with balls enough to do it" (218), he insisted. However, when he comes to the attempt, pistol in hand, and when we remember his earlier fondling of his prized .44 Magnum, we can well wonder just where he carries his self-vaunted sexuality. Wherever it is, she gets him in both places. J.L. knees him in the groin, grabs the gun, and threatens to blow his balls off. His abject cowering, as Mackenzie arrives on the scene, prompts the question of whether he's "got any" (221). Much the same point is also made another way. "He tried to rape me. Not very good at handling a woman and a gun at the same time" (222), J.L. observes. One form of Jerome's sexuality (the gun, his means) got in the way of the other (his erection and its intended end), leaving him both disarmed and very publicly unmanned—in short, doubly symbolically castrated. Or switching from the Freudian to the feminist register, we can see the pistol as a shifting signifier that, passing from his hand to hers, proves her to be the better "tentpegman," when she nails him and with his own gun at that.

Yet J.L., aiming at Jerome's genitals and having him in her power, doesn't shoot. To do so would be both a deserved retaliation (he could be "hoist with his own 44," so to speak) and an expression of sexuality in the Jeromian (i.e., degenerate) masculine mode, a claim of one's own power advanced by engraving another's "inferiority" into the other's body. On the textual level, too, sexuality in the obvious male register is resisted, and there is no conventional climax enacting "the end" of the work. Instead, *The Tent Peg*, like *Judith*, diffuses and extends, through several subsequent episodes, the female protagonist's triumph, which becomes, thereby, more an ongoing revisioning than a concluding resolution.

In the first of these episodes, a kind of flashforward, Franklin tells how, after the expedition was over, the men all found little sachets of tundra that J.L. had secretly sent back with them, and smelling the "faint lemony scent of the tundra" they also smelled her and knew, in an effective merging of retrospect and prospect, they would "never be able to forget either her or [that] summer" (224). Those sachets of tundra conflate and compromise their earlier concepts of both woman and wilderness. For the "explorers" in this book, a number of them ironically bearing the names of famous explorers of Canada (Mackenzie, Franklin, Hearne, Hudson, Thompson), have not discovered much about either woman or wilderness, and what they retain is mostly a mockingly faint whiff of each. But then, as Annette Kolodny has argued at length in *The Lay of the Land*, the very terms of exploration and expropriation applied to a "new" land are taken from an older male rhetoric of female subjugation, so it is appropriate that a sign of the nonpossession of the one here also signifies the nonpossession of the other.[33]

J.L. sends the men back with the sachets and with something more as well. The novel concludes with the striking of the camp as described first by J.L. and then by Mackenzie. Everything that will not be carried out is being burned including J.L.'s worktable. Only then does she don women's clothes. With the fire flaming up, she decides not to be another "encindered" Joan of Arc: "Instead, I'll play siren, put on the gypsy skirt that has been collecting creases in the bottom of my knapsack these three months, gather it in my hand and jump atop that sagging table to give them one last word, one final invocation to send them on their way" (225). That last word is a whirling dance on the burning table, and in her "transfiguration" they are "themselves transformed, each one with the tent peg through the temple" (226). This evocative scene is doubly narrated, first by J.L. and then by Mackenzie, to dramatize its ongoing status as an ending extended through subsequent recountings. This ending is also a staged and restaged carnival scene in which J.L.'s final "disguise" is her ostensibly "proper" dress. The reversals of the book reversed again, cross-dressing corrected to yield carnival, the woman masquerading as the woman, the paradigms of gender are here doubly undone, all of which drives home the final metaphoric tent peg the men all take away with them. J.L. unmanned Jerome. The rest she more subtly unwomaned, depriving them of that convenient construct (their earlier view of woman) whose postulated limitations conveniently warranted their claims and excesses.

In *Judith,* a farm (significantly, a *different* farm) stays in the family; the daughter takes up her father's former role but does not return to his former rule. At the end of the novel the women have claimed the space of the breeding pen, which, like the cutting shed, was where they were traditionally not supposed to be, and what they say once there—comments on sexual performance and, even worse, laughter at male sexuality—show why they were formerly excluded. Those comments also allow them to claim a previously precluded space in narrative, the right to last words in matters textual as well as sexual. And although that right is not exercised in *The Tent Peg,* J.L. has clearly altered the terms of male discourse and altered them most, as Mackenzie's last words (and the last words of the novel) attest, with her resumption of female dress and her final dance, a "wildly sensual movement to an unheard music, that of tambourines and golden trumpets" (227), a dance perhaps archetypal in origin but endless in extension as Mackenzie envies Sisera the literal tent peg that at least consigned his predecessor to peace. Mackenzie's tent peg, ever "lodge[d] in [his] skull" (227), is his inability to reconcile J.L. in female dress with J.L. in male dress with J.L. in no dress (itself an experience that moved him to wonder and a memory that continues to do so). But at least he is addressing the problem with a higher part of his anatomy instead of trying, like Jerome, to "write" women into a crude and self-serving definition of what he would prefer them to be.

Both "last words," then, provide a final parallel between the two novels and help to define van Herk's feminist accomplishment as a writer of Westerns, which is, simply put, to restage the very literary/gender war out of which, Tompkins suggests, the traditional Western originated by claiming total male victory. "Smile when you tell me that," van Herk, in effect, says. More explicitly, she acknowledges that she "like[s] tough women, women who can act," and that she is "also interested in the woman as trickster figure, women who can trick to get what they want."[34] The trick of both texts is the textual/sexual reversals on which they turn, whereby the author, as a western Canadian woman, insists that women can stake their claims (as J.L. at one point does in *The Tent Peg*) in whatever realms they please, in the Western itself. If men cannot accept that new order, there are always (for the Lacanian male) knives and (for the Freudian) tent pegs.

6 The Gynocentric *Journey*

Anne Cameron, like Aritha van Herk, persistently subverts the Western's traditional phallocentric ethos to produce fictions of female empowerment. That empowerment is most obviously signaled, in Cameron's work as in van Herk's, by scenes of castration. But whereas van Herk explores the implications of symbolic or substitute emasculation, Cameron portrays the real thing. In one other way, too, Cameron goes considerably further than van Herk. In contrast to muted portrayals of covert female homoeroticism, Cameron, in *The Journey* (1986), celebrates an explicit lesbian love affair between her two protagonists. Indeed, most of the novel charts the flight of these two characters from patriarchal control to the possibility of some community of women. It is a long journey, and with *The Journey* the Western itself has come a long way from its partial origins in James Fenimore Cooper and such subsequent authors as Owen Wister and Zane Grey.[1]

Even more than van Herk, Cameron early asserts her intention to revolutionize the Western. Her dedication is, in part, "for all the little girls who always wanted to be and never could grow up to be cowboys."[2] One of the epigraphs reads:

> I see by your outfit that you are a cowboy
> I see by his outfit that he's a cowboy true,
> I see by their outfits that they are all cowboys,
> If I get an outfit can I be cowboy, too.
>> (as sung by those of us tied for
>> too long to trees and stereotypes) (n.p.)

Equally germane and appended to the dedication and epigraphs is a suggested genealogy for the novel. Here Cameron notes how integral to childhood the Saturday Western movies were and how "the boys could identify with the heroes" whereas the girls had "Dale Evans" who herself had "no guns" and "the slower horse, [and] who rode behind Roy just in time to catch the mud flying from his gallant steed's hooves." Because of the standard iconography of the movie Western, the author caught a certain amount of "mud" too: "And so, because I had long hair, worn in pigtails, and the stereotype did not allow me a six-gun, a rifle, or a knife, I spent many hours tied to trees, the captive Indian. Perhaps that was the beginning of this story" (n.p.).

In that "beginning" we can read the novel's "end" as well, which is to untell more standard accounts of how the West was won/one. Foregrounding other stories typically suppressed in the dominant discourse of the Western, *The Journey* requires the reader to recognize how much those other stories have been there all along and how their recognized presence undermines the ethos that would silence them. For example, give one of the Chinese coolies working on the railroad a chance to recount his own tale, and the heroic task of creating a nation by traversing it with steel rails also becomes, as it no doubt was, an extended exercise in brutal exploitation. Or, similarly, let a conventional dance-hall encounter be described by the woman participant whose present prostitution is a painful detail from her story, not simply a pleasant interlude subsumed into his:

> "I'm not very experienced at this," she lied again, "and I know you probably are."
> "Not too," he contradicted, beginning to feel less awkward and stupid. "Not too much." (22)

In those lies—his and hers—we see the much larger lie that requires them both, the myth of male mastery. It is in this sense especially that the novel provides more than the obvious reversals inherent in a lesbian Western.

The reversals, in fact, begin before the novel itself. Notice, for example, in the last line of the parodic "Streets of Laredo" epigraph, the difference between "be cowboy, too" and the expected and more grammatically correct "be a cowboy, too." It is a difference that highlights dress as determining essential selfhood which thereby becomes merely a matter of dress (a circular proposition also implicit in the original song in which, it will be remembered, we do see by one's "outfit" that one is a "cowboy"). Being or bootedness? Or, when it comes to cowboys, is there any difference between the two terms? In short, is cowboyhood contingent on essence or outfit? And although cowboys would answer the question one way, is not that predictable response mostly a demonstration of the prerogatives of cowboy dress—cowboys being real men of course—which is to say that discourse across the dividing line of gender tends to cloak claims of sexual superiority in assertions of natural order.[3] Such suspect readings of nature illustrate, naturally, the power structures of the society that makes them.

That men have long been misreading their own outfit as essence and correspondingly designating women as fundamentally misoutfitted is suggested by another of Cameron's epigraphs, one that pointedly invokes still other possibilities of sexual misreading: "If you don't know how . . . fake it; who'll know the difference, anyway?" (n.p., ellipsis in the original). That last derisive comment is more a Shere Hite question than, say, a Luke Short one. Would a true cowboy even be caught in the presence of a fake orgasm? Still more to the point, would he know it if he were? Moreover, if men can be deceived about women's sexuality even during intercourse, should they really have the full and final word on just what that sexuality, in the abstract, signifies (masters of the stereotype if not the orgasm)? Sexuality is very much at issue in this text that reverses the usual sexuality of textuality and particularly the sexuality of Westerns.[4]

As Barbara Johnson argues in her intriguingly titled essay, "Allegory's Trip-Tease: The White Waterlily": "It is not the life of sexuality that literature cannot capture; it is literature that inhabits the very heart of what makes sexuality problematic for us speaking animals. Literature is not only a thwarted investigator but also an incorrigible perpetrator of the problem of sexuality."[5] Cameron's title and first epigraph suggest that she will do some tripping and teasing too, and both, moreover, will not be without allegorical significance as well. For if the complicity of textuality and sexuality cannot be, as Johnson and others have argued, fully untangled, it can at least be looked at from different angles. More specifically, if "Western discourse as a whole," to again quote Johnson, and particularly the discourse of the Western, indulges in "repeated dramatization of woman as simulacrum, erasure, or silence," then "it is not enough to be a woman writing in order to resist the naturalness of female effacement in the subtly male pseudo-genderlessness of language."[6] By implication, a resisting woman must look for different differences, which is precisely what Cameron promises in still another section of her prefatory material:

> Dedicated critics and committed historians will quickly find that this novel does not pay particular attention nor give much respect to the recorded version of history.
>
> —*Pickypicky!*

> When one is re-inventing the world one cannot be concerned with minor details, and when one has become convinced, over a number of years, that the privileged patriarchal perspective is sick, one looks for alternatives. (n.p.)

As its prefatory material implies, the sexual politics asserted in *The Journey* are as direct and forceful as a slap to the face—or, a more appropriate comparison, a kick in the balls. For testicles, in Cameron's Western world, do not fare particularly well on the literal level largely because their symbolic function is regularly disputed in the text:

> Halfway down the street, a figure lurched from a doorway and a hand reached out to grab her arm.
> "Hey," the voice slurred, "you wanna celebrate New Year with me?"
> "No," she said shortly, pulling her arm free.
> "Don't be like that," the man coaxed, reaching again.
> "Okay," she said agreeably, smiling up at him. He smiled back, and she stepped forward quickly, slamming her boot hard on his instep, bringing up her other knee and driving it viciously into his crotch. He gasped, gagged and slumped to the ground. (87)

An anonymous male here gets exactly what he unwittingly requested, for she ceases to "be like that," a woman who only verbally turned him down, and proceeds to do so physically as well. That "no" in action illustrates the poetics of violence informing the text. Men who would enforce their self-serving definition of women must be resisted. As in van Herk, a symbolic order represented by the phallus can be countered by another symbolic order represented by the knife.

Although the cutting that asserts the symbolic order of the knife does not take place until near the end of the novel, that resolution is hinted at from the very beginning of *The Journey*. In even the first episodes substitutions and elisions undercut both paternity and male sexuality. The novel, in fact, begins with "a young girl and a weary woman" (1) standing over the grave of their father/husband and contemplating the difference that his death has made in their lives. The main difference is the presence of the dead man's brother, Uncle Andrew, who has arrived on the scene to be the "man in the family" (4) and who brutally exploits the women by working them, under constant threats of beatings, to the limits of their endurance while claiming both the scanty profits from their labors as well as the credit for taking care of them.

At first the fourteen-year-old girl only dreams of retaliation, "of being big enough, strong enough, hard enough to just kick Andrew where it would hurt the most" (5). She is forced to do more than dream, however, when her mother presently dies under Andrew's harsh regime (he was too cheap to send for a doctor until it was too late), and on the very night of the funeral he sets out to teach the daughter a further lesson as to what her future with him will entail. Alone with her uncle, under his heavy stare, and with the threat of sexual violence hanging in the room, she drops a cup. He slaps her and then, when she answers back that it was only an accident, viciously straps her with his belt. It is a beating prompted partly by his own only slightly deflected sexual desire—"Just because your hard little titties are pushin' against the front of your dress don't mean you're a full-grown woman" (13–14)—and partly by a pedagogical program intended to preclude any need for subsequent deflection:

> "That's just a sample, Missy. From now on, whatever I tell you to do . . . you do! You do it and keep your mouth shut to the neighbors or you'll get more of this." He reached down and took her chin in his hand, his big fingers squeezing cruelly. "You're a big girl now. Time you learned your place. Time you learned what a woman's place is. And I'm gonna teach you. Damn quick!" (14, ellipsis in the original)

Her place, he would have it, is subservience and silence no matter what he might do to her, and we note the obvious hints of rape and incest implicit in his ominous ellipsis.

Uncle Andrew's lesson is premised, of course, on her having already learned it, on her knowing her "place" and accepting his right to consign her to the still more brutal version of that place he is in the process of imposing. Experiencing the nature of his teaching and anticipating its end, she learns a lesson rather different from the one he thought he was enforcing. Later that same night she splashes kerosene over the cabin and barn, conducts all the farm animals to safety, sets fire to the buildings, and, dressed as a boy, rides off on her uncle's prize stallion. Cross-dressed and cross-lessoned too, she escapes subservience and sexual tyranny by transgressing a gender boundary to claim a freedom regularly accorded only to the male protagonist. Particularly in the popular American Western the mistreated adolescent boy has long asserted the right to strike out on his own to achieve, as a personification of America, his own destiny.

The iconography of a youth in flight from civilization and its constraints validates individualism over community, self-reliance over responsibility; in a word, freedom (American style) over commitment. Implicit in those privileged terms—individualism, self-reliance, freedom—however, is a hidden adjective: "masculine." Freedom and flight, as noted in the previous chapter, are coded "male"; what is fled from is implicitly "female." Huck Finn can always "light out for the territories" to escape the civilizing mission of his Aunt Sally as well as the "feminization of American culture" aided and abetted by popular nineteenth-century domestic fiction.[7] So when Anne sets her uncle's house on fire and lights out for the Canadian equivalent of the territories, she not only curtails (symbolically and actually) the perverted abuse of patriarchal power, she also proposes a model of female power different from the stay-at-home domesticity championed by the sentimental novel.

Her alternative model, however, begins with her disguised as a boy, which is no alternative at all. Unlike van Herk, who in *The Tent Peg* employs crossdressing to highlight the contradictions of the gender essentialism that requires it, Cameron focuses on the contradictions inherent in cross-dressing itself. Thus Anne's boyish flight is at first an oxymoronic escape. In order to define who she is, she must deny who she is. To remain true to herself, she flees under false colors. She can appear to have died in the fire she set, yet her surviving female body means that before she can find herself she will have to return to the girl she was and come up with a better way to integrate gender and ideological paradigms. Anne must recover herself *as woman* and, in the process, she must also forge from the ideological oppositions of the traditional Western a new vision (Western? Canadian?) in which the individual flourishes within the community—self-reliant, free, and responsible both to others and herself. Only women, Cameron strongly suggests, can achieve this balancing of seemingly opposite imperatives.

In her quest for herself conducted as a wilderness escape, Cameron's protagonist has numerous Canadian role models. Although, as Annette Kolodny has shown, there was a substantial body of frontier fiction and memoirs written by U.S. women, that writing was largely lost from United States narratives of "How the West Was Won," and names such as Caroline Kirkland or Mary Austin Holley are only now being recovered through feminist scholarship such as Kolodny's *The Land Before Her*.[8] In Canada, however, accounts of women finding themselves in the "wilderness"—from Catharine Parr Trail's *The Backwoods of Canada* (1836) or (her sister) Susanna Moodie's *Roughing It in the Bush* (1852) to Margaret Laurence's *The Stone Angel* and Margaret Atwood's *Surfacing*—are staples of literary history. As Heather Murray argues, "both women authors and characters are excluded" from the American "frontier [which] is by definition the place which is far enough away to leave women behind." In Canada, however, a different myth of a "pseudo-wilderness" mediating a city-wilderness continuum undercuts the "'frontier' . . . nature/culture dichotomy which casts woman as either nature (land) or culture (society) but invariably constitutes her as other, as part of either force against which the lone [American] hero must set himself."[9] Borrowing partly from Elaine Showalter's "Feminist Criticism in the Wilderness" and Showalter's mapping "of the 'wild zone' of women's culture" as partly outside "the dominant structure" of male space and language and thus the privileged site for a "double-voiced discourse" that knows both the heritage of the center and of the margin, Murray superimposes Showalter's "always imaginary" wilderness on a Canadian landscape to postulate a crucial physical/imaginary space for Canada's women writers and women characters.[10] In Canada, "women in the wilderness" (Murray's title) speak from a place doubly marginalized—as wilderness and as Canada—to perform a "mediating function" that, for Murray, is "at the heart of English-Canadian literature."[11] Consequently, even a Canadian lesbian writer produces, in Murray's apt phrasing, "a literature of dangerous middles," not one of dangerous margins.[12] Coral Ann Howells has similarly noted how Canadian women writers' "appropriation of wilderness as feminized space . . . unsettles the boundaries of male power" and "provides the textual space for such imaginative revision" as "the rehabilitation of the feminine as an alternative source of power."[13]

Consistent with this Canadian tradition, Anne's venture in the wilderness is an evolving exercise in self-definition starting with her repudiation of Uncle Andrew's views of who she—and how things—should be. Both female subservience and female labor had underwritten his complacent sense of superiority, all of which he loses in the fire. Only then does the community, that never objected to his previous treatment of Anne and her mother, condemn his failure to be a "man." As a neighbor who soon arrived at the charred ruins observes, "he saved himself and left that poor child to perish," whereupon they "all stared at him . . . grim faced and disgusted" (17). One of the small ironies of the scene is the belated rightness of this wrong communal judgment. But the chief irony is that the girl thwarts the man and makes her escape on his stallion taking his rifle and knife with her. The Freudian significance of the two weapons is obvious, while the stallion especially embodied, for Uncle Andrew, male sexuality in action. She has evaded his control, his sexuality, and she has also taken its signs and most of its substance with her. No wonder he will henceforth implacably pursue her in his own inept fashion, a paradigmatic representation of, first, the implicit violence whereby women, Natives, "Others" have always been consigned to subordinate status in the traditional Western and, second, of the fraudulent nature of that enterprise.

The novel's first parable of female victimization and escape is immediately paralleled by a second one which also devolves from another episode of a woman ostensibly being "taken care of" by a man. Chapter one launches Anne on her journey and chapter two launches Sarah. The site of that second launching is a saloon where Sarah serves as a dance-hall girl and prostitute under the steady gaze of Keno, the polished, handsome gambler who is also her lover and pimp. In that last capacity, he is also another male supported by female labor. She earlier took up her profession to save him from jail, and after she has paid his fine, "without either one of them ever saying anything, Keno worked the tables and she worked a back room and turned her money over to him" (46). Raised without parents, used and abused by being handed from relative to relative, Sarah fled this servitude at sixteen to enter another similar one, to be handed on from man to man, exchanging sex for room and board. Keno has simply accelerated the process of being used that has hitherto constituted her whole life.

Working the back room, Sarah occupies a representational space regularly assigned to women in the standard Western, but she occupies it with a difference. The narrative focus on Sarah's successive setbacks as setbacks deromanticizes that old war horse of male romance, the prostitute with the heart of gold. This figure's accommodating nature always was a male attribution. Since her profession supposedly gives her so much pleasure, she need not expect matrimony—or even money—in return for servicing men. Particularly in the Western, her profession serves men in another sense too. The prostitute, as a woman to bed but not to wed, becomes a safe and saving pal. By polarizing woman as promiscuously available (the hero need never marry her) or virtually unassailable (the hero would never want to), the Western effectively cancels women out of men's ongoing lives, yet avoids the "danger" of their total exclusion. The prostitute still mediates, in Eve Kosofsky Sedgwick's terms, homosocial desire, and so shows that there is nothing suspect about men who, for the most part, prefer the company of other men.[14]

Furthermore, if patriarchy constitutes itself through the circulation of women, then Keno as the pimp is the representative figure of that patriarchy. Or if women should not circulate, if they are going to be kept at home, then Uncle Andrew—and incest—become the norm. Neither alternative will appeal to women; neither reflects particularly well on patriarchal society either. Both, however, largely situate each female protagonist. Sarah's choice is prostitution or laundering at slave wages. Anne's choice is to stay properly at home (which would still be a form of prostitution, submitting to Uncle Andrew in return for bed and board) or to circulate improperly (as Sarah has already done). Not surprisingly, under the options set forth by Keno and Uncle Andrew, woman's either/or turns out to be more a matter of both and neither. From her perspective, the very categories that supposedly define her are the bankrupt ploys whereby the Kenos and Uncle Andrews of her society would both possess and dispossess her.

In short, her society is not hers at all. As a woman, she is marginal, expendable, and she is even more so if she is already publicly defined as a marginal woman, a prostitute. For example, when Luke Wilson, a newly elected local sheriff pathologically opposed to sexual sinning, comes with a posse to clean out the town and in the process accidentally kills the teenage cowboy who was with Sarah in the back room, Sarah is conveniently blamed for "tempting" this youth to his demise. She is tarred and feathered, then tied to a half-broken horse and run out of town. Like Anne, she, too, rides away from the scene of her long continued victimization, even as, again like Anne only more so, that ride is an extension and a continuation of her victimization.

With such a similar beginning despite their different starting points, it is not surprising that the two female protagonists soon come together, become friends, and in the course of their travels jointly learn better to know themselves (and one another) and to help each other (and themselves). Neither is it surprising that they eventually become lovers and by the end of the novel have established a small cross-racial lesbian homestead utopia. Like Huckleberry Finn and Jim, they have traveled, in best picaro fashion, through much of their world, have seen how it works, and have seen that it does not work particularly well for them. They therefore choose not to give civilization, so to speak, a second chance but remain in the "territories." Nor is it their lesbianism that takes them largely beyond the reach of their society. Rather, it is leaving that society behind that brings them to their lesbianism.

As its title implies, *The Journey* is, again like *Huckleberry Finn,* a fiction of the open road. The two wandering women witness the Caribou Gold Rush, the building of the trans-Canada railroad. They experience the proprietary behavior of men in the settlements and on the trail. Various characters are encountered and reencountered, as when the arrival of both Uncle Andrew and Sheriff Luke ends Anne and Sarah's early brief attempt to live a more settled life, and they must set forth again. Also in standard picaro fashion, various characters bring in their own stories, as when the reappearance of the sheriff leads to an account of how he began—and ended—his career of sniffing out female sin.

This embedded story especially mocks both the traditional Western and male sexuality. Determined to be different from his "milksop" father, Luke signs on to a cattle drive and immediately finds in the foreman "the man [he] most wished his father had been like" (105). The attraction is apparently mutual. The foreman invites the youth to join a late evening celebration during which he is first plied with drink and then pressed, not entirely unwillingly or willingly, into sexual activities seldom hinted at in Hollywood renderings of cowboy life. Luke's reaction: "He never again touched whiskey, he never again went out behind the wagon, and he never forgot that if there had been women around, his hero wouldn't have even looked at him twice" (106). His homosexual seduction/rape is blamed on the absence of women, and so an action entirely between men still "proves" women's sexual sinfulness and launches him on his career of searching for female scapegoats. When, for example, Luke soon chances upon a cowboy buggering "a bewildered, frantic and securely tied heifer," he immediately "shot the heifer" (106).

That shooting can be read as something more than Luke's ludicrous apportioning of sexual blame. With these three participants, we have an odd example of the triangulation of desire that René Girard has extensively explored.[15] As Sedgwick observes:

> Although the triangles that most shape [Girard's] view tend, in the European tradition, to involve bonds of "rivalry" between males "over" a woman, in his view *any* relation of rivalry is structured by the same play of emulation and identification, whether the entities occupying the corners of the triangle be heroes, heroines, gods, books, or whatever [including cows] (emphasis in the original).[16]

Luke and the cow as rivals for the cowboy's favor? The cow and the cowboy as rivals for Luke's? Strange doings down home on the range! Or perhaps not so strange. The Girardian perspective does illuminate the oedipal triangle that Luke reenacts, first in his violent overrepudiation of everything feminine, and, then, in his renouncing the service of the law of the father to serve, instead, the mother in the bountiful form of matronly Belle. *Cowboy* and *lawman* are here cast not as absolute or even adult conditions, but as inherently unstable and childish mediations of oedipal identity.

Belle, as a motherly madame, has a propensity for taking in waifs such as Anne and Sarah and even Luke too. The pursuit of Sarah presently brings Luke to Belle and her girls, who have temporarily sheltered the two wandering women and, at Anne's insistence, given them honest work. But this lawman, instead of killing, as he intended, all the women, is himself disarmed and then bested in a sexual duel with a woman that is an obvious send-up of the more traditional saloon shoot-out. When Belle wagers that one of her girls can get a rise out of him, Luke can rise to her challenge only by not rising. The sign of male sexual superiority would be, here, a flaccid penis, a pistol, so to speak, still in its holster.

There is a certain verve to Cameron's parodying of the conventional Western climax. Certainly, the overtly high-camp concretizing of Freudian symbolism (the pistol here really *is* a penis) reminds us of how much sexuality, desire, even, is excluded from the Western tradition. That exclusion is further emphasized when Luke's "pistol" fails him by not failing him, and his erection, instead of attesting to his male mastery, transforms him, according to the terms of the travesty duel, into Belle's boy and the passive object of her sexuality. Furthermore, Belle's victory (which even Luke soon comes to enjoy) affirms life and so questions, even as it parodies, the death-dealing ethos of the more usual (i.e., masculine) Western confrontation.

As Linda Hutcheon has recently argued at length, such parody is a crucial feature of contemporary Canadian fiction:

> Canada's own particular moment of cultural history does seem to make it ripe for the paradoxes of postmodernism, by which I mean those contradictory acts of establishing and then undercutting [i.e., parodying] prevailing values and conventions in order to provoke a questioning, a challenging of 'what goes without saying' in our culture.[17]

Moreover, if the country as situated at "the periphery or the margin" is an appropriate site for "the postmodern ex-centric," then so, as Hutcheon also acknowledges, is the writing woman, and parody thus becomes one of the "major forms of both formal and ideological critique in feminist and Canadian fiction alike."[18]

Cameron, however, partly delimits her parody by limiting its effectiveness in the text. She suspects that—contrary to the conclusion of van Herk's *Judith*—the rule of the father is not likely to be laughed into abrogation. And, indeed, Luke's unlikely conversion into fancymanhood does not at all end the pursuit of the two women. Far from it. Uncle Andrew is still on their trail; Luke is replaced by Simon, a former member of Luke's posse and an advocate of the same patriarchal power implicit in the posse. All that Luke's comic defeat allows is for the two women to hit the road again to follow it to the edge of the Pacific and the limits of westward expansion. There they find an abandoned house still more in the realm of the Indians than in the world of whites and again try to settle, a little ahead of encroaching civilization.

Anne and Sarah have already "adopted" Ruth, a ten-year-old girl in revolt against her own intolerable father, and Sarah has had a baby. Soon two more members are added to their family. The house had belonged to Negro settlers, which partly explained why it was so far out of the way. The parents had died, leaving a young son and a still younger daughter, who were taken in by the local Indians. The Indians come, bringing the children, and communicate through the boy (who speaks English as well as the Natives' language) that only "family" should use the possessions of the dead. The two women realize that they are being asked to take in the children and, in effect, become their family. Still more to the point, Anne especially sees that she and Sarah have here been cast in the same role originally occupied by Uncle Andrew when he moved in and "just *took over*" (232, emphasis in the original). With that realization, the novel begins to circle back to the beginning, a circle completed when Uncle Andrew arrives on the scene, accompanied now by Simon, Luke's successor who is even more misogynist than was that "lawman." The law of the father stands ready to be imposed again.

Brutally imposed: the two men find Sarah in the cabin with two of the children—Jennifer, her own baby (a token of her last affair before she and Anne became lovers) and Lin, the adopted black toddler. Sarah is beaten and raped. Lin is callously killed when she tries to defend Sarah, whose screams bring Anne, and the two older children rushing back to the cabin. Anne shoots Simon but cannot, much as she wants to, kill the other attacker once she recognizes who he is. Ruth, however, has no such qualms and, with her own rifle, blasts Uncle Andrew away.

Something more than parody was required to repudiate male rule and something more than killing is apparently required too. Before the two men are disposed of by being hauled out to sea to sink, weighted with rocks, James, the adopted boy, insists on treating them "Indian fashion," taking all of their possessions so that they will go into death stripped and empty-handed, unable to "lie [their] way into the good place" because all already there will "just look at [them] and know" them (281) for what they are. What they are is also engraved on their bodies when James removes and burns certain parts: " 'They don't get sent over with their dings,' he said coldly. 'If they got their dings, even if they're naked and got no presents or treasures, they might fool some spirits who were never very smart, any-way. . . . These naked things with no dings . . . everyone'll know they're nothin' but driftwood. And they won't ever get to come back again!' " (282).

With this act the novel enacts a version of the violence that it has condemned men for practicing. Simon and Andrew ostensibly "deserve" to be marked as trash—here and hereafter—mostly because when they inflicted their definition of woman onto Sarah's body they exercised much the same authority that is now being exercised on them. In short, the excision of the men's sexual parts is, like rape, an inscribing of "Otherness" on the body thus "Othered." These different inscriptions are different writings and different readings of social power, and power, Elaine Scarry warns in another context, "is cautious. It covers itself. It bases itself in another's pain and prevents all recognition that there is 'another' by looped circles that ensure its own solipsism."[19] There is another contradiction here too. To symbolize the male genitalia as the sine qua non of value is to reinscribe the rule of the phallus in the very act of removing the penis.

On the level of plot, however, a case can be made for the castration. The episode does sum up the sexual politics of the novel and shows where that earlier knee to the testicles was ultimately aimed. In the appalling metaphysics of women-hating expressed during and enacted by the anal rape of Sarah, we see how much violence underpins the circulation of women whereby patriarchal society constitutes itself and, in the process, produces such representative specimens as Simon and Uncle Andrew. What she is ostensibly justifies what they say and do, and so they act to make her what, for them, she must be. It all hangs together—patriarchy, projection, a violent and perverted sexuality, a rankling hatred for woman's role in the procreation of life—and the only thing to do with it is to counter it with a different defining violence. Because they kill, they must be killed. The removal of the sign of their power, in this context, becomes the sign of the powerlessness to which they must be reduced for others to live.

The implications of castration in *The Journey* differ, too, from the implications of castration as it is more usually rendered in texts, which is to say metaphorically, as "castration-writing." Dianne Sadoff has argued that such writing "enables a ritualized sacrifice, the cut or mark of circumcision [or "hanging" or "beheading" or some other wounding] which inscribes castration while allowing it not to take place."[20] Sadoff's focus in "*Locus Suspectus*: Narrative, Castration, and the Uncanny" is the fiction of Dickens, but the Western could certainly provide equivalent examples of "manning" and "unmanning" woundings, of ritually enacted scenes of violence and sacrifice whereby a rigorously patrilineal order is maintained. As Sadoff concludes: "Castration-writing, then, serves not only to confess a son's narcissistic desire, to turn castration against the castrating father, . . . but also to mediate the struggle between fathers and sons and so to facilitate the binding of both to cultural and patrilineal law."[21]

As even the brief quotations from Sadoff attest, castration-writing in the phallocentric mode depends on substitution and displacement. Cameron, however, employs different substitutions and displacements and employs them to a different end. One obvious substitution is to literalize figurative castration. Another is to give women a larger role in the resulting primal scene. The climactic action is not then entirely between men. Neither is it just men who are sacrificed. As one example of Cameron's deployment of substitutions, notice that Lin is, at the time of her death, about the same age as was Anne when her uncle first came into her life. As we have seen, what he previously had in mind for his niece was a kind of protracted figurative death and later he intends to inflict on her the real thing. So Simon as a stand-in for Luke is also a stand-in for Uncle Andrew when he (Simon) kills Lin as a stand-in for Anne. One side of that series of substitutions sets forth the ongoing working of the law of the father; the other the perpetuations of that law's chief victims, who are not sons, for sons can succeed to father status. By much the same logic, when Anne shoots Simon she shoots, too, Simon as Luke as Uncle Andrew. But, significantly, she cannot kill Uncle Andrew as Uncle Andrew. He still stands in the place of the father and she still is partly bound by the father's law as here embodied in her real substitute father, whereupon Ruth, as another stand-in for Anne and a young girl in flight from her own father, kills Uncle Andrew as a substitute for that father. Furthermore, that second killing represents a belated substitute for the opening action of the novel. The girl escaping in the guise of a boy is here re-represented as the girl as girl confronting her oppression. It is in Ruth, then, that Anne finally returns to herself as a young woman and sees another way to oppose the gender and ideological paradigms that forced— but were not altered by—her flight. Simply switch paradigms and an action previously unthinkable becomes almost as easy as breathing (and almost as essential to survival).

Still another suggestive substitution occurs when the symbolic cut (that depotentizes even as it establishes the two men as embodiments of the law of the father) is inflicted by James, another male, instead of, as we might well have expected, by one of the women. That act is done, moreover, according to the teachings of another male, Ap-jei, the young Native man who has taught James Indian ways. When a stand-in son (James as Anne's son) castrates a stand-in father (Andrew as Anne's father) according to the teachings of another stand-in father (Ap-jei as James's father), it is hard to sort out just what the Freudian and Lacanian implications might be. And does the male on male nature of this action represent Cameron drawing back from the feminist implications of a woman-performed castration or moving beyond them? If the father-son symbolism, whether in the Freudian register or the Lacanian, here seems to stumble over itself, perhaps it is because the disjunctions in that symbolism oppress men even as they serve men, and so carrying out a symbolic castration might ultimately be doing the work of men as well as of women. Or perhaps only the work of some men; James, it will be recalled, is black and has been raised Indian; the patriarchy opposed is white; there are imbalances other than those of gender to be redressed.

Yet those other imbalances, effectively evoked at the end of the novel, are not at all thereby resolved, and the sexual journey enacted in this text is rather longer than the social one. *The Journey,* in part, begins with the author re-presenting herself as a young girl "tied to trees, the captive Indian." It concludes with the two female protagonists set free—from their pasts and from various attempts at patriarchal control and definition (such as the rape of Sarah). At the end of the novel, however, the Indian is still captive, which is to say that the male construct of female has been disputed but not the white construct of Indian. Admittedly, James, as noted, disposes of Simon and Uncle Andrew according to the teachings of Ap-jei, and the women end up living more in the realm of the Natives than of the whites. Yet just as the mutilation of two white men does not attest to a triumph of feminism, neither does it mark any vindication of Indian ways. Also, and even more to the point, although the feminist utopia finally established in *The Journey* is situated at the margins of both Indian and white society, its very success will further marginalize only the former. Already pushed to the edge of the Pacific, the Native, like the novel, is running out of room.

The last action and words of *The Journey* especially displace the Indian. The two women rest from work with a brief dip in the ocean and "then, together, they swam lazily toward the shore, toward their home" (307). The text insists that this land is now "their" land, and that same point is also made by the labor from which they are resting. The final cedar rail had just been put "into place" and "the fence was finished" (305–6). The last rail here signifies much the same as would the last spike in a more conventional Western, with railroad or rail fence serving as a synecdoche for the imposition of white order. And "rows of beets, turnips, parsnips, carrots, an entire plot of potatoes, rows of lettuce and tomato plants tied to strong sticks" (306) do show that the prediction of its truck-farm future is already being written on this West Coast land. In effect, a feminist utopia here serves as an unlikely advance guard for the advent of "civilization," a role more commonly assumed by exploring expeditions, trading ventures, military or missionary outposts, and other such primarily male incursions into the realm of the Native. But changing the sex of the new settlers does not alter the dispossession of the original inhabitants.

"A central factor in all of the literature on the indigene is that his role is invariably that of the indigene. There are novels in which a woman is not Woman or a plumber is not Plumber but there are none in which an Indian is not INDIAN."[22] One can, of course, wonder whether representation is ever ideologically innocent, if woman is not always to some degree Woman and plumber Plumber. Even designation can be programmatic and problematic. In the foregoing passage, for example, does not the conjunction of woman and plumber serve to Womanize woman? Nevertheless, Terry Goldie's analysis, in *Fear and Temptation,* of how consistently "the image of the indigene" (to borrow part of his subtitle) serves white interests is convincing and certainly accommodates *The Journey.* In this novel, too, Indians are adjunctive to white designs and can be held in reserve until their presence is required in the text.

Sarah, for example, finally recovers from the rape only after the Native women come and ritually bathe her, have her drink a tea made from a "sacred and healing" plant (297), and burn other leaves and herbs to make smoke that induces a kind of dream state—all of this administered by a matriarchal old woman who mothers Sarah through the ceremonial purification and back to health. The essence of that process is the vision whereby the white woman's individual pain is subsumed into the far larger catastrophes the Natives have suffered for centuries. As Sarah envisions "ships in the fog and men with fierce eyes, glittering chestplates and metal helmets" (the arrival of the Spaniards from across the Atlantic) or "entire villages emptied and the ravens of death fat in the cedars" (the decimation of the Pacific coast cultures), she also sees the "lined face of the old woman" becoming thousands of women's faces over thousands of years "and all of them enduring" (298–99). That last "them" clearly includes Sarah. As her suffering merges with theirs, she ostensibly becomes one of "them," a daughter and disciple of Old Woman. Thus the violence of rape is undone and so also is the violence of dispossession. Through the ceremony, Sarah is "indigenized" (Goldie's term) into Old Woman's ultimate heir and can thereby claim her wisdom as well as, it would seem, her land. No wonder neither guilt nor Natives figure in the novel's conclusion, and this oversight is even more problematic than the contradictions inherent in the defining castration that "legitimizes" the lesbian utopia with which *The Journey* ends.

"The lesbian traveler in patriarchy," Bonnie Zimmerman has recently argued, "exits from the mainland through suicide, through madness, or, more positively, through riding away" to some place "beyond the boundaries" of the patriarchy where "women's community and lesbian culture" might be established.[23] That place, in this novel, was already the Natives' place. It can be possessed only by dispossessing them. The sad paradox of *The Journey's* end, then, is that, radical as it is in one respect, it is in another still the same old story of enforced dominion that it purports to controvert.

Part IV   Native Affairs

7 Epic and Extinction

"As a literary genre, the epic was particularly well-suited to the portrayal of the conquest and colonization of the New World," writes Earl E. Fitz in his recent assessment of *Inter-American Literature in a Comparative Context* (his subtitle), and so it is not surprising that works as geographically and temporally separated as Alonso de Ercilla y Zúñiga's *The Araucaniad* (1569–89) and E. J. Pratt's *Towards the Last Spike* (1952) share a common epic ancestry.[1] From Chile to Canada, Fitz concludes, from the mid-sixteenth century to the mid-twentieth, "European models" would be shaped "formally, thematically, and stylistically to both the extraordinary realities and the vast potentialities of the New World experience." Of those models, the epic especially served writers "who wished to give heroic proportions to the immense achievement that was the conquest and colonization of the New World."[2]

One can hardly quibble with European settlers or the descendants of those settlers for employing ancestral literary forms to commemorate what they choose to see as heroism. And if the pattern of heroism was already there in one available genre, the epic, so much the better. But the casting of "conquest and colonization," in the previously quoted sentence, as an "immense achievement" evinces a Eurocentric bias that can no longer pass without question. Achievement for whom? Both the muted nature of the recent five hundredth anniversary of Columbus's crossing of the Atlantic, as compared to the grand festivities a century earlier, and the spate of revisionary studies such as Kirkpatrick Sales's *The Conquest of Paradise: Christopher Columbus and the Columbian Legacy* or Irving Rouse's *The Tainos: Rise and Decline of the People Who Greeted Columbus* attest to a growing awareness that the "immense achievement" initiated with Columbus's first voyage was also an immense calamity.[3] Considering the five centuries of injustice and worse that Native peoples have now endured, there is, Stephen Greenblatt points out, "something inherently debased about . . . accounts of glorious conquests."[4] Moreover, and as Abdul R. JanMohamed has argued at length, the asserted "glory" of the right triumph by the right side depends on "a Manichean allegory of white and black, good and evil, salvation and damnation, civilization and savagery, superiority and inferiority, intelligence and emotion, self and other, subject and object"—dubious dichotomies that give us not the "reality" of any colonial encounter, but the colonizers' "self-contained fantasies" that underwrite claims to the right to rule.[5]

In Canada, as in other New World countries, any Native "opposed to white control, orthodox Christianity, and ordered landscapes" was regularly cast "as a savage antagonist" who had to be defeated in the course of the settlers "ordained mission to bring civilization to the New World."[6] But Leslie Monkman, in his assessment of *Images of the Indian in English-Canadian Literature* (his subtitle), also notes some countering tendencies such as an English Canadian propensity to cast the French and Americans, too, as savages "in the conventional demonic red" mode.[7] In best Canadian fashion, English Canadians, I would add, were early a little unsure of their own identity in terms of that defining civilization/savagery boundary. For example, in John Richardson's *Wacousta; or The Prophecy: A Tale of the Canadas* (1832), the savage leader of the Indians, Wacousta, turns out to be an Englishman in disguise but still no worse than his former rival in love and present rival in war, Colonel De Haldimar, the ostensible representative and defender of "civilization." This novel especially calls presumed definitive differences into question.[8] Furthermore and as Monkman points out, Dave Godfrey's definition of "a Canadian as someone forced to choose between being an American and being an Indian" and Northrop Frye's postulation of a Canadian "quest for the peaceable kingdom" both express long-standing Canadian attitudes that underlay the attempt, in "many poems, plays, and novels [to] envisage an integration of red and white cultures," to see not just "Indian Antagonists" (Monkman's second chapter), but also "Indian Alternatives" (his third).[9] The Indian as Alternative allows for a Canadian alternative to the more conventional Western rendering of the Indian as implacable enemy.

Two Canadian novels, Peter Such's *Riverrun* (1973) and Rudy Wiebe's *The Temptations of Big Bear* (1973), especially reverse the Eurocentric epic of heroic conquest and do so by transferring the heroism to the losing side. But Wiebe's reversal turns on a counter reversal, the way Big Bear, the great chief of the Swampy Cree, in resisting white encroachment and the ongoing attempt to consign him and his people to a Reserve, also rigorously adheres to his own vision of nonviolence to become, paradoxically, the truest Christian in the whole tragic affair of the Frog Lake Massacre and its aftermath. As such and as even the title suggests, Wiebe's history of cultural conflict is also a parable about religious apotheosis in terms, finally, more European than Native, and Big Bear becomes the measure of what we should have been. Such's account of the complete extermination of the Beothuk of Newfoundland, however, is not tempered with hints of possible Christian transcendence for either the defeated Natives or the surviving whites. Moreover, the very finality of the defeat suffered by the Beothuk foregrounds the problems inherent in any attempt to portray this history as anything other than "the horror, the horror" of colonialism at its worst.[10] An epic of extinction? How can acknowledged genocide be rendered heroic? *Riverrun* particularly poses that question. So even though Wiebe's novel, transversing (like the railroad) the Canadian prairie, is more clearly a Western, the Eastern setting of *Riverrun* does not rule it out of consideration and can even be a pertinent provenance.

The West always was a state of mind and a state of history rather than a specific geographical location. It was a New World of perceived possibility on the moving western edge of European expansion, and at one time the far western edge was Newfoundland and the Atlantic seaboard. Indeed, the Western as a literary form began in what is now the East, and *Riverrun,* centering on the decimation of the Beothuk down to one final survivor, could well have been titled "The Last of the Beothuk." But the novel is hardly a Canadian parallel to Cooper's *The Last of the Mohicans.* As Dana D. Nelson has pointed out, in American nineteenth-century frontier romances such as Bird's *Nick of the Woods,* Simms's *The Yemassee,* and *The Last of the Mohicans,* "the Indians are guilty of their own demise" and most obviously so in Cooper's novel in which "the end of the Mohican race in the narrative comes at the hands of a Mingo and is lamented by every 'white' person present—including the French aide of Montcalm."[11]

Dialogically deploying "romance" and "reality" to partly counter the Manichean imperatives of colonial discourse, Nelson, in her chapter "Romancing the Border: Bird, Cooper, Simms, and the Frontier Novel," asks of these three writers: "What are the cultural implications of the 'romance' imposed by members of the dominant culture on the 'reality' of the American frontier?"[12] On a different border and in a different century, free from the historical imperative of forging (in both senses) a new collective national identity and from "the monologic drives of American tradition-making" as well, Canadian writers can romance a different reality.[13] They will register the "excesses of American claims" (Nelson notes John Quincy Adams's

1811 prophecy—echoed in 1820 by Henry Clay—that "the whole continent [was] . . . *destined by Divine Providence* to be peopled by one *nation,* speaking one language, professing one general system of religious and political principles")[14] and will deploy, as Margaret Atwood points out in *Survival,* "a superabundance of victims in Canadian literature."[15] The Manifest Destiny of conquest, of dispossession will not be so readily affirmed north of the forty-ninth parallel. Or, more simply put and on the level of two paradigmatic texts themselves, as we move from one century and one country to another, Natty Bumpo, the mature white man who, in *The Last of the Mohicans,* is at home in both the white world and the Native and who serves as the advance figure for and agent of an ongoing white victory, gives way to Shawnadithit, the young Indian woman who, in *Riverrun,* is finally at home in neither the white nor the Native world and who serves as the final proof and victim of a total Beothuk defeat.

There is little agreement as to just who those Beothuk were. They may have been the indigenous inhabitants of all of Newfoundland or only of part of that large island; their population before contact has been estimated as high as 50,000 and as low as 500; they have been described as another (although widely divergent) Algonquin tribe, as the last marginal survivors of an older "archaic" Indian culture that once occupied much of Northeastern North America, or as the product of earlier Viking/Native contact; they were reported to be sometimes brown-haired or even blond and to be often exceptionally tall, but such reports have also been deemed exaggerations or fictions. What is agreed on is that they did have a number of unique customs, such as covering themselves with red ochre, which may or may not (this, too, is debated) be the origin of the term "Red Indian."

Neither is their history any clearer once we get to the arrival of Europeans and the beginning of recorded accounts. There is some evidence that numerous Beothuks may have been early enslaved; that policies of extermination were perhaps pursued by the early European settlers themselves or by Micmac Indians brought to Newfoundland by the promise of a bounty to be paid for every Beothuk killed; that as many as 400 Beothuks might have been massacred on a spit of land still called Bloody Point. Each of these postulates has also been vociferously denied. Again, there is little more that can be agreed on besides a few bare facts. Whatever the early contact might have been, the Beothuk soon decided that they wanted little truck or trade with the encroaching whites and for some two hundred years held themselves apart as much as possible, not even borrowing, as other Eastern tribes did, the use of the gun. When they were clearly near extinction early in

the nineteenth century, the measures officially intended to save them spec-
tacularly failed. Shawnadithit, the last known surviving Beothuk, died of
tuberculosis in St. John's in 1829, leaving little besides a brief word list and
some drawings she did illustrating traditional Beothuk life as well as scenes
of her captivity, a few of which are used to illustrate *Riverrun*.

Set in Newfoundland and setting forth the final episodes in a longer story
of conflict between white settlers and Red Indians, *Riverrun*, the most eastern of Westerns, is anomalous in other ways too. Westerns rarely invoke the
name of James Joyce, yet Such takes both his title and his epigraph from
Joyce's *Finnegans Wake* (1939). He also produces a book which, although
brief and starkly simple, still justifies that borrowing. As John Moss has observed, Such "writes with a nearly mystical sense for the People, the Beothuk
of Newfoundland, who were extinguished entirely from the earth; he is thus
able to give them a lasting voice, to tell their story in a song of prose fiction
that will rise above their death in time; singing, as they yearned, of how
it had been for them once, and in their final years."[16] But there is more
to the song of the story than the enduring tragic lament of an otherwise
lost people, than the writing of their history that was never written down.
As the Joycean title suggests, there are always unlikely countercurrents,
undercurrents, in any river's flow, and even time runs out in unsuspected
eddies.

Indeed, Such's first complex cross-current begins with his borrowed title
and the irony of that borrowing. "Riverrun," the epigraph conveniently reminds the reader, is of pivotal significance in *Finnegans Wake*. This first word
in Joyce's last novel begins a narrative fragment that completes the partial
sentence with which the work concludes. By thus conjoining beginning and
ending, Joyce transforms linear to circular narration and casts his novel as
a circle, thereby evoking and imitating the Viconian cycles that he sees as
constituting human experience. Summarizing that pattern by reproducing
as a one-sentence epigraph the two fragments that bracket and complete
Finnegans Wake, Such opposes the larger cycles of human existence as perceived through Old World eyes to the smaller and more obviously natural
seasonal cycle grounded in the ecology of a specific New World land.

The Beothuk Indians, before white contact, adhered to a mode of existence that was perfectly adapted to their large island. To exploit various
food resources as those resources became available at various times and
places, they traced out a "'yearly round' from deep in the interior to the
coast and back again [that] was approximately three hundred miles."[17] But
after European fishermen more and more claimed the choice fishing sites on
the coast and asserted those claims by force, the Beothuks "remained inland

year round, never venturing to the sea-coast except in small food-gathering parties which were almost always immediately set upon by the whites."[18] Thus the circle of their "yearly round," the traditional way of life on which the Indians depended, was broken by the global curve of European man's materialistically oriented westward expansion.

Even then the Natives might still have survived despite the loss of one of their chief food supplies. European fishermen, however, were followed by their furrier brothers who, penetrating the interior of the huge island, proceeded to deplete the woodland animals. To protect their traps and trapped prey from "thieving" Indians, the furriers, in ostensible self-defense, also continued the informal policy of extermination. The two main currents implicit in the title of the novel are, then, complementary actions imaged in the ebb and flow of a tidal river. The river is lost in the ocean; the ocean flows back into the land, claiming even the river bed. Whites, identified in the novel with the ocean, overrun and obliterate the Beothuk, identified with the river.

Consistent with this symbolism, the white men, so far as the Indians are concerned, are merciless creatures from the ocean, worse than the "furious whitebears" sometimes brought to them on "massive ice-rafts" (3). Or, near the end of *Riverrun,* one of the last surviving Indian women wonders: "Weren't the whitemen from the sea, their huge ships with wings like gulls," really the "monsters" that, in old stories, came "from the sea" to punish "evil men?" Yet she cannot imagine what "great evil" her people might have done to justify their present suffering (135). She asks this question, it might also be noted, immediately after the drowning of her "husband." He dies when a small party of four, attempting to reach the coast and bring back mussels for those unable to make the journey, is attacked by furriers. Following a river and a trap line set by the white men, the Indians had taken a few animals but had left the pelts, hoping that the trappers might not "bother to track us down" (125). Nevertheless, they are pursued, and as they try to escape across the thawing river, Osnahanut, the one man in the party, falls through the ice when he turns back to help his wife's fallen mother. Shawnadithit, his "wife" (the two were too closely related to be proper mates—one of the consequences of decimation), tries to save him, but as the sheet of ice to which he clings breaks again, she can only watch him drown: "His hair, like eel-grass, lifted in the water and drifted under a downstream ledge of ice and gently away. . . ." (134, ellipsis in the original).

Osnahanut's physical death by water is itself an objective extension of an immediately preceding metaphoric drowning. When he and Shawnadithit make love in a long-abandoned brush hut in which the near-starving

Beothuk briefly find shelter, he asks himself "why was it he and Shawna-dithit could build no babies? . . . The lake, the river, the forest paths, all empty. The mamateeks all empty and decaying like this one. Only the People's spirits would be there. . . . But there would be no breathing, hunting person to bear their memory" (128), and breaks into a "fearsweat": "She said nothing. He held her tightly. . . . She slid under him and spread herself like a fish split for drying. Frantic he pounded himself into her, fighting the darkness, fighting. But at the end it caught him and he cried in her arms like a child . . . Adrift. He was drowning" (128–29). The figurative drowning precedes the literal one. Both foreshadow a still larger symbolic and literal drowning even then well underway.

The image of a rising ocean obliterating the final reaches of a tidal river is a potent symbol, but it is also partly flawed in that it too much naturalizes the event it represents. Neither does it adequately represent other "currents" of *Riverrun*, for each of the predominant flows (to victory, to extinction) examined in the novel also entails its own cross-current. In this context, we might first consider the opening "Proclamation" which also serves as a kind of second epigraph to the novel and further ironizes the first Joycean epigraph. In appropriately formal language "and on behalf of His Majesty King George III," the governor of Newfoundland announces that "ALL PERSONS" shall henceforth be "enjoined and required" to treat "the native Indians of this island" in a "kind and amicable [manner]." The current state of informal war will be succeeded by peaceful trading relations. To encourage that desired end, anyone who "shall succeed in establishing on a firm and settled footing an intercourse so much to be desired, he shall receive One hundred pounds as a reward for his meritorious services." Conversely, those who "exercise any cruelty, or be guilty of any illtreatment towards this inoffensive people, they may expect to be punished with the utmost rigour of the Law" (n.p.). As earlier noted, these belated measures did not forestall extinction.

The hostilities continued, as is indicated by the first episode in the novel, dated September 1818, some five years after the supposed declaration of peace had been signed by Governor Keats in Saint John's. And in the final episode, another five years later, the three Indian women captured when Osnahanut drowned are returned to the woods to establish, finally, peace with the surviving Natives. None have survived. "A way a lone a last a loved a long the/riverrun, past Eve and Adam's, from swerve of shore to bend of bay" is longer and loner for the three women who, in the novel, are given "a little boat . . . [to] go to look for the Indians and bring them down" (142). Their river and their time has run out. Adam and Eve as the first Old World couple can still in some sense survey the ongoing course of their progeny. In the Beothuk context, and after the death of the last surviving Beothuk woman (an inverse Eve), all that remains is the shore, the bay, "the speaking rivers that run to the sea forever" (144), but no speaking people (and, indeed, except for a few word lists compiled shortly before Shawnadithit's death, even the language of the Beothuk was lost).

Not restrained by the governor's rhetoric nor by any fear of "the utmost rigour of the law," those who encountered the Natives were carried on another current which continued until the Indians were exterminated. Yet the Beothuk's total defeat also derived from the fact that they, unlike the nearby Micmac, first heroically attempted to fight on in a losing war and then would not surrender even after they were too decimated to continue any form of effective resistance. But this futile holding out cannot be seen as a way of conveniently blaming the victim for being victimized. The Indians had their reasons for not trusting themselves to the mercy of the victors.

From the imagined Indian point of view, the white men had no mercy. They lacked (and here the echo is from Conrad, not Joyce) restraint. Thus several episodes contrast the Beothuk mode of hunting to the practices of the furriers. Nonosabasut, another main character in the novel, early notes that a partridge hunt could easily have been more successful: "But it wasn't a good thing to take too many. During the difficult springtime they might not come your way because the spirit who ruled them considered you greedy" (16). This same character remembers, soon afterward, the shock of first witnessing what the white men could do: "His father had said, *Now you are ten years old, this summer you can come and see for yourself.* And that was the first time, at the sealing, he'd seen a horizon of skinned carcasses, soft boulders from the sea, piled where the white hunters had left them" (20–21, italics in the original). The same—from the Indian's perspective—senseless and sacrilegious killing is extended to the Indians too. The previously quoted passage continues: "Towards the season's end, he saw a beach again littered, but this time with the shot-down bodies of the People, his father's lost somewhere among them. . . . Would the whitemen have skinned those carcasses also?" (21).

The Indians do not retaliate in kind. Even the historic episode of the killing of two white hostages—which, for the settlers of the time, completely proved Indian brutality—proves no such thing. This event, frequently referred to in the novel, took place shortly after a truce was arranged between a group of Beothuk and a small expedition of whites. Hostages were exchanged, supposedly as a pledge that peaceful relations would continue. However, one of the Indian hostages escaped and returned to warn his people that the whites were not going, as promised, for presents for the People, but would return with reinforcements and attack the unsuspecting Indians. Even then no one wished to punish that breach of faith by killing the white hostages held by the Indians, for "there was no honour in it" (8). Finally a young widow, with "no one to stand up for her," was required "to cut off the whitemen's heads" (127). Under the circumstances, two decapitated men do not conclusively demonstrate Indian savagery, especially when contrasted to a beach "littered" with the bodies of shot Beothuk. Or, in a more minor key, Such quotes a missionary who witnessed the three women loading themselves down with "pots, kettles, hatchets, hammers," etc., in preparation for returning to their people and saw only foolish greed: "the sick woman . . ., not withstanding her debility, was determined to have her share in these valuable treasures" (141). It simply does not occur to this man that the sick woman's obvious overload might be in service of her people. With such episodes we see how easily, how humanly, the whites dismiss the humanity of the Indians, who do not behave in reciprocal fashion. Yet the author does not oppose the cliché of the Native as wild savage with the countercliché of the Indian as nature's nobleman. Neither portrait, at this point in time, can be taken very seriously—which is precisely why Such avoids the rhetoric of either perspective and also employs, almost as a leitmotif, the story of the hostages who were both brutally murdered and reluctantly executed.

The seemingly natural, naturalistic flow of *Riverrun* does not correspond to the narrative complexity of the work from which it takes its title. Nevertheless, Such's epigraph from *Finnegans Wake,* reverberating with multileveled implications, still hints at the shape and content of the novel it precedes. The epigraph also suggests that readers must listen attentively if they would hear, in a phrasing from the novel, "the speaking river." Surfaces are not always what they seem. The killing of the hostages was not just an act of Indian savagery. The proclamation for peace was an empty gesture that changed nothing and well may have hastened extinction as whites tried to capture a woman or a child to claim the reward and killed Beothuk men in the process. We might also here consider the first action portrayed in the book, the last real victory of the Indians, a victory in which little was won. This opening episode can be seen as simply a standard in medias res beginning. Occurring near the end of the hostilities, it summarizes numerous earlier engagements and sets the stage for the final ones which follow. But this minor and mostly symbolic (symbolic of what the Indians have lost) token triumph still serves to suggest to the Natives that they might prevail again in the future or at least negotiate from a position of some strength peace with the whites. So one countercurrent in the Beothuks' extermination is the sustaining illusion that they are not yet totally defeated. Ironically—but consistent with the water imagery—that crosscurrent only adds to the undertow that soon carries the last of the people away. They were all the more lost in that they understandably attempted to believe that they were not.

There is still more to this first episode in which a small raiding party makes what might be, the participants realize, their "last journey to these shores" (3). On the coast that was entirely "the People's place once" (6), four Indians succeed in stealing a large boat loaded with a summer's catch of fish. A minor robbery is thereby contrasted to a major one; the taking of the boat and its cargo is the Beothuks' answer to the theft of the whole seashore. The Indians' raid, in the fall of 1818, is also compensatory retaliation in a more immediate sense, and rather modest retaliation at that. The commander of the robbed fishing party had led, in the early spring of the same year, a party of furriers in an attack on an Indian camp. Seeing this enemy, Nonosabasut, the leader of the Indian party, remembers his tribe's most recent defeat:

> After the raid, Longnon had taken them to where Osnahanut's and Demasduit's mother lay. The river's water and the river's air were still like this, that early spring. . . . His own heart was beating anger as it beats within him now. He heard Demasduit his wife and Osnahanut his marriage-brother break the silence with their mourning. Their mother who had died stone lonely apart from the People, her blood let from her by the furriers' longknives. . . . (5, second ellipsis in original)

The two raids do not really balance. Killing one old woman is rather less heroic than stealing a boat from under the very noses of those who guarded it.

Just as the overall structure of the novel is controlled, as previously discussed, by the central contrast implicit in the title, so too are the various episodes individually structured and jointly interrelated through a multiplicity of calculated comparisons and contrasts. Thus the spring raid of the whites is succeeded by the fall raid of the Indians to be succeeded, another half-year later, by another raid of the whites. That second early spring raid is further linked to the first one in that an Indian is unheroically killed during the course of each of these "punitive" expeditions. But the later encounter, which becomes the central episode of the novel, is also significantly different from the former one. The minor current implicit in the governor's proclamation has come into play. The raiding party, composed of the men whose ship was stolen, will make good their previous loss by keeping the woman who falls into their hands and collecting the promised reward. Nonosabasut's heroic attempt to gain freedom for his captured wife must consequently prove futile. Contending unarmed against armed men, he is immediately killed.

Some members of the second white party apparently believed that they were seriously pursuing an exercise in mercy and attempting to assure the Indians' survival. One of the leaders even laments the death of the Indian man who had approached bearing a sign of truce and who, after speaking at length to his wife's captors (who did not understand him) and shaking hands with most of them, had attempted to lead her away. The tragic melée which ensued is retrospectively described by this regretful participant who employs, unconsciously and unaware, the very dichotomy on which the novel is structured. Indeed, the details of his account well might seem too loaded if they were contrived by the author. But they are not. According to the first chronicler of the capture of Demasduit, renamed Mary March partly after the month in which she was seized: "He ['the ill-fated husband'] strove to drag her from them; one of [our] men rushed forward and stabbed him in the back" (81). The wounded Nonosabasut then felled two assailants and seized a knife from one of them, but, shot twice, he died before he could reach the man who first wounded him. In the further words of the historian of this unheroic combat: "the noble Indian . . . lay a stiffened corpse on the icy surface of the limpid waters" (82). Appropriately, the killing took place on a frozen lake from which a river flows to the sea.

The subsequent actions of the whites further emphasize some contrasts already suggested in the novel. One of the furriers uses his marked stick to determine the size of their "catch"; the body "measured as it lay, 6 feet, 7½ inches" (85). Another is even truer to his profession and attempts to strip the fallen man of his beaver-lined deerskin winter coat. Two leaders of the party "bitterly reproached the man who first stabbed the unfortunate native," and one of them even "declared that he would rather have defeated the object of his journey a hundred times than have sacrificed the life of one Indian" (87). This speaker's unconscious hypocrisy, a proclaimed reluctance to kill the husband in order to capture the wife, stands in obvious contrast to the honest brutality of the man condemned. "The fellow merely replied, 'It was only an Indian,' and he wished he had shot a hundred instead of one" (87). It is also still deemed "best" to keep captive "the poor woman" so recently bereaved, for, treated kindly and shown the benefits of civilization, she "might, in the course of time, be returned to her tribe, and be the means of effecting a lasting reconciliation between" the whites and the Indians (87). With such a noble end in view—and we hear nothing here of the promised hundred pound reward—who could doubt their good intentions?

This whole episode illustrates, first, how the program intended to be a countercurrent to the general practice of extermination soon added, as did the other countercurrent of a few Indian victories, to the prevailing flow. Sid Stephen has argued that the plan intended to save the Beothuks actually served "to seal [their] fate," since family bands were massacred as a means of safely capturing a few females and collecting the reward.[19] But there is a still greater irony in the almost predictable failure of this mission. Nonosabasut is portrayed as the only Indian who perceives that his people must make peace with the whites, as the one leader with prestige enough to persuade the Beothuks to trust the whites. When his wife is held hostage instead of being immediately killed, he thinks he has his chance. He "will go to speak to them" and "tell them . . . how we shall be friends with them and will share our lands with them in peace" (80). He is consequently arguing for precisely what the best men on the ostensibly peacemaking expedition believe they want when he is killed.

An expedition intended to establish, finally, peace with the Beothuk ends up taking one woman captive and killing one man. The discrepancies between proclaimed purpose, actual action, and predictable effects are so glaring that Frederick W. Rowe, in *Extinction: The Beothuks of Newfoundland,* observes that "we are entitled to wonder why it was that the authorities were so obsessed with the formal semi-military expedition and the 'capture' of Beothuks as a means of establishing friendly intercourse with them."[20] But even admitting how "incredibly stupid and ill-considered" the Peyton expedition was and that "no person, even in 1819, should have sanctioned the violent seizure of this young woman," Rowe can also maintain that "without doubt the Governor was motivated by a genuine desire to do something to ameliorate the condition of the Beothuks." Thus, for Rowe, "of all the episodes connected with Beothuk-European relations, the Mary March one bears the closest resemblance to a Greek tragedy."[21]

This strained reading of both local history (Rowe is from Newfoundland) and Greek tragedy effectively serves to reduce the whole sorry episode to an unfortunate accident whereby "the most propitious opportunity ever available to white settlers to express friendliness and good will was lost forever."[22] In the very act of advancing this covertly apologetic interpretation, Rowe, however, cannot himself accept it.[23] He acknowledges that the promised bounty for capturing a living Beothuk virtually assured the scenario that followed. He notes that the governor of Newfoundland, with perhaps "some trepidation about his own role in the affair, went through the motions of having the matter referred to the Grand Jury where it was 'minutely investigated.'" The subsequent report—blaming the Native's death on his "obstinacy" and finding "no intention on the part of Peyton's party to get possession of any of them by such violence as would occasion bloodshed"—is judged "one of the most flagrant pieces of coverup in the annals of British colonial history,"[24] which is no doubt as much an overstatement as the earlier imputing of tragic innocence to the whites.

As Rowe's own history of white/Beothuk dealings makes clear, the "stupidity" of the 1819 expedition was hardly unique. For example, in 1808 another governor "sought and got approval from the English government to have a painting prepared depicting friendly intermingling of Indians and Europeans." The plan was to leave "the painting, together with appropriate presents totalling in value £100, at some place where the Beothuks were likely to find them."[25] Unfortunately, the officer commissioned to carry out this mission could not find such a place and returned, with picture and presents, to St. John's. "Thus ended in failure another well-meant, somewhat naive, and certainly expensive effort at effecting relations between the two peoples."[26]

Neither is the 1819 plan to abduct a Beothuk the better to establish contact with them really that surprising. As Greenblatt observes: "From the very first day in 1492, the principal means chosen by Europeans to establish linguistic contact [with Natives] was kidnapping."[27] Europeans preferred not to put themselves in the subservient pupil position of learning from the Natives their language, but, rather, to put Natives in the still more subservient position of prisoners/pupils forced to learn their captors' language in order to serve them as translators. "Contact," indeed, was mostly envisioned as an imposed learning of European ways on the part of those hitherto deprived of the benefits of Christianity and civilization, benefits to be paid for, of course, with desired products of trade and/or labor. The double flow of cross-cultural exchange thereby becomes a one-way lesson in mastery, with the whites determining both what they would give and what they would take. Neither is it really surprising that a belated desire to save probably hastened the process of extermination. Roy Harvey Pearce has convincingly argued that, when it came to the Indian, "philanthropy and humanitarianism would not work. He on whom it was to work was in fact no Indian but an image which the civilized conscience had created just for the protecting, which the civilized intellect and the civilized imagination had earlier created just for the destroying. Civilization," Pearce continues, "had created a savage, so to kill it. The need was to go beyond image and idea to the man."[28]

Which is precisely what the whites in the novel cannot do. The only way they can get to Nonosabasut is with the knife in the back of their construct of the savage.

Carried away after her husband's death, Demasduit, renamed Mary March, is intended by her captors to be the salvation of her people. Held prisoner for a year, she will experience firsthand the benefits of Christianity and civilization. And she does. The brief section of the novel which describes that process gives us a traditional New World literary form strikingly inverted, a captivity narrative narrated by an Indian captive. What this prisoner views is, from her perspective, mostly unhappy, inhuman constraint, as even one brief excerpt indicates: "This then is the white people's mamateek which they call HOUSE. A place for the fire. A special room to sit in. A different place to sleep. Large boxes where things are hidden so you have to remember where they are. And parts of the house where some people are kept separate from others" (94–95). Her captors cannot imagine that she might see them as cramped, cabined, and confined. The fact that she dies from tuberculosis while she is being sent back to the Beothuk is not particularly considered either: "I considered it still desirable to prosecute the original design," wrote the commander of the expedition charged with returning the woman to where she had been captured one year earlier, "and . . . to have the corpse conveyed to the place of her former residence" (116). Adorned "with the many trinkets that had been presented to her" (117), the body is left to achieve "the desirable object of producing to those poor creatures the blessings arising from civilization" (115–16). One wonders what "blessings" they thought they had demonstrated when they return dead the woman they took away alive, the woman whose husband they killed so that they could take her away.

Demasduit, returned dead, completes the "circle" of extinction that her husband saw all around him on the frozen lake as his blood ran out "like riverwater" (82). The last leader is joined in death by all his family. The wife is removed from the wooden box in which she was left and is placed beside the remains of her husband and child. "Then the People decided to abandon the lakeshore, cursed as it had become" (121). This decision balances the earlier recognition: "*Soon we shall have to leave the fresh sea-islands to the whitemen entirely and make our life only by the great lake*" (19, italics in the original). The lake, with the river that flowed out of it, was to sustain them after the loss of the sea. Now even the lake has been lost. Nonosabasut and Demasduit will soon be followed by the few still surviving Beothuks.

The end of this process begins with the scene earlier considered, the desperate journey to the ocean and the death of Osnahanut. We might now note how that episode contrasts to the earlier ocean-edge adventure, the successful stealing of the boat. The four participants in that opening triumph are balanced by the four participants in the final disaster. But the first party—two young men, an old man, a young woman—is inversely mirrored by the second—two young women, an old woman, a young man—and that reversal attests to the continuing decimation of the Beothuk. The earlier venture concluded when the young woman rowed the canoe in from the ship (which had been taken from the harbor to the open ocean) in order to tell the other People of the prize they had seized and what they must do next. The victors were all "laughing" and "alive" (11–12). The latter venture ends with the young man swept, drowned, out to sea. The grieving captured women are the prize. There is nothing that can be done for those left behind who now will not survive. To emphasize further the connection and the contrast, Such has Shawnadithit, as she mourns the death of Osnahanut, sing "Nonosabasut's song about the taking of the whiteman's boat" (135); he has her, at the end of this episode, arrive at a site that "she hasn't seen for years" (137), the site of their last success. Left briefly alone, she climbs the cliff to a tree from which they earlier watched for their chance to steal the boat. She even sees that there "are still faint ochre stains" on the branches. She also sees a "huge ship . . . blowing its heavy way across the bay" (139), the ship that will carry her and her mother and sister away to Saint John's.

Like Nonosabasut's vision, the novel has come full circle. In this beginning returned to—another hint of Joyce—is the Beothuk's end. Yet for them there are no Viconian cycles even though Shawnadithit's concluding song, mourning the death of her mother and sister, begins "where the riverrun ends" (144). The final circle of *Riverrun* is a maelstrom, not a life-sustaining flow, and the novel concludes with the total extinction of the People. A starkly factual final postscript balances the opening "Proclamation" that came to nothing. Shawnadithit, the last surviving Beothuk, "died in St. John's on June 6, 1829. . . . Her grave, originally in the Church of England cemetery on the Southside, St. John's, was lost when the cemetery made way for a city street" (145). The muted irony of that last statement is the final note in the Beothuk's death song—as if the lost grave could matter after the whole People had been lost.

The final tragedy, is, of course, that it did not have to end that way. In *Marvelous Possessions* Greenblatt assesses at some length "an unusually detailed (and impressively modest) account of the tentative establishment of trading relations [between the Beothuk and the English] through the manipulation and interpretation of signs."[29] In November 1612 a few Englishmen, led by the Bristol merchant John Guy, come onto a small and temporarily deserted Beothuk dwelling site. They note the few goods that grace the Beothuk camp, particularly a brightly polished copper kettle, whereupon, under Guy's orders, "everything was removed out of his place, & broughte into one of the cabins, and laid orderlie one upon the other, & the kettle hanged over them, wheearin thear was put some bisket, & three or fower amber beades," all of which "was done to beginne to winne them [to trade, not conquest] by fayre meanes."[30] As Greenblatt points out, the signing here is far from the fatuous claims of total linguistic and cultural mastery that characterized most early contact starting with the first, Columbus's "fantasmatic representation of authoritative certainty in the face of spectacular ignorance" as he "reads" the first "Indians" he encounters.[31] Guy imagines how the Beothuk might read him and textualizes his entry into their place accordingly; signing his temporary presence; oversigning his intention to have that presence noted; signing, with the small gifts, that this intention attests to his peaceful purposes. The signing is read rightly; the Beothuk send two canoes after the English ship, and now Guy can demonstrate that he is a shrewd reader of signs as well. When the ship's boat is rowed toward the canoes, the Natives retreat. The English see that they should not seem to pursue and bring the boat "to anker, which pleased them [the Beothuk], & then they stayed." The Beothuk land, from one canoe, two men; the English land one man. As the Natives approach, the Englishman imitates their actions until the three meet and exchange gifts, whereupon another Englishman comes ashore bearing and receiving gifts. "Then all fower togeather daunced, laughing, & makeing signes of ioy, & gladnes, sometimes strikeing the breastes of our companie & sometymes theyre owne."[32] As Greenblatt concludes: "For a simple moment—two Indians and two Europeans imitating each other, exchanging small gifts and dancing together on the shore—there is something like a secular communion."[33] Such moments of epiphany were, however, rare and fleeting, and even this one was not quite the innocent encounter it seems to be. Guy's success with the Beothuks partly resulted from him being also a deliberately bad reader of his own culture and disobeying the commission that ordered him "to assay by all good means to capture one of the savages of the country and to intreate him well and to keep him and teach him our language, that you may after obtayne a safe and free commerce with them."[34] Nevertheless, the fact of this brief dance does emphasize the large tragedy implicit in the more salient fact that most whites could not question their self-justifying construct of the Native as savage or the consequences of that ordering.

The epic of white conquest, of European success and achievement in the

New World, is more satisfying to read than the counterepic of Native resistance or the anti-epic of European perfidy and/or stupidity. The heirs of the victors in a four-hundred-year war for the possession of North America produce and consume most of the accounts of that long engagement. The stories told will necessarily serve their interests and will continue to do so even when the occasional narrative of conquest is, like *Riverrun,* strikingly idiosyncratic.[35] For one claim of Such's novel is that we are at last "man" enough to confront honestly what our predecessors did, to admit even genocide and the stupid or hypocritical (you can take your pick) measures whereby it was finally fully accomplished largely through the very designs instituted, ostensibly, to prevent it. For the most part, however, white narratives will not venture into these dangerous waters but will cast Natives as subhuman beings deserving their fate; as opponents in some respects admirable but still rightly defeated, or as, for all practical purposes, not there, leaving an empty land ready to be claimed.

The first of these ploys is the most common. Thus Columbus, even on his first voyage and despite a sporadic rhetoric of having encountered "the best people in the world and the most peaceable" (16/12/1492), can convert those very terms of praise, particularly the "peaceable," into reasons for conquest: "They are fit to be ruled," he writes in the same journal entry. And soon he is suggesting that "cannibal slaves, fierce but well-made fellows . . . wrested from their inhumanity [to make] the best slaves that ever were" (30/1/1494) could be sold to support the cost of European settlement.[36] Such cannibal slaves double serve: as slaves they add to the profit of white enterprise; as cannibals they justify it. The savage Indian has been in service now for a very long time.

As Columbus's early observations attest, it is a small step from the Other as "noble savage" to the Other as "potential slave." The reason for this easy slippage, Tzvetan Todorov goes on to point out, is the "common basis" for both constructs, "which is the failure to recognize the Indians, and the refusal to admit them as a subject having the same rights as oneself, but different."[37] With this slippage in mind, white renderings of the Native are not somehow redeemed by individual heroic Natives recognized as worthy opponents. Thus, in Zúñiga's *Araucaniad* the Araucan chief, Caupolican, can be clearly the better man, as in some ways Hector was in the *Iliad.* But technology (i.e., muskets) necessarily wins over nature (i.e., bows and arrows), and the Natives can be simply savages again when convenience and the gold and silver mines require that they play the more debased role instead of the more elevated one. Similarly suspect are works such as *Towards the Last Spike,* Pratt's epic poem in which the Native is mostly missing. Violence can then be enacted, harmlessly, on the land itself as it is tamed and claimed, beaten into place and into "Canada" by the driving of all those railroad spikes.

All three of these related approaches give us different versions of the vanishing Indian. But, as Leslie Monkman wryly notes: "The assumption that the Indian would inevitably disappear grows less pervasive in twentieth-century literature as his continued physical presence demonstrates his obvious survival."[38] Columbus, Todorov claims, "discovered America but not the Americans."[39] It was a long-continued nondiscovery, and it well may be that the real epic of contact (not of conquest) is the survival of Native people in the face of fictions whereby they regularly were not human and often were not even here. In this context, the epic achievement of *Riverrun* is that it forces us to recognize the humanness and the hereness even of those exterminated in keeping with earlier fictions of who and what they were. As the Beothuk come back into white and Native consciousness, the Viconian and Joycean cycles set up in the novel spin in a larger and more complicated fashion.

The "postscript" ending of the novel is a brief and dated ("March 13, 1973") account of Shawnadithit's death that itself concludes by noting how her "grave, originally in the Church of England cemetery . . . was lost when the cemetery made way for the city street" (145). From "riverrun" to city street. But again there are countercurrents, ironies, and Shawnadithit's final loss also has its positive aspects. Through further desecration, she is at least free from the confines of the Christian cemetery and the care of the Church of England and can retrospectively doubly haunt the novel that tells how her peoples' death ended in hers. Scattered throughout that narrative are a few of the illustrations drawn by Shawnadithit herself, illustrations that definitely tell a different story than any white rendering of her story.[40] Then, at the end of the white account, she escapes the place where we (as whites) thought we had conclusively put her in our first ordering of her life. Appropriately, the last words in the novel itself are in Beothuk. They are Shawnadithit's death song for her mother, Doodebewshet, and they are not translated.

8   Lessons on Perspective

If Carlyle Sinclair, the protagonist in W. O. Mitchell's *The Van-ishing Point* (1973), had more perspective on himself and knew what he wanted, he well might have published a personal ad such as the fol-lowing: "Widowed white male, thirty-something, disillusioned with civili-zation and its discontents, desperately seeking bright young Native woman (18 to 25) to broaden horizons, restore faith in humanity, and, in general, make him feel alive again. Please send writing sample and recent photo." Not until late in the novel, however, does he recognize how much—and how—he desires Victoria Rider, the first student to graduate from the small Indian school where he is the sole teacher, the one graduate whose ongoing academic success might validate his pedagogical career. And Victoria does go on to Calgary and to nursing school, but soon gets pregnant and drops out. Her academic failure precipitates in the protagonist a personal crisis resolved only when he finally comes to see that she is the woman he loves, not the girl who let him down. He thereby resolves, too, the longer crisis that has constituted his life up to this crucial turning point. In short, the romantic impetus of the novel's plot is perilously similar to the parodic thrust of the imagined personal ad, and that conjunction foregrounds one of the crucial questions on perspective implicit in *The Vanishing Point*.

What is the connection between disillusion with civilization (coded male) and desire for the Native female (coded nature)? One partial answer might derive from the early "initiated . . . habit of mind that came to see the Indian woman as a kind of emblem for a [new] land that was similarly enter-taining the Europeans 'with all love and kindness and . . . bounty,'" those last words taken from Arthur Barlowe's "First Voyage Made to the Coasts of America . . . Anno 1584."[1] How tempting to read both the Native woman and the new land in terms of one another to find welcome mats spread out everywhere. The Native woman thus institutes and mediates "what is probably America's oldest and most cherished fantasy: a daily reality of harmony between man and nature."[2] Small wonder that "the frontiersman's association with Indian women is viewed as a natural occurrence that bolsters his masculinity without weakening his morality."[3] But natural to whom and on what grounds? Why is his masculinity a central consideration? Why is it not also natural for white women to be correspondingly associated with Native men? There is something forced in this governing construct of the Native woman as embodying nature, as other than—and justifying—the civilized white man. Such "Othering," as numerous critics of colonial writing have noted, represents "projections [and] self-contained fantasies that are entirely indifferent to [the Other's] reality."[4] As such, they tell us nothing real about those Others but something about the psychic needs of those who formulate them.

Also germane is O. Mannoni's argument that the "divided" and "ambivalent" (especially with respect to his "unconscious . . . attitude towards his memories of his own early childhood") nature of "civilized man" leaves him torn "between the desire to 'correct' the 'errors' of the savages and the desire to identify himself with them in his search for some lost paradise (a desire which at once casts doubt upon the merits of the very civilization he is trying to transmit to them)."[5] Sinclair, significantly, is both agent and teacher at the *Paradise* Valley Stony Reserve (emphasis added). Mannoni's formulation fits this protagonist personally too, with his repressed Victorian upbringing, his Blakeian yearning as a child for tigers on the prairie (ironically realized later in Gloria Catface, the beautiful Stony prostitute). But it hardly sums him up. Divided is not necessarily the mark of civilization, but the mark of difference, and particularly in the complex colonial context of Canada (English/French/Ethnic/Inuit/Indian) "any statement of identity is an assertion of difference."[6] Moreover, Victoria—desperate to please Sinclair, destined to disappoint him—is obviously divided too, perhaps more problematically than he. How odd, for example, that she is named Victoria, after the queen whose adjective he would have her countermand. Yet her story is told only as it impinges on and is perceived by him. Why, indeed, should nursing her own Native baby be "failure" whereas nursing dying white patients in a Calgary hospital would be "success"?

As Marianna Torgovnick argues in *Gone Primitive*, "within Western culture, the idiom 'going primitive' is in fact congruent in many ways to the idiom 'getting physical,'" and since the constraints on getting physical especially bear on Western ideals of self-contained and self- (and Other-) mastering manhood, it is no surprise that "the lure of the primitive" regularly turns "out to be something" that allows an escape from "the confines of masculine identity as we know it."[7] Of course, the missionary falls for the Samoan maid and the cavalry captain for the young Apache woman. Yet masculine identity retains its claims to mastery even as it flirts with other possibilities. Of course the story of his temptation, whether resisted or succumbed to, is his story, not hers. And "the difference" between her story and his—especially when she is woman, Native, Other—Trinh T. Minh-ha concludes, is simply this: "He does not hear or see. He cannot give. Never the given, for there is no end in sight."[8]

The point of *The Vanishing Point*—the point that vanishes because it seems so natural—is that such details of Native life as are presented serve primarily to show how a white man is changed through his encounter with that life. It is in his perspective, his growth, that the locus of value lies. So although the narrative is ostensibly about perspective, we see that perspective is also mostly fixed and that Sinclair's point of view prevails from beginning to end. Novels have their necessary provenance and do not erase cultural divides by pretending to cross them. Even in portraying a "particular ethnographic encounter" and even one that ends up in bed, "the text creates the reality of the Other in the guise of describing it," and thus, "although [it] can operate as ethnography, . . . the literary text . . . is not the site of shared mental experience, and should not be seen as such."[9]

As Sinclair saw as a boy, two parallel lines neither really disappear nor totally merge. It is a lesson he must later translate into the register of race to dispute (another implication of the title) the conventional white view that Indian culture is conveniently passing irrevocably away, either through extinction or assimilation.[10] But even in exposing the limitations of the basic "white" perspective on the "Native," Mitchell also necessarily reaffirms just that power relationship—white over Native. This inequality, too, is partly reaffirmed by the plot. Sinclair determines, at the end of the novel, to marry Victoria, to legitimize the child—not his own—she will presently bear. In some ways, this desire to make her an "honest" woman is as Victorian as her name and hardly affirms his escape from white constraints. But more to the point, making her "honest" will necessarily diminish her. Marriage to a white man will not make her white—but it *will* (by the racist and sexist Canadian law of the time) make her "non-Indian" by depriving her and her children of all treaty rights.[11] In short, Sinclair, at the end of the novel, can modestly "go Indian."[12] It is a standard white male ploy, one that Robert Kroetsch satirizes in *Gone Indian* (published the same year as *The Vanishing Point*). Victoria, however, cannot "go white." Passing, the most she can do, is a different proposition entirely and requires the total repudiation of one's own heritage in order to assimilate into the dominant culture that necessitates such denial. Married to Sinclair and living with him, unassimilated, on the Reserve, she becomes not his *best* student but his *second* wife and an Indian wife at that.

Mitchell can be applauded for attempting to describe the possibility of love between a white man and a Native woman. Such love, however, has been a feature of North American literature since the time of Captain John Smith and Pocahontas and does nothing to destabilize established power relations of race or gender but, instead, doubly reifies them. Her desire affirms both her subordinate position and her society's (which is why an inverse tale of, say, a Miss Joan Smith falling in love with and rescuing Chief Powhattan from a Puritan-inflicted death just would not do the same social work at all). Thus Sinclair can claim as his own the woman who has previously claimed him, and his last act—looking forward to marrying Victoria—is precisely what makes him, finally, in his own eyes, an admirable man. In the context of the novel, it doesn't take much. Yet it should also be noted that *The Vanishing Point* does not work toward Victoria's erasure, to the usual end of the miscegenation plot in the Native woman's death or abandonment. Moreover, Mitchell explicitly shows that Victoria, not Sinclair, initiates a clearly consensual sexual relationship, whereas, as Terry Goldie points out, "the normative sexual relationship of the white male with the indigene female is rape."[13]

A final casting of the hero as hero is not the whole story either. The perspective of the novel is applied to Sinclair as well as (more dubiously) through him, and a series of comic contrasts serve to illuminate this protagonist in a less than flattering light. For example, Sinclair's predecessor at the Paradise Valley School, the Reverend G. Bob Dingle, in his three-year tenure, apparently taught the children little more than to sing "Bringing in the Sheaves" in Cree. Not in their own Stony language or in English but in Cree, because the Reverend G. Bob believed that "lyric Cree might soften their ["guttural" Stony] speech."[14] Retired from teaching, he remains the minister to the Reserve, in which capacity he can continue "to help these people in [their] progress" to a more Christian life, that "help" mostly taking the form of opposing unsanctified and irregular unions even though, as another character points out, "the fine old Stony Institution of trial marriage . . . works out pretty good—when they hit on the right combination . . . they remain faithful—even monogamous" (153). But the wrong kind of faithfulness is not the right kind of progress. Certain of his own categories and with an easy faith in natural goodness, especially his own, this smarmy Christian regularly bestows on those all around him the one Stony expression he has learned to pronounce in his years with the Indians. But what he has been told is a high compliment signifying "you please me very much" actually means "bullshit." And bullshit, Sinclair sees, is what the work of most of the whites on the Reserve amounts to, especially after the Stonies like him enough to tell him what the "No-watch-es-nichuh" he has picked up from Reverend Dingle really means.

Another Reverend, Heally Richards, who has come to Calgary to practice some farm-team pitching in preparation for more major league evangelical hucksterism, provides an even more pointed and sustained parallel to Sinclair. Both had an often unhappy childhood presided over by a missing mother and an imperfect father. Both aimed at a profession—Sinclair at being a doctor, Richards at being a dentist—that each early found he could not afford. Both came to their present occupation through an attempt to escape the unhappy consequences of an early marriage. Both are caught up in their feelings for a young Indian woman but neither will admit to himself the real nature of those feelings. Both fail in a crucial plan and equally lament that failure in similarly overstated terms: "Oh God—Oh God. . . . Why would He ask Heally Richards . . . to lift this weight—not ten or twenty or a hundred pounds beyond his strength—but tons!" (360); and Sinclair: "Why—oh, God, why had he been asked to accomplish impossibility so far beyond his strength—beyond all human strength" (366). The Reverend Richard's dubious desire to "save" Gloria Catface (whose selling of sex is itself paralleled to his selling of salvation) is further conjoined with Sinclair's desire to save Victoria when Sinclair envisions, with unlikely imagery, a "fallen" Victoria as a future and still more fallen Gloria: "Little lost lamb soliciting—little lost lamb screeching Stony hate and obscenity on city streets . . . vomit[ing] in alleyways" (367). Although he here dubiously confuses the lamb of proclaimed innocence with the tiger of perverted experience, Sinclair also more accurately admits that, with Victoria, he has been, all along, a fool and a fraud, "not one bit different from Heally Richards" (366).

Sinclair's admittedly melodramatic disappointment and grief are comically compromised by still other structuring contrasts. When, early in the novel, as teacher and agent at Paradise Valley Reserve, he comes to report the problem of the missing Victoria to his supervisor, Ian Fyfe, director for the Western Region of the Department of Indian Affairs, he observes a bee in one of the orchids Fyfe breeds, comments on that fact, and then notes Fyfe's "violent" reaction, "snatching up a spray can from one corner of the bench, nailing the bee in a bitter cloud, so that it had tumbled out of the

blossom and dropped to the tiles" (94). Fyfe had special plans for that particular specimen. He was going to cross it with his General Eisenhower
orchid, but a bee has intruded and "spoiled it for General Eisenhower" (95).
Fyfe's disappointment, however, is not the flower's. Sinclair can muse that
his superior should "listen to the orchid . . . let her tell her own delight and
need" (86). But that is before he discovers that there has been, so to speak,
a bee in his orchid too.

To what the orchid might aspire does not enter into the plans of those who
devote themselves to the propagation of orchids. Neither does the Native's
perspective particularly concern those who run the Reserve. But just how
much and how dubiously the Indian is discounted is shown in the novel by
Sinclair's recounting of what at first seems an oddly placed minor episode
from two years earlier. Sinclair at one point recalls how he and Archie Nico-
tine, the most independent Stony on the Reserve, returning from Calgary in
a sudden December blizzard, came on the signs of an unfolding tragedy—
an empty Volkswagen on the side of the road, blood and tracks in the snow.
A hunter had obviously wounded an animal and set out to follow it, not a
smart move when the wind-chill factor was heading for sixty below. Archie
had gone after the man; tracked him to where he was already lying dead,
frozen in the snow; propped him up so that he could be found again; and
then frozen both his own feet in getting back alive himself, a task that he
accomplished only by striking the proper "balance between too much effort,
which would make him sweat [and then freeze], and the not enough that
would lead to capitulation and death" (106).

It was a heroic effort, but when Archie returned he was hardly welcomed
as a hero. Quite the contrary. A Mounted Police constable soon visits the
Reserve and makes it quite clear that the official suspicion is possible foul
play, as one sample of Archie's questioning amply indicates:

> "But how did you know he was dead?"
> "Mainly by him being dead."
> After a moment the constable said, "You say his tracks were cov-
> ered up?"
> "Hey-uh." ["Hey-uh" can mean yes.]
> "Well—were they?"
> "Hey-uh."
> "That you followed—to him."
> "Dead."
> For several ticks of the kettle on the stove the constable stared at
> Archie. "Just how—do you follow tracks—covered with new snow?"

"It's difficult," Archie said.
"Wouldn't it be impossible?"
Archie shrugged.
"Wouldn't it?"
"For you."
"Or for anybody."
"Hey-uh." ["Hey-uh" can mean no.]
"You mean impossible for anybody?"
"You do." (219)

Archie goes on to observe that not all tracks are covered equally: "If you climb under dead-fall on your belly you will make a pretty big track" that "it will take one hell of a lot of snow to cover," so "I would track you by now and again to where you were lying froze to death—on your face and all your fingers split open and that is the whole situation" (220). But it is hardly "the whole situation" for the police constable. The bruises on the dead man's face . . . ? The missing gun . . . ? He cannot make as much of these matters as he wants because Archie, in the policeman's scenario, no doubt tampered with the evidence. Thus the one charge of which he is certain:

"You are not supposed to touch the body! We want to see that body first—exactly as it was!"
"By spring it would be a lot different, you understand."
"I am telling you . . ."
"High."
"Do not—ever again—touch or move—a body!"
"Next time I won't," Archie promised. "To please the R.C.M.P."
The constable stared at him for several long moments, then consulted his notebook again.
"And the spring bears," Archie added. (221–22, ellipsis in the original)

Exasperated, Archie finally has some questions of his own: "what happens to a person when they fall all over dead-fall and hitting himself on his face and head?" And "why will I waste my strength and make myself sweat to club him to die which he will anyway. Write down—it don't hurt much to freeze to death so I would not have to kill him to save him some suffering" (223). The questions are valid. Nevertheless, Archie has it all wrong. He can imagine the police suspecting him of killing a dying man to end his pain. They suspect, however, cold-blooded murder, not mercy killing. Might not Archie have come on the man while he was still alive? Only very fresh tracks could be followed in the falling snow. Might not he have taken the gun? It is, after all, missing, and Indians are notorious thieves. Might not he have then killed the victim to cover up the first crime? There were those bruises. Although these hypotheses are not explicitly articulated, the whole exchange still epitomizes one of the major lessons in the text and shows how pervasively whites can pander to their own distorted view of "Indian."

This episode also suggests that later it will be Archie, not Sinclair, who goes after Virginia to bring her back to Paradise Valley, forcing Sinclair into still other unflattering comparisons: "How could [I] have left Victoria on that city street. Archie hadn't" (385). The teacher begins to see, too, that he failed his pupil far more than she failed him, and with that realization the novel devolves to its predictable comic—and colonialist—close. Victoria, back on the Reserve and attending a tribal celebration, invites Sinclair to join her in the Prairie Chicken Dance and then dances him home and into bed. The muddling-through-midlife white man finally knows—and has—what he wants.

In other ways, too, the story is mainly Sinclair's. As the Blake references make clear, one structuring polarity of the novel is innocence versus experience. Yet for all the lamb imagery directed toward Victoria, the chief candidate for innocence and inexperience is the older man, not the younger woman. Sinclair, for example, at the very beginning of *The Vanishing Point,* can think of himself as a "thirty-six-year-old adolescent" (4) because he is one. He wakes, in the first paragraph, to the sound of "a ruffed grouse drumming out again and again its invitation to join the living whole" (3). Not until the very end of the novel does he deign to join that whole living world, to enter the dance, and even then he has to be asked by the eighteen-year-old girl who is, socially and emotionally, hardly the "child" he had postulated just a few weeks earlier. At the final Prairie Chicken Dance—"certain as birth or death or love" (386)—he finally gets the message that he did not receive when the grouse first drummed, and at least a modest tiger begins to stir in his veins and—presumably (the action is not described in the text)—his bed.

What partly keeps this happy conclusion from being merely another white commoditization of Native sexuality is, first, the fact that Virginia chooses him much more than he chooses her and, second, the consideration that her choice significantly changes him. He is forced to revisualize the course of his previous life and the way he has failed the people he has lived among by seeing them wrongly, by mirroring them as "backwards people." Significantly, he now can use their terminology to assess how he has distorted his—and their—view of who they are. Indeed, the novel ends with Sinclair answering

Archie with Archie's usual answer: "'Hey-up!' Sinclair said," (393) employing (although slightly mispronouncing) the wonderfully ambiguous Stony word that can mean, depending on the context, yes, no, or maybe.

In *The Vanishing Point,* Natives, and particularly Archie and Victoria, resist the Otherness whereby white society would define them and, instead, image back to Sinclair a definition of himself as other than he wants to be. But there is still, finally, something suspect in the positive power of this mirroring, particularly when Sinclair, after spending the night with Victoria, goes for an early morning walk during which he encounters various textual underwritings of his own recent revitalization. The stream along which the Native settlement is located had earlier gone dry but is suddenly in full flow again. Archie is engaged in his own cross-cultural negotiation, starting his dilapidated truck with a team of horses and starting a horse stampede with the explosive backfiring of the truck. Or Sinclair observes and apostrophizes a half-dressed urchin playing in the overflowing Beulah Creek flooding the very cabin in which the child lives:

> Dear little bare-bum shaman, I am here—I'm standing here. Oh, let me show you to you—I want to mirror you so you may be more nearly true! Please perform your marvels for me—surprise me. Astonish me with your accidents. Trust me now. I promise you I won't destroy you with distorted image. I will not turn you into a backward person. At least I will try not to. Let's you and I conjure together. You watch me and I'll watch you and I will show you how to show me how to show you how to do our marvelous human tricks together! (389)

One of the tricks is that the teacher still does all the talking, claiming the humanistic high-ground and the meaning of all this reflection that is itself ambiguously reflected in the text by still other details of this same scene. The boy plays in the rising water, digging miniature canals through which he floats chips and twigs, and if one of them momentarily stalled, "the child's touching finger freed it to moving life again" (389); the truck emits a "great blue back-fart" (391) as it also begins to move again; each is mirror and metaphor for Sinclair's upsurge of sympathy and feeling, the other movement with which the novel ends. "Hey-uh" indeed!

The whole novel also partially undercuts the optimism of its ending, an optimism based on the unlikely premise that whites might suddenly see the errors they themselves have committed in their previous dealings with Natives, change their views and behavior, and that all problems would thereby be resolved. Mitchell knows perfectly well that this is not going to happen. He has, in fact, already shown it not happening. Thus, Ian Fyfe, Sinclair's superior, is also concerned for the Indian children, but his concern takes the form of a Scotch faith in oatmeal. He has concocted a fortified oatmeal "Minimal Subsistence Cookie" that the school children are given each day but mostly crumble on the floor because they find it simply inedible. When Sinclair figuratively rubs his supervisor's face in the mounded crumbs, Fyfe still cannot admit the futility of his endeavor. Doubt oatmeal and the very foundations of his world would collapse. But bannock and boiled elk are quite another matter. Of course they should instantly give way before the superior merits of his cookies. And the children just as resolutely refuse the cookies even though many of them are clearly in need of the minimal subsistence Fyfe attempts to provide. In effect, in this interaction, and in much of the novel, imperfect songs of innocence (each side's faith in its own ways) are played out against other songs of imperfect experience (the collision of different ways), which is to observe, again, that the work is deeply Blakeian. That stream is not named Beulah for nothing.

Beulah, it might also be remembered, was in the Bible the promised new name for the redeemed land. What was "termed desolate" would "be called . . . Beulah" (Isaiah 62:4). It was, for John Bunyan, a valley beyond the Shadow of Death, beyond the reach of the Giant Despair, the last resting place before reaching the Celestial City. For William Blake, Beulah was a female counter-Eden, a spring realm of light and creativity, and "the ideal within our sexual reach."[15] So when Beulah Stream flows through Paradise Valley, the landscape is overencoded with white myths and metaphors for sex and salvation, for physical and metaphysical deliverance.[16]

That overencoding suggests that the key issue in the novel is not the problem of the Native's social marginality, but the problem of an individual white man's psychic marginality, of his alienation from himself and his culture.[17] Sinclair desperately needs something "other" to hold on to. Devolving from this need, The Vanishing Point can articulate a powerful critique of white culture. Sinclair is rightly running from its prudery, its hypocrisy, its deflections of sexuality (Fyfe and his orchids), its dubious drive for mastery (the privileged perspectives of and in his narrative). But the novel does not suggest any "what next," any new name for a redeemed land. In Paradise Valley, what can Sinclair and Victoria do other than teach white lessons to Native kids? Ultimately, then, The Vanishing Point does not change our readings of "white" or "Native" even as it questions those binary terms. "I must Create a System, or be enslaved by another Man's," William Blake famously observed. The ironic failure of this Blakeian novel is that, in the register of both race and gender, it can only hint at a system other than the old polarity of "us" and "them" but cannot envision what this different system might be.

A different and in some ways bleaker reading of the Native as Other is provided by Philip Kreiner's *People Like Us in a Place Like This* (1983), a collection of short stories all set in the North and all also documenting the difficulties of negotiating across racial and cultural as well as sexual differences. One of these tales, "We Collide in Our Dreams," even inverts the ending of *The Vanishing Point*. For Kreiner, a relationship with a young Native woman serves not to alter a white male protagonist's life but to confirm it. The affair between the two becomes public; her relatives condemn him for the injury he has done to her and to them; he is now unwelcome in the village. Threats are first scrawled on the door of the Inuit shack in which he has been, incongruously, trying to live like an Indian so that he can "honestly" write about it, and then the building is burnt down. Forced to leave, he refuses to take her with him, even though he had earlier thought to stay forever, to "get married and have children who would never go south."[18] As he finally insists: "It wouldn't work. People like me, we're transient. We don't stay long in one place. We don't have roots. We're tourists. You couldn't live like me out of a suitcase, in a hotel-room. You might think you could, but you couldn't. I know" (71). That "knowledge," of course, did not keep him from trying to live Native. Nevertheless, she cannot be allowed any attempt to reverse the cultural transition he has not accomplished, for her projected failure cancels out his present one and leaves him the unquestioned questioning subject, a tourist still complacently surveying his realm even as he is being kicked out of it.

With deadpan irony the text also notes that the protagonist's "whole life had been a rehearsal for this speech" and that "he wondered when he would have to say it again" (71). Even as he plays out the opening performance, his anticipated tragedy of love foiled by cultural difference is repeated into farce, both by having been so assiduously rehearsed and by its anticipated second run. The reader might notice, too, how much his departure is a restaged *Casablanca* ending, repetition once more conducive to farce:

> She said again, "Take me with you."
> He knew she hadn't heard him. It was always like that. He turned to the airplane. The entrance was small and black. He tried to picture himself going through it. "I'll write you a letter," he said. Walking slightly faster than his normal speed, he left her there. (71)

Such parodic reenacting of Humphrey Bogart heroism constitutes a hollow claim to both superior male rationality (women simply cannot understand these matters) and morality (what might look like selfishness is really self-sacrifice). Furthermore, the hackneyed role he here enacts happily excludes any other possible scenario, and especially one in which she might play a larger part. Indeed, he notices her only once and only briefly in the part in which he has cast her (more his audience than his fellow actor), and then it is only to be surprised at how small and sad she looked, as, suitcase in hand, she walked toward him and the plane: "Seeded with sorrow was the way he framed it. He liked the image" (71). It is an image that serves him well, obscuring her as a person even as he pretends to acknowledge her pain, covertly voicing yet not acknowledging his hope that he might be leaving her pregnant.

The poetic ring of the protagonist's phrasing—and he does pride himself on being a writer despite writing singularly little during the course of his wilderness sojourn—partly echoes the poetic title that the author gives the story. Moreover, "We Collide in Our Dreams" tends, as much as the protagonist's summation and dismissal, to reduce the human significance of whatever has happened/is happening to her. Who seduces whom in a dream? How much can a dream conjoining or a dream parting matter? In short, in this story, as in much of Kreiner's fiction, it is hard to separate author and protagonist. After all, the protagonist is a self-proclaimed "writer . . . writing a book about life in a northern Indian village" (53). And *People Like Us* is just such a book. Moreover, who is "us" in that title? White readers, white protagonists, and the white author all seem reflections or versions of one another. Such mirroring is more metafictional than Mitchell's, yet, like the Indians in *The Vanishing Point* (but, again, with starker implications), it still serves to show *us* what *we* are in being there.

Much the same lesson is somewhat more explicitly drawn in the volume's title story, a title that only half conceals the question that the tale itself largely addresses. What are people like them (us) doing in a place like that? At first they are mainly trying to avoid any substantial encounter with the locale and its permanent inhabitants. The whites sojourning at Little Whale River spend most of their time holed up in a government housing unit aptly misnamed "the six-unit motel" because "its occupants . . . have a tendency to stay only for a short time" (6). During their stay they mostly keep boredom at bay through reading, quarreling, dinner parties, and, especially, sex. One of the small ironies of the text is the way the male narrator, a visiting anthropologist, resents being shanghaied into one of the resident teacher's sexual scenarios: "I'm not me anymore. I'm anyone. I'm not sure I like that"

(20), he can complain, without drawing a parallel to his comparable attempt to name, without knowing, the Indians of the area.

There are numerous parallels he does not draw. Early in the story he objects to the assertiveness of another visiting expert, a man from Turkey whose obnoxious authority in the service of the Ministry of the Environment soon leads the narrator to wonder "how [that individual] got into Canada" (9) in the first place. It is a question that the locals well might ask about the anthropologist and the Arctic. Or even more obviously, the only doctor in the area is the spoiled daughter of an oil executive sleeping her way through virtually the whole Native community. Each "new boyfriend," one of this woman's "friends" reports, has been "more important . . . than the last" until "she's worked her way right to the top" and is "having an affair with the chief" (19). "A bit of an anthropologist" herself (17), she, too, intrusively wants to know and disguises, even from herself, a dubious drive for mastery as a commendable openness to new experience. In much the same vein, the main objective of the anthropologist's study is to discover the Native's "secret names." He wants to go beyond the designations "by which they will allow you to know them" to uncover the different ones "by which they know themselves" (11), and so pries with his notebook much as the doctor does with her body.

Neither, of course, thereby comes to know the Natives. When a few Indian women arrive at the hospital, the physician did not recognize that one of the group was the chief's wife. She tells them that they will have to wait until she is free to attend to them. They, however, have come to attend to her, and there is no need to await her convenience to do so. Neither does she really "know" the chief. Beaten up, her apartment wrecked, forced to leave the village, she insists he will leave with her: "He said he would. . . . He loves me. I know he does" (36). She is wrong on both counts, and he too sends her on her way, refusing even to see her before she departs because she "embarrassed him in the village" (36). Similarly, when the anthropologist narrator is finally taken into the bush and stays at a Native camp, he cannot "recognize" those there encamped. As he significantly admits: "I know them as numbers on the census role, but not by their faces. My research didn't go that far" (43). Nor did it go far enough to prepare him for the shock of what seems a threat on his life.

"People Like Us in a Place Like This" concludes with the narrator hiring four Natives to take him to an isolated river mouth where, in 1917, a trading post was burnt to the ground, killing the traders stationed there. It was a soon forgotten small massacre. Such things should not have been happening in 1917, and, besides, the country was then totally preoccupied with larger killings occurring elsewhere. The narrator, having stumbled onto this bit of hitherto lost history, wants to put himself "in the place" of the murdered men, "to see what they saw when they saw it for the last time," and so "have [his own] taste of the end of the line" (39).

The anthropologist experiences rather more than he bargained for. When, as they embark on the excursion, he quibbles with the Natives about the price he had agreed to pay, he is warned that he can easily be dumped "into the bay and no-one [especially him] will be the wiser for it" (42). Once they have arrived, his jokes and questions elicit further threats, both implicit and explicit: "They died squealing, worse than animals," one of the Indians, speaking in English, notes about the narrator's predecessors, just as he is falling asleep. "We could kill you, you know," this individual continues, "But we're not going to. It wouldn't do any good now. Not like before. We'd like to, but we won't. You can sleep now" (47). The next morning, just before they start back, the same Native solicitously covers the narrator to protect him from the rain and then, in the last words of the story, "says, 'Don't tell lies about us,' pauses, and then says, 'Too bad you don't understand'" (50). This ending gives another answer to the question implicit in the title. For the most part, in a place like that, people like us are reading it wrong.

The wilderness, Dawn Lander has argued, can be portrayed as the place "where the white man will have the best sex of his life" because the exclusion of the white woman and the presumed radical "otherness" of the Native woman allows for "a sexuality which is [at least for him] without responsibility."[19] Caren J. Deming has similarly maintained that "the most womanly" Native woman can be cast as the perfect partner for "the most manly" white "mountain man" precisely because she is "portrayed as everwilling" and also as "making no demands that might restrict his freedom."[20] Much the same accommodating Native woman is encountered, only slightly modified, in both Mitchell's novel and Kreiner's stories, and her long heritage of service suggests something about the program that requires it. For the white man's valuation of the Native woman—"the natural woman," "the most womanly woman"—does seem part of a larger process that devalues women generally and, as such, bears out Sherry B. Ortner's thesis "that the universal devaluation of women could be explained by postulating that woman is seen as 'closer to nature' than men, men being seen as more unequivocally occupying the high ground of 'culture.'"[21] As Ortner also points out in her seminal essay, "Is Female to Male as Nature is to Culture?" "the culture-nature scale is itself a product of culture," and so, particularly in a patriarchal culture, women will be caught in "a vicious circle."[22] Culturally assigned "naturalness" will consign women to the roles men want them to play, as is, indeed, exemplified by the previously quoted passage from Deming in which the Native woman is "most womanly" simply by virtue of her imputed free sexual availability. Such a fantasy figure is, of course, neither Native nor, for that matter, woman. "She" is, in best "Othering" fashion, entirely his construct, which, as such, has nothing at all to do with what any woman, Native or white, might, in her own terms, be.

In this context, we might notice how excluded the Indian woman warrior is from white portraits of the West. Although the existence of the *berdache*, the Indian male who preferred to live as a female, is generally admitted, the equivalent female figure is not.[23] Yet the historical existence of the "manly" Native woman is well documented. For example, Valerie Sherer Mathes, in "Native American Woman in Medicine and Military," assesses the lives of such Plains Indians as Woman Chief (so named because of her capabilities as a warrior), whose success at hunting and war allowed her to " 'take' four wives to keep house, prepare food, and tan hides," or Pine Leaf, who "vowed not to marry until she had killed one hundred of the enemy," who had killed her brother, and who in one battle "counted six coups and killed four [Cheyenne warriors]."[24] This is not what Mitchell's and Kreiner's protagonists had in mind at all. As Mathes concludes, "historians recounting the Indian past must reject white assessments of Indian women as slaves and thoroughly explore the ethnographic data instead."[25] So, too, might novelists.

The conventional construct of the Indian woman as abused drudge of her Indian husband but happy sexual partner for the white man passing through posits the white man as preferable over the Native even for Native women, who can thereby be seen as both sexually accessible and grateful to be so. The same construct also doubly served the interests of the white man in his own domestic sphere. First, and as Deming notes, it "play[ed] white women and women of color off against one another" as rivals for his favor.[26] The white woman was thereby cautioned to take care because he had an alternative. And second, it denied her the alternative it granted him. If she chafed at the restraints placed on her life, she should not look to Indian ways for an escape. Of course, she occasionally did. Despite much prompting to the contrary, "neither fear of the landscape nor aversion to miscegenation [were] of necessity feminine traits."[27] As Arabella Fermor, one of the female characters in Frances Brooke's *The History of Emily Montague* (1769, and both the first Canadian novel and the first novel written in North America) at one point observes: "Absolutely . . . I will marry a savage, and turn squaw . . . never was any thing so delightful as their lives; they talk of French husbands, but commend me to an Indian one, who lets his wife ramble five hundred miles, without asking where she is going."[28] A different picture of the pleasures of a squaw's life can forestall such female ramblings, both the character's and the author's. But as numerous studies of Western women's writing have shown, actual captivity narratives regularly do not fit the conventions of the fictional ones. You are, in fact, not a captive at all when you write "I began to think much of him [the Indian husband] for his kindness to me, and when they brought the news that there were two white men in the camp, I did not care to see them."[29]

The white woman could also be constrained by denying the possibility of such kindness, and thus, despite remarkably little historical evidence that female captives were sexually assaulted (until that practice was picked up from whites), the Native male is regularly portrayed as a "bloodthirsty savage" particularly prone to raping his enemies' women.[30] This construct, too, conveniently served white male interests.[31] It gave the white hero an occupation beyond cavil or question, as he regularly found himself called on to (in the wonderfully mixed metaphor of Natty Bumpo in *The Last of the Mohicans*) "save these tender blossoms from the fangs of the worst of sarpants."[32] In the name of that occupation, even genocide could be justified. Projecting "the urge to violence onto the Indian provided a splendid rationale for white retaliation"; and thus, as Susan Armitage observes, "protection of white women, the symbols of civilization, and the extermination or removal of Indians went hand-in-hand."[33]

Neither *The Vanishing Point* nor *People Like Us* deploys the full panoply of sexual and social mythology out of which the Native, both male and female, has been constructed. Despite the contrast between Mitchell's buoyant optimism and Kreiner's pervasive cynicism, both authors share a concern with perspectives and pedagogy. They want to communicate to an implied white audience not a standard fiction of Native life nor a truer account, but something of the problematics of any white narrating of any account. This second "story," however, necessarily derives from the much larger and more entrenched first "story," an already in-place discourse on the Native that has been worked on and worked out now for a full five centuries. Small wonder the first story regularly threatens to swallow up the second.

Mitchell and Kreiner, perhaps inevitably, deploy the very stereotypes they intend to examine, the "differences" they want to present differently. In *The Vanishing Point*, for example, Archie saves Victoria from the city streets, but Norman Catface, another Stony, put her there and pimps for Gloria Catface too. "Just sell your sister, Norman" (370), Archie advises as he slits Norman's face open and with Norman's borrowed knife at that, acting as an obvious agent for Sinclair and revenging the sexual sullying of Sinclair's lamb. Or we might notice how Kreiner's chief, talking love, is, like any married white man on the prowl, after sex, and so exploits his wife and the female doctor as much as the doctor exploits him. And once the wife arrives to extract revenge, the result is not a woman warrior asserting her rightful claims, but a catfight, a different matter entirely. Such episodes illustrate Kreiner's ploy of demonstrating the alterity of the Natives with episodes in which they act surprisingly like us (which is, on second thought, hardly surprising given their long history of colonial subjugation).

Mitchell's ultimate retention of "us" and "them" is problematic, but so are Kreiner's suggestions of a larger "us." I have previously read his title as if "people like us" are necessarily white, a dubious premise only partly supported by the obvious limitations of his white protagonists. A title "us," however, can certainly take in all present characters, and one of the stories, "That Year My Father Died," is explicitly told from a Native protagonist's perspective and recounts the consequences of the loss, in the same year (and the same sentence) of "my father" and "our land" (72). Indians and whites, males and females, are we all "us" together, people in the novel's present and really no different? Suggestions of such universalism are as suspect as obvious Othering. Universalism, moreover, flies in the face of much of the specifically colonial critique that both novelists offer, a critique that partly accounts for the actions of the Natives in terms of a history of subjugation in the past and a pervasive racism in the present.

Kreiner and Mitchell both aim at a new perspective, at an understanding beyond the entrenched stereotypes and clichés. But for the white writer trying to grasp a vision of a nonracist society or, even more, of an Indian-centered rather than a Eurocentric Canada or text, the next step—an envisioning of an alternative model of existence—is almost impossible.[34] One can only wonder, for example, what kind of new narrative might have emerged in either book were the Native women represented not by Victoria or that sad woman with her suitcase, but by a figure like Woman Chief. That novel hasn't been written yet. Nevertheless, it haunts both Mitchell's and Kreiner's fiction and suggests that the most important lesson on perspective in each text is the lesson—"Too bad you don't understand"—that calls entrenched white perspective into question.

9 Representational Rites

From Brooke's *The History of Emily Montague* and Richardson's *Wacousta* down to the present, Natives in novels have been predominantly portrayed according to interests and agendas other than their own. The Indian feared, the Indian desired, or the Indian somewhere in between—as natural being, as natural curiosity, as marginal survivor, as misfit in the world of white society—is, to borrow both Robert Berkhofer's title and argument, *The White Man's Indian*. The white man's Indian is not likely to be the Red man's much less the Red woman's. And conversely, can Natives adequately represent themselves in the borrowed forms and languages of French or English fiction as opposed to traditional oral tales in their original indigenous languages? Would not even these tales be substantially co-opted if they were novelized, Anglicized, or Frenchified?

Borrowed forms, moreover, do not necessarily have the same status in the new context as in the original. When a coalition of Native writers, the Committee to Re-establish the Trickster, presents to the Premier of Ontario a one-sided treaty written in Cree and claiming the Provincial Parliament Buildings because of the greater good those buildings would serve if taken over to house the homeless as compared to the scant and dubious value of their present utilization, that treaty is hardly comparable in its force and effect to a similar treaty then being forced onto the Teme-Augama Anishnabai whereby their land could be taken from them largely because of the logging value of the old-growth forest it contained. The discrepancy between the two treaties is precisely the point that the Native writers wished to make, and this point is probably better made through the Cree treaty than in an English novel about the injustice of treaties. That novel, *The Temptations of Big Bear,* had already been written, and no treaties were renegotiated in its aftermath.

This is not to say that novels of Native life are to be left to sympathetic non-Native authors such as Rudy Wiebe. The Native case for exclusive rights to their own stories, and to their own representation of themselves, has been powerfully argued by Lenore Keeshig-Tobias, an Ojibway poet, storyteller, and a founding member of the Committee to Re-establish the Trickster. "Stories," she insists, "are not just entertainment," they "are power" and "they reflect the deepest, and most intimate perceptions, relationships and attitudes of a people," so much so "that, in Native culture, one storyteller cannot tell another's story without permission."[1] Whites, she also points out, have a long history of taking without asking. "The missionaries stole our religion and the politicians stole our land and the residential schools stole our language," while "archaeologists used to rob our graves for museums."[2] Any belated white attempt to relate a more honest story of the Indian, so far as Keeshig-Tobias is concerned, only extends this history of dispossession; it does not at all redeem it. The one honest way to have access to Native story, she concludes, is to share Native experience:

> As [Maria] Campbell said on CBC Radio's Morningside, "If you want to write our stories, then be prepared to live with us." And not just for a few months.
>
> Hear the voices of the wilderness. Be there with the Lubicon, the Innu. Be there with the Teme-Augama Anishnabai on the Red Squirrel Road. The Saugeen Ojibway [and the Mohawk at Oka she would have later added]. If you want these stories, fight for them.[3]

Canadian non-Native writers have not taken up this challenge and this fight. Instead, they have, for the most part, responded to charges of "cultural theft" with ringing affirmations of the need for artistic freedom. Thus Neil Bisoondath, a Trinidadian-born writer of fiction living in Montreal, can "reject the idea of cultural appropriation completely." This author would put no "limits [on] the imagination" and insists that "no one has the right to tell me who I should or should not write about, and telling me . . . that amounts to censorship. I don't believe anyone can steal the culture of another." For Bisoondath, "fiction is an exploration of the other, and the only thing that matters is whether you do it badly or well, not whether you collaborate or ask for any kind of permission."[4] This declaration of literary independence, however, suppresses completely the pertinent question of just who—you or the other—gets to decide whether that "exploration of the other" was done "badly or well."

Still more suspect is the response of W. P. Kinsella, perhaps because his fiction is rather suspect too. Starting with *Dance Me Outside* (1977), this writer has set a number of short-story collections, narrated by Silas Ermineskin and collectively titled the Ermineskin Tales, on the Hobbema Reserve in Alberta, where the actual Cree Ermineskin band lives. A partial founding in fact—and Kinsella regularly uses real names—is doubly offensive in fiction that also depends on standard derogatory stereotypes. When Frank Fencepost, for example, in the title story of *The Miss Hobbema Pageant* (1989), decides to enter the local competition and then goes on to win the Miss Indian America title as well, the comic focalization of the work entails more than its safe send-up of beauty contests. Frank claims that his moustache is no problem because "half the girls in Hobbema got mustaches, and those are the good-looking ones"; he suggests that there is no need to come up with a second dressing room because he has "been to bed with all but two of the contestants anyway," and so they have "no secrets from each other."[5] The point of this humor seems to be the consideration that they are all, including Frank, comparably ugly as well as comparably promiscuous. Frank well may be "Kinsella's version of the trickster in Indian tales," but he is also a version of the racial Other as clown/criminal/incompetent in demeaning white tales.[6] Thus, for the pageant's talent competition he "could show how I stuff five-finger bargains down the front of my jeans and boogie out of a store."[7] As Gerald Vizenor, a Chippewa author and critic, observes: "Ermineskin is a fictional narrator, but imagination does not absolve racialism; humor is no excuse to exploit negative preconceptions about tribal people. The author plays Indian for a white audience."[8] Ruby Wiebe even more specifically condemns Kinsella for his "reprehensible" and repetitive use of "the stereotypes of the Indian as uncomprehending child, the Indian as total nonachiever in white society, the Indian as chronic liar, the Indian as buffoon"—stereotypes that serve "to fictionally deface a particular race of aboriginal Canadians."[9]

Kinsella, in his own defense, has maintained that "if minorities were doing an adequate job of (telling their stories), they wouldn't need to complain [but] they don't have the skill or experience to tell their stories well. Indian writers tend to retell myths and legends. And that, to me, is boring and repetitive."[10] Not only does the white author here claim, in the name of his greater experience as a writer, the right to tell the Native's story, he also claims the right to determine just what that story should entail (none of those boring myths and legends, thank you). Moreover, although his greater experience as a writer is very much at issue, the question of his experience as an Indian is apparently so immaterial that he can admit he has, for all practical purposes, none. He "knows only one Indian personally and has never visited the reserve."[11]

Kinsella also elsewhere insists that "stereotypes are reality. The few people who don't like my work," he goes on to observe in one of the interviews scattered throughout Don Murray's *The Fiction of W. P. Kinsella,* "presumably want to see Indians with doctorates."[12] He claims, too, that conditions on the Hobbema Reserve and particularly "the general meanness and viciousness of life," which is "mostly due to alcohol," are much worse than anything he depicts.[13] "If there's anything wrong with showing a drunken Indian," Kinsella thereby concludes, "I fail to see it because it is reality; and yet, as I've said, I hardly touch that aspect of life."[14] He knows the "reality" of the Reserve without ever being there; he remains blissfully oblivious of how much that "reality," much less his perception of it, is socially constructed; he totally ignores the way his literary work demeans Natives and consigns them to some marginal place; yet he still congratulates himself, in the name of that same "reality," on both his honesty and his restraint. The man just doesn't get it.

Not all Canadian writers and institutions remain so invincibly ignorant. Anne Cameron, for example, has agreed "to stop using Native culture and sacred stories in her books and to move over and make room for Native writers who are writing out of their own experiences and traditions."[15] The Canada Council, the major government agency for funding in the arts, is "moving slowly towards a position that collaboration with minority groups must be increasingly recognized if those voices are to be effectively used."[16] Joyce Zemans, the director of the council, maintains that collaboration and consultation "is a more appropriate way to work" and is also "one way of avoiding the stereotyping that has existed," but she declines to comment on the more problematic matter of what restraints might reasonably be placed on fiction's "imaginative exploration into other cultures."[17] And "the Writers Union of Canada, whose membership is actively involved in the creative 'appropriation of voice' at various levels, has taken no stand at all on this issue."[18] But increasingly non-Native writers are recognizing that cultural appropriation entails real questions, questions that cannot be simply dismissed with claims of artistic freedom, and are incorporating that awareness into their fictions of white/Native interactions.

Particularly germane in this respect is Philip Kreiner's *Contact Prints* (1987), a novel that partly records a white attempt to appropriate Native Otherness and turn it into art. Iris Bickle, a long-time art teacher at a small Indian community school on James Bay, achieves signal success with her primitive masks only after she begins marketing them as products of an "authentic" Cree princess. As she insists to the at first indignant narrator, a young white male teacher newly arrived at the same school:

> I was making masks when you were in diapers, and do you think I ever made a buck? . . . Not one. Not one lousy buck. Not fifty cents. Not one penny until I became Winnie Beaver. Now I'm in some of the best private collections in the country. They even know me in Germany. They're crazy for Indian art over there. What does it matter who I am? My work is good and it sells now. It has integrity. It possesses truth, and it deserves to be seen, even if I have to lie.[19]

Here and throughout *Contact Prints,* Kreiner conflates representation, ethnicity, and imposture.

Indeed, the comic highpoint of the novel occurs when two German reporters from *Stern* come to do an article on the artist, and Iris has to hire a local Indian woman whom she dresses up in war paint, a duck-feather headdress, a fortune in furs, and "enough beadwork to supply the Montreal tourist trade with a year's worth of Indian jewelry" (147). Interviewed, the "Princess," speaking in Cree, tells one of the blondly handsome reporters "what she would like to do with him in bed," all of which Iris "translate[s]" into a disquisition on how the artist finds it "problematic" that her masks "hang in galleries all over the world, contributing to the white man's aesthetic discourse" (149). The whole show proceeds in much that same vein and presently concludes with an assemblage of girls from the school doing a "faithful imitation of an Indian dance performed by Puerto Rican actors in an old movie recently screened in the parish hall" (154). Devolved from her "basic collage principle," what might well be termed the Masque of the Red Princess is one of Iris's more impressive pieces and soon brings the narrator to admit that he had previously "undervalued her talent" (147).

Iris's art and anticolonial rhetoric hardly reverse the usual direction of the colonizing process. Neither does her subsequent career. The "price of fame"—that is, the German interview—is still more media attention. A Canadian film crew is coming to do another feature on Winnie Beaver, and, Iris suspects, they might be harder to fool than were the Germans. She flees to Mexico where she soon begins to "market authentic Mayan silkscreen prints and batiks" (214). A different culture and locale but the same old enterprise of ripping off the Natives in the name of "authenticity" but with an art which emphatically isn't.

The title of the novel, *Contact Prints,* puns on Iris's art, both "Cree" and

"Mayan," which pretends to facilitate some contact with Native traditions while totally failing to do so. It is also a punning reference to the photographic record of contact, the white attempt to fix and appropriate the image of the indigene. The narrator of the novel, Joe, a young man on the loose who has come north to teach because that was the first job that presented itself to him after he came back to Canada broke from Jamaica, photographically documents his own belated first encounter with Natives who "weren't what [he'd] expected" (2). Of course his innumerable photos do not show him who these people are either; they only attest to how he wishes to see them. The title of the novel, too, explicitly alludes to the manipulation and the "mistakes" of any photographic rendering: "those failed shots, the ones spoiled by a dog running through or by the subject moving, or worse yet, the shots that captured some nasty quirk best left in the dark, I never bothered to blow up. I left them in the contact print stage" (14). In this sense, contact prints attest to the agenda of the objectifying eye and thus demonstrate that the photographic record exists as a contrived white artifact, not as a rendering of natural Native facts. So Joe's photographs parallel Iris's masks as another dubious white appropriation of Native culture.

The parallels and variations on contact prints worked out in the novel also subsume the novel, which, after all, presents itself as a *print* depiction of various *contacts* (most of which prove abortive) across a doubly divided dividing line, not just white/Native, but also French/English on the white side and Indian/Inuit on the Native—two further divisions that seem, incidentally, as difficult to negotiate as the larger one that contains them.[20] The novel thus breaks down, even as it asserts, the governing polarity of Native versus white. But it also reaffirms that polarity by incorporating into a work portraying cross-cultural contacts two failed white attempts (both Iris's and Joe's) to cross a cultural dividing line in order to portray Native culture in ostensibly unmediated form.

As Iris herself regularly acknowledges, her art is premised on imposture. The novel, for example, ends with a postscript, a letter from Iris offering Joe a chance to make "B-I-G M-O-N-E-Y" in her new venture, "Under The Volcano: Artesanías Indígenas Mexicanas" (243). She also reminds him that she is now Maria del Flores, not Iris Bickle, and that he is to bring the right kinds of commercial dyes and wax when he comes for a visit. A postscript to that postscript letter also tells him he is to say, if asked, that he is her brother. Deceit on every level, starting with the fact that silk screening and batiking are hardly indigenous forms of Mayan art, just as mask-making was not a Cree tradition either. Yet the narrator himself is hardly less dubious. Iris early observes that "with [his] damn pictures" he is "just like" her (45).

The reader regularly sees him using his photographs to achieve distance and control and missing much of what goes on around him in his effort to catch it on film. His retrospective realization, "I didn't see," is almost a refrain running through the novel. Two such portraits of the artist as a conniving and/ or duped recorder well might call into question the larger portrait provided by the text itself.

The white artist, in Kreiner's novel, does not stand in for the Native artist but, rather, leaves the Native artist no place to stand. Winnie Beaver's success preempts the field and establishes what "Cree art" should be—not Cree but Western. It is in this sense that Winnie Beaver herself is Iris's "best creation" (141) and makes possible the creation of the masks by defining the context of those artifacts as a white concept of Native, not any native expression of anything.[21] Thus even the Cree students, when they play their minor role in Iris's Winnie Beaver show, are cast as Hollywood Indians. Similarly, when the governor general comes, after Iris has left, to visit the tribe, he is presented with "a *grande folie indienne* so similar to [Iris's] Winnie Beaver tableau" that both must have originated from "the same newsreels and movies" (232) or—a more likely explanation—from the same white construct of the Indian, from the same "Indianism."[22] To break out at least in part from the constraints of that "Indianism," Kreiner problematizes his novel by questioning its ontological status and by portraying more the process of misportraying across a cultural divide instead of pretending to present an accurate rendering of another way of life.

Does "Indianism" leave any place for the Native artist? Joan Clark, in *The Victory of Geraldine Gull* (1988), suggests that it can but does so by inverting the question to ask what place the Native artist leaves to Indianism. In a number of ways *The Victory of Geraldine Gull* both reflects and reverses *Contact Prints*. There are, for example, two figures of the artist in each work, but in Clark's novel these two are a Native and a white and are cast in roles that serve to privilege the former's art, not the latter's. More specifically, Willa Coyle, Clark's white artist, is a young woman who has come, much like Iris Bickle, to a Hudson Bay Indian settlement to teach art and to work on her own art. But when Willa encounters the prints and paintings of the now dead Alexander Bear, she immediately recognizes their superior merit and soon agrees to "act as [a] dealer" for this art even though "the whole effort will cost" her "time and money [she] planned on spending on [her] own work."[23] Moreover, she achieves some small recognition on her own only through working with and for the Indians. The gallery that purchases most of Alexander's art subsequently mounts "a show of [Willa's] entitled 'Sketches from Niska'" (288), drawings she did while helping to found a new Native community with its own small gallery displaying some of Alexander's work. It is as if she can portray Natives only because the very circumstances of that portrayal indicate that she knows they do it better. Or differently put, Alexander Bear produces Native art; Willa Coyle sketches Indians.

In each of these two novels the figure of the Native artist also prefigures (but again differently) the text of the land. In *Contact Prints*, Cree land, like Cree art, is subject to appropriation and transmogrification. The setting is a James Bay river valley that is itself the site of a massive hydroelectric development. When the narrator reluctantly visits the company town and the amenities of civilization (a shopping mall the hydro company has situated in the north), he specifically notes the sudden transition when he passes through the company gate to a "world . . . reduced to rubble, albeit rubble arranged neatly in rows" (82). The gate is significant too. Access is restricted. Officially, restriction is denied; nevertheless, "a 'whites only' town [occupies] land which had been Indian since the end of the last Ice Age." To do business there, Joe observes, "would be like shopping in South Africa" (74). This assessment does not prevent him from doing business, although he does refuse to go in on his second trip when the Indians with him are crudely and insultingly refused admission.

Loss and its consequences extend outward from the company town. Back in the Native community, Fort Henrietta Maria, Joe's relationship with his Cree "friend," Simon Blueboy, founders on the fiasco of the aborted shopping trip:

> "You white men," [Simon] said, applying pressure to my neck. "You come here and you take our land and then you tell us we can't go on it. . . . What do you have to say for your people?" . . .
>
> "It wasn't me. I didn't do it. I'm just a teacher," I found strength to reply, the words tearing out of my throat like fishhooks.
>
> "Nice try, white man. But that won't do," he said, again dropping his hand to the base of my neck. This time he squeezed hard, making me wince. "I could kill you, you know. Right now. It would be so easy," he whispered, putting his mouth to my ear and blowing lightly just before he released me. (226–27)

Neither does the Native village, although down river from the dam, survive that new development. The flow of the river has been altered; the large island on which Fort Henrietta Maria was situated is being washed away; the community must be relocated. During that relocation, the narrator's other

Native friend is killed at the novel's conclusion. To record the removal of the village, Joe persuades a reluctant Pauloosie, the outcast Inuk who lives on the edge of the Cree settlement, to take him out onto the river, and once more not seeing what is happening even as he photographs it, Joe directs Pauloosie to bring their boat closer to the barge carrying the first building being relocated, the church. The barge tips; the building collapses; the boat is broken in two by the toppling steeple. Caught in the wreckage, Pauloosie drowns.

In this final parable of progress, the church (the building itself) kills Pauloosie, just as the church (imposed Christianity) had figuratively killed much of the original Inuk and Indian cultures. Pauloosie, moreover, is bribed to his death with the promise of a rifle, and guns were, of course, a major trade commodity as well as the telling proof of white technological superiority. To the very end, then, *Contact Prints* presents (another pun of the title) the form contact was forced to take as scripted, both in action and in narratives of that action, by whites. Kreiner, however, gives us a different version of the great matter of the Western, the story of how the West was won (i.e., how what was theirs became ours), and the difference is that, unlike most versions of this master narrative, his novel does not valorize the taking.

The Victory of Geraldine Gull does not valorize the taking either and even advocates a certain taking back. In other ways, too, this novel both resembles and goes beyond *Contact Prints*. It also ends with a flood, a forced relocation, and a Native death by drowning. Yet the flood is a natural one (the product of a particularly rainy spring and summer), not the by-product of a hydroelectric project. The forced move is forced partly by the flood and partly by the Natives themselves. A few of them have decided that a site some twenty-five miles upriver would be a better place for their village: "There's good fishing, lots of timber for houses. It's high enough above the river so we don't need to worry about being flooded out of our beds" (209). Their present location, a far less suitable river-mouth muskeg, was chosen by the Hudson Bay Company as the site for a trading post. Indeed, between the post on one side and the church on the other, the very layout of the village speaks its colonial origins. In contradistinction to a line of flimsy cabins scattered along a decaying boardwalk linking the two sites of white administration, the Indians plan a different structure, a "village center" consisting of a cooperative store, a church and a school, a radio station, a meeting hall, a band office, and a clinic, all "arranged in a U, with the space in the middle being left for sports—ballgames, powwows, things like that" (209). To encourage the move, Geraldine burns down the Hudson Bay store, the one tie to the old location that some of the community could not imagine giving up, and soon, again following her lead, they are on their way. The novel then concludes with a brief account of the building of the new community. Natives are drawing their own map of the land and claiming their place on it.

Although *Contact Prints* portrays how Native art is effectively denied any public place and status, it nevertheless acknowledges the existence of such art. At one point Simon invites Joe to come along on a Blueboy family hunting excursion into the bush. The first night out, Simon's father tells a traditional Cree story of how once, in "the old days," when all forms of existence had special capabilities, "the shit in one camp . . . was tired of always being left behind when the people moved" and so "formed" itself into a "very handsome man" who "walked to the new camp and went in" to impress all the girls (193). But then it entered a teepee to sit before the fire where it soon began to smell as it started to melt back into shit. Fleeing this disgrace (and unmasking?), pursued by the young girls, it drops one of its gloves, which one of the girls finds and also finds "full of shit" (193). Running after the young man again, his female admirers round a corner to find only "a pile of shit" (193). Joe can recognize in the "lulling singsong quality" of the narration that it had "obviously" been intended as a kind of lullaby, and that is precisely its effect (192–93). The children are all soon asleep. But he also suspects a personal reference, for, earlier in the day, suffering from a particularly explosive case of "bush fever," he had relieved himself in the nearest clump of bushes, rather closer to the camp than his hosts consider proper. The story bothers him, so much so that he cannot sleep and presently he wakes one of Simon's brothers (Simon has not yet joined the hunting trip and has turned Joe over to this brother) to ask what it means. "It's just a story," he is told, "It doesn't mean anything. Stop thinking like a white man" (194).

Of course the Cree narrative can sustain a number of interpretations. One obvious possibility is that certain meanings and values are themselves full of shit (a reading suggested by the fact that the women of the Blueboy family find Joe attractive). But the main point here is that Joe would place himself as totally outside the hermeneutic of the story and cannot even voice to himself the probable source of his unease, the possibility that he has been cast as the shitman. Insisting on being the viewing subject and never the object viewed, he marginalizes Native life and Native art as much as does Iris or, for that matter, the hydroelectric company. The author portrays this process of claiming privileged status—or allowing it to be claimed for one— and he also shows Joe's partially redeeming sense of bad faith as the protagonist plays his white man's part. But Kreiner does not suggest how the disjunctions he charts might ever be bridged. In this sense, *Contact Prints* resembles a latter-day all-Canadian *Passage to India*. Even the setting of Joe's and Simon's attempt to connect—and especially as that setting is itself being obliterated by the dam and the rising water of the hydroelectric company— is still saying, "No, not yet."[24]

Contact Prints contains but does not incorporate into any dialogical structure the Cree story just considered. The overall print division of the novel itself is here indicative: almost two hundred and fifty pages for white narrative; just half a page for Native. In pointed contrast, *The Victory of Geraldine Gull* demonstrates that the division seen in Kreiner's novel is not the only way of deploying white and Native narrative. Far from it. The one novel substantially devolves from the very synthesis that the other denies, and that synthesis is integral to its structure. Furthermore, whereas the final flood in *Contact Prints* emphasizes division and separation, the concluding flood in Clark's novel foregrounds that text's dialogical synthesis.

The cross-cultural intertextuality in *The Victory of Geraldine Gull* does not obviously privilege white texts. This intertextuality is especially emphasized by the beginning of the final section in which brief narratives of other inundations precede the recounting of the climactic flood that resolves the plot and action of the novel. The first of these, from Cree Trickster Tales, tells how, at a time when "the world was drowned," Wesakaychak had various animals dive to "the bottom of the world," but only Muskrat surfaced with a "little bit of mud" whereby the "land [could be] reclaimed and Life multiplied again" (254).[25] The second is the Biblical story of the flood, which is itself given in three versions: from Genesis in English, from Genesis in Cree, and in the local priest's simplified redaction. The third narrative is from the village chief's notebook and briefly recounts the near disasters of major floods in recent decades. Taken together, these three narratives of three floods give an immediate historic background to the present of the novel as well as two contexts, one Western and one Native, whereby that ongoing present can be mythologized.

Furthermore, the two mythological analogues to the concluding inundation inform the whole narration. As a latter-day Noah, and that is exactly how he sees himself, Gerald Gull (Geraldine's husband) first saves himself from alcoholism through the task of building himself an ark, and then, when that project is completed just before the river rises, he saves his people by taking them, in the words of Father Aulneau's telling of the Biblical story, "away to a better place" (255). And what Gerald does physically, Geraldine does metaphorically. The flood in which she is first drowning and that she is fighting against throughout the text (thus her defiant abrasiveness) is the continual inundation of Native ways by white civilization. In resisting that inundation, Geraldine becomes a version of Muskrat in the Cree story. Her life of degradation—alcoholism; arrests; loss, even of her son, who is taken from her for his own "good" after one of her arrests and who eventually dies as a partial consequence of that show of white concern—is her dive to the bottom. What she comes up with, Alexander's art, which she saves after his suicide, is the little bit of that which would otherwise be buried out of which land and life can be reclaimed. The Native text is not, then, subservient to the white, even on the anagogical level. If the latter-day ark can be seen as the work of God and thus the proof of his existence (the white perspective), that same working can itself be seen as the work of Wesakaychak and thus the proof of his existence (the Indian perspective). In short, just as Alexander's art takes precedence over Winnie's, so, too, is the Christian story of the flood subsumed in the Cree story, which is itself retold in a Western novel.

The privileging of Native art and narrative in *The Victory of Geraldine Gull* is, admittedly, an admirable gesture, but it unfortunately remains little more than a gesture, and for several reasons. First, Alexander Bear's better art did not save Alexander Bear, and Willa Coyle profits more from his success than he did. Why, moreover, must the lesser white artist somehow serve to validate the superior merits of the other? Alexander, despite his paintings, still seems a "'them' [who] is only admitted among 'us,' the discussing subjects, when accompanied or introduced by an 'us.'"[26] Neither does the consideration that, in one particular case, a Native artist is deemed superior to a white change the fact that the rules of judging and the judges remain mostly white. But the main problem with Clark's solution to the problematics of Native representation—white art and artists happily playing second fiddle to their better indigenous counterparts—is the inescapable fact that this solution hardly reflects the larger social context in which it is set. The river of representation and the flood of acculturation still flow pretty much the same old way. Alexander's art does not change the place of Natives in the ethnic hierarchy of the country, no more than does, to borrow the title of the novel, the victory of Geraldine Gull, his mother. Indeed, her concluding death by drowning, with the final defiant gesture of her beret remaining, in the last words of the novel, "a bright red banner, a brave and tattered flag" (287), suggest at best a Pyrrhic victory in a campaign still far from concluded.

Something more than defiance in defeat—than even victory in defeat— is required. Not surprisingly then, and as Margery Fee has pointed out, "recent works" by Native writers are "aimed" mainly "at strengthening Native readers' sense that there must be a better way to think about themselves than that presented by the dominant discourse."[27] In "Upsetting Fake Ideas: Jeannette Armstrong's *Slash* and Beatrice Culleton's *April Raintree*," Fee assesses how both of these novels undo the simplistic and self-denying dichotomy typically presented to the Native protagonist. As Slash early notes in the novel of the same name, whites "really . . . wished we would all either be just like them or stay out of sight."[28] Two ways of disappearing that both serve the same end: whether marginally making it by passing in white society or not making it, in white terms, on the Reserves or on city skid rows, the Indian is consigned to "the economic and social margin, the margin whose major purpose is to affirm the centrality and superiority of white culture."[29]

The choice and no choice of assimilate or vanish especially structures *In Search of April Raintree* (1983), the story of two Métis sisters taken early from their parents to be differently raised by (mostly) different white families and who then go, as young adults, in seemingly quite different directions. One, who looks white, marries the man of her dreams, a rich businessman from Toronto who ensconces her in the family mansion with his racist mother; the other, more obviously Native in appearance, sinks to alcoholism, prostitution, and suicide, but also, before her death, points out to the more "successful" sister that she has sold herself just as much and perhaps more dubiously. The novel is also of particular interest because of the way it uses the Western for purposes the Western typically did not serve, to represent the Native "Other" as other than Other. As an example of this reversal, it is the Native children who are held captive by white savages, savages that twice in the novel literally scalp their victims. And one of these children, grown up, embarks on a Western quest to find and save her missing sister, a quest that also turns, in best Western Canadian fashion (vide Anna Dawe), into the searcher's search for her self.

The reasons for both losses, of one sister's life and of the other's sense of identity, are dramatized by the novel's Native I/eye point-of-view.[30] Portraying how the protagonist sees whites seeing her represents not just the Native from another and unexpected perspective (i.e., that of the Native represented), it also presents from that same subversive perspective the whole panoply of self-serving white ploys and devices whereby the Native is more commonly presented. The novel, in short, is partly a representation of a misrepresentation and of who pays the cost of that misrepresentation. In this context it might also be noted that the author and her sisters were taken from their parents to be raised by white families (kindly in her own case, Beatrice Culleton acknowledges) and that she began *In Search of April Rain-*

tree after the suicides of two of her sisters. As even this tragic biographical grounding of the novel attests, the "authorities" went years without recognizing that the policy of forced acculturation which supposedly benefited Native children by teaching them to be white regularly killed them. The "mismanagement" of the last of the Beothuks need not "stagger one's credulity"; similar mismanagements were commonplace and totally acceptable to white society well into the second half of the twentieth century.[31]

The ignorance and obliviousness of white expertise on Indian affairs is effectively dramatized when Cheryl visits her married sister in Toronto and attends the family's large New Year's party. During the course of the festivities (festivities slightly dampened because Cheryl, unlike April, is recognizably "Native"), a particularly revealing exchange takes place: "Then two men came over and one asked Cheryl what it was like being an Indian. Before she could reply, the other man voiced his opinion and the two soon walked away, discussing their concepts of native life without having allowed Cheryl to say one thing."[32] Even the present Native has no voice in the discussion on what being Native entails. This little episode repeats as farce what is already in the process of being enacted as tragedy.

Cheryl is not heard here exactly as earlier neither child was ever heard when they tried to tell of the conditions of their lives. At one point, for example, when they are both with the worst family and after a "prank" of enticing Cheryl into the bull pasture could well have killed her, they decide to run away. They have almost made it to Winnipeg when they are found by a policeman and turned over to their regular social worker who immediately criticizes them first for hitchhiking and then for lying when they insist they walked all the way on their own. It is much easier for this woman to see them as dishonest and ungrateful—"Mrs. De Rosier is worried sick. Don't you know how much she cares for you?" (65)—instead of mistreated and desperate. They can, indeed, be themselves blamed for any problems: "You girls have had a very bad influence on each other" (65). The fear of another forced separation was one of the reasons for running away. Now they will be so separated and supposedly for their own good. Supposedly for their own good too, Mrs. Semple, the social worker, goes on to give them her "native girl syndrome" lecture predicting that they will soon be making "accusations that everyone in the world is against" them which soon leads—an odd domino effect here—to "alcohol and drugs" and then "shoplifting and prostitution." Neither child has a clue as to what "drugs" and "prostitution" actually are, but they do realize that they and their parents have been "insulted," and Cheryl presciently can "guess I'm going that syndrome route, huh?" (67–68). Warning is, here, recipe and social work is professional malfeasance, although no one, not even Mrs. De Rosier, is ever punished for child abuse when the truth of what the children suffered at her hands and in her house does finally partly come out.

The whole process of dispossession and mistreatment forced onto the children well may have begun with another case of self-justifying misreading similar to Mrs. Semple's. A third daughter was born sickly, hospitalized, and then, despite the misgivings of the parents, released to their care. When the baby subsequently dies, the authorities conveniently see this death as demonstrating Native parental neglect rather than, possibly, a white mistake such as sending the infant home from the hospital too soon. With no prior visits on the part of social workers to determine just how they are being treated, the two surviving children are removed from their home, as if that removal alone constitutes ample proof of parental unfitness and white concern. In pointed contrast, Mrs. De Rosier is an unfit mother even to her own biological children whom she is raising to be moral monsters, but no white social worker is going to look into that matter (despite the ample evidence at hand) or move to remove white children from this white mother's care.

The same one-sided circular formulations are deployed throughout the novel and are shown as such. Thus Cheryl, at school, can be beaten into silence when she objects to the history—"savage" Indians and heroic explorers and missionaries—she is being taught at school. "Giving me the strap isn't going to change the fact that your history books are full of lies" (58) she observes, but she gets the strap anyway and then, back at the De Rosiers, her hair (as well as April's) is cut off as further punishment. In much the same vein, the De Rosiers, mother and daughter, regularly assign April all the household work because she is supposedly a lazy half-breed. Their work is to see that she does hers, and, doing that work, they can claim moral credit for improving her even as she is brutally exploited. Or when April does better at school than Maggie De Rosier, Maggie can retaliate by telling lies about April's "promiscuity," lies that even April's favorite teacher and her one friend both at first believe because Natives are like that.

Small wonder April dreams of getting "free of this place" and being able to "live just like a real white person," not like a half-breed, "ugly and stupid," "poor and dirty," "weak and [drunk]" (49). She painfully hates the Native in herself and even more so in her darker sister whom she also loves. At her first opportunity, she tries to flee the whole problem of being Métis for the life of a wealthy white matron in Toronto. Racism, however, is not left behind when one opts for the rich life in the big city, as Cheryl's Christmas visit clearly attests, suggesting also that April is not really included in the "*we* Radcliffs" whose social success she so proudly asserted (116, emphasis added). When she hears her mother-in-law "dread[ing] being grandmother to a bunch of little half-breeds" (126) and encouraging another woman, white, of course, to continue being her son's mistress so that she might become his second wife, April finally recognizes just how excluded she has been. "And thank God I didn't become pregnant by your son. I wouldn't want the seed of your blood passed on to my children," April can proclaim, giving a reversed valuation and a new validity to that standard line from the miscegenation plot (127). She also demands a divorce and then returns to Winnipeg to find Cheryl beaten, hospitalized, far more a victim than April herself, who comes back with a large settlement from her now ex-husband.

One painful experience with false definition—marriage as a way to pass as white—is followed by an even more devastating one in which April is in no way complicit. Attempting to help her sister get her life back together without any knowledge of just how fallen apart that life is, she goes to Cheryl's previous residence to pick up some few personal belongings. While there she is abducted, raped, urinated on, called a savage and a squaw. During the subsequent trial, the larger story comes out, including the fact that Cheryl has been a prostitute. Three men were out to punish Cheryl in retaliation for a dispute with another prostitute. During the rape, one of them could insist, "I know you want it so quit pretending to fight it, okay? Or I'm really going to give it to you" (141). At the trial they can all claim that an honest mistake has been made, that they thought she was a prostitute and would not object. But the point of these "mistakes" is the pattern implicit in the crucial act of the rape itself, as they forcibly cast her in the role they have written for her and then act to confirm her as deserving of that role. In this sense, there was no mistake at all. She was Native; she was Cheryl; the rape was a grotesque reenactment of all the abuse that has long been heaped on both sisters and done in the same terms but now to a different effect. April begins to learn how and who to hate, to hate them for who and what they are and for what they have done to her, instead of hating herself for being cast into the role of validating her oppressors' oppression.

As Lynn A. Higgins and Brenda R. Silver observe in the introduction to *Rape and Representation,* "who gets to tell the story and whose story counts as 'truth' determine the definition of what rape is."[33] In this context, it must be remembered that April, mistaken for Cheryl, can present on the witness stand a story that Cheryl, in the same place, but as a "prostitute," could not tell. The rape was intended to put Cheryl in her place because even as a prostitute she had not "fallen" far enough. So although the rape is deemed rape and punished—because the three men violated the "proper" sister who looked white, not the "prostitute" who looked Native—the same rape also functions as ritual in the sense that, as Mary Douglas emphasizes, "rituals enact the form of social relations and in giving these relations visible expression they enable people to know their own society."[34]

Or to know the society that disowns them. The rape, as a culminating representation of the white representation of the Native, is also a representation of white society. Seeing whites in this stark perspective, April can begin to give up her earlier desire to "live just like a real white person" (49). She also begins to own up to the family she had earlier largely disowned, but not in time to save Cheryl, who, blaming herself for what has happened, commits suicide much as their mother had earlier done. Yet the novel can still end on a substantial note of redemption and promise. April discovers that Cheryl left an infant son and in that son she can see for "MY PEOPLE, OUR PEOPLE" the promise of a "tomorrow," a "better" tomorrow. In the last words of the novel: "I would strive for it. For my sister and her son. For my parents. For my people" (228).

Margaret Atwood wryly describes what she terms "The Great Canadian Baby" or "the Baby Ex Machina" as a "literary institution" that has "a lot to do with the Canadian habit of predicting great things for the future (since the present is such a notable failure)."[35] The baby at the end of In Search of April Raintree, like the baby at the end of The Double Hook, does at first seem to serve mostly as a promise for that better tomorrow. But the baby signifies somewhat differently in the Native text than he would in a white one with much the same plot. First, in Cree kinship terminology, he is April's son as much as he is Cheryl's and so is not a substitute for the family she does not have only in white nuclear family terms (terms that did not prevent white society from depriving her of her immediate family). And second, he is not going to be so deprived. The cultural genocide integral to the whole program of separating Native parents and children will be reversed, and with that reversal April can finally reproduce and represent herself as one of her people, working for their cultural and biological survival.

The Native baby in Thomas King's Medicine River (1989) makes a more timely appearance and, born early in the novel, not at its very end, does not so blatantly signify "resolution." But that baby arrives to take on much the same tasks carried out by little Henry Liberty Raintree in In Search of April Raintree. South Wing Heavyman, named after the wing of the hospital in which she was born, allows Will, the half-Native male protagonist of Medicine River, to get a better fix on his life and to begin to resolve thereby large questions of representation that have long troubled him. Yet the differences between these two obviously similar parables of uncertain identity partly resolved through the re-presentation of the Native baby is more than the matter of timing and the switch in sexes, as even the names of the babies imply.

Patrick Henry's ringing "Give me liberty or give me death" hovers behind the name of Henry Liberty Raintree and resonates back through the novel itself as another difference between the two sisters. Cheryl has already been given "death," leaving "liberty" and Henry Liberty to April. The borrowed claim to freedom, borrowed from a man who did not voice it on behalf of Native people, is therefore compromised by both the way that claim has worked itself out in the novel, providing a real and present death but at best a hope for future liberty, and by the way it is embedded in the English part of the name, Henry Liberty, not the more Native part, Raintree.

In contrast to the calculatedly loaded name of Henry Liberty, South Wing derives from a mistaken identity and a joke mistaken for earnest. The nurse, assuming that Will, at the hospital with Louise Heavyman when she is having her baby, is the husband and father, has it all wrong when she comes to tell "Mr. Heavyman" that his wife has just had a daughter, to let him hold the baby, and to ask what name the parents have "picked out for her":

> All I could see was the big sign outside the maternity ward. "Yeah," I said, feeling really good with the baby in my arms, "we'll probably call her South Wing." I guess I expected the nurse to laugh but she didn't.
> "Is that a traditional Indian name?"
> "I was just joking."
> "No, I think it's a beautiful name."[36]

The mother had intended "Wilma," after one of her grandmothers, but it is "South Wing" on the birth certificate. Will has named a baby not his own, and he has done so through the white nurse's Indianism, through her seeing a beautiful traditional Indian name in his little joke. Yet it is a beautiful Indian name, and the real Mr. Heavyman, the baby's grandfather, heartily approves. Thus—the final implication of the name and the fortuitous result of the mistakes which lead to it—South Wing, as the white designation for a fact of white life, is changed totally as it is translated into a Native context, much as "Manitoba" and "Saskatchewan" have lost their original Native reference to become designations of parts of white Canada. The signifier can be totally resignified by Natives as well.

Naming as representation is deployed differently in these two novels because, despite their similarity, they fall into different categories that King himself has cogently named. In "Godzilla vs. Post-Colonial" he argues that the very term "post-colonial" cannot fit the Native writer's concern with ostensibly post-colonial concerns: "centres, difference, totalizing, hegemony, margins."[37] Although "post-colonialism purports to be a method by which we can begin to look at those literatures which are formed out of the struggle of the oppressed against the oppressor, the colonized and the colonizer," King points out how "the term itself assumes that the starting point for that discussion is the advent of Europeans in North America."[38] This assumption thereby "cuts us off from our traditions, traditions that were in place before colonialism ever became a question, traditions that have come down to us through our cultures in spite of colonization."[39] King, "as a contemporary Native writer," is "quite unwilling to make these assumptions . . . to use these terms."[40]

In their place he would put other terms that are less centered, less Eurocentric, and less suggestive of some supposed "progression" from primitivism to sophistication. The terms he suggests are tribal, interfusional, polemical, and associational. Tribal literature designates those works in the language of the tribe and intended for the members of that linguistic community, not for any larger audience. Interfusional literature comprises narratives adapted for wider circulation (i.e., written down, often in English) but that still retain, as much as possible, the Native voice of the storyteller as well as traditional oral tale narrative devices and subject matter. Polemical literature "chronicles the imposition of non-Native expectations and insistences on Native communities and the methods of resistance employed by Native people," particularly "the championing of Native values over non-Native values."[41] Associational literature, in contrast to polemical literature, "avoids centering the story on the non-Native community or on a conflict between the two cultures, concentrating instead on the daily activities and intricacies of Native life." It eschews the stereotypes, both positive and negative, of Native life in favor of a "rather flat narrative" largely devoid of "heroes and villains," "judgements and conclusions," "climaxes and resolutions."[42] As such, this literature allows non-Native readers a limited association with a Native world but reminds them they are not part of that world nor in possession of its truths. Non-native readers are, in short, not the primary intended audience. Instead, Native readers are, and for such readers:

> Associational literature helps to remind us of the continuing values of our culture, and it reinforces the notion that, in addition to the usable past that the concurrence of oral literature and traditional history provide us with, we also have an active present marked by a cultural

tenacity and a viable future which well may organize itself around major revivals of language, philosophy, and spiritualism.[43]

The major difference between *In Search of April Raintree* and *Medicine River* should now be clearer. The former is one of Canada's paramount polemical Native novels. Henry, the name of April's and Cheryl's father, conjoined with Liberty, demands for the grandson a life different from that endured by the grandfather. The novel is necessarily set mostly in the white world because that is where the Native problems addressed in the text— matters of dispossession, stereotypical misdefinition, rape both literal and figurative—originate. But published only a few years after Culleton's novel, King's presupposes quite a different intercultural context, one in which Natives are much more free to go about their business, in which the assumed—and portrayed—alignment of the two cultures is more a matter of parallels (problems of family violence in both, for example) than of hierarchy. Even the white nurse's Indianism here takes the relatively benign form of seeing "South Wing" as a beautiful Indian name.

This is not to say that basic problems of racism have already been solved or are resolved in the novel. They definitely are not, and King shows standard stereotypes still operating at full force. For example, in one of the last episodes, the *Medicine River Herald* prints "the story" of how "Ray Little Buffalo had been shot in the stomach" and David Plume "had been arrested" for that attempted murder (251). Ray's injuries, Will subsequently discovers, did not happen that way at all. He slipped and fell on a bottle he had in his pocket, but "the papers sort of got [things] mixed up" (254). Yet King himself originally wrote the episode as the newspaper, in the novel, misrepresents it and then, in the course of revising, realized that "I was falling into the very trap [of "assumptions and stereotypes"] I thought I had been able to avoid. A very sobering moment."[44] Such sobering moments are worked into the novel itself; thus Harlan Bigbear's friends all assume that he has succumbed again to alcoholism instead of recognizing that he has merely come down with a serious case of the flu.

The stereotype that is not the picture but is part of it is particularly thematized in a novel with a Native photographer protagonist. As Percy Walton, partly borrowing from Terry Goldie, argues:

> Photography generates an image from a negative, a negative which is reversed to project the desired picture. Similarly, in order to project its image, *Medicine River* plays upon and reverses the negative semiotic field of the indigene, with its connotations of drunkenness, violence,

dishonesty, and mysticism, nature, nostalgia. By constructing a presence upon the absence of the native Other, the text avoids prioritizing native culture over other cultures [just as it also] rejects the culturally exclusive endeavor that has marginalized the native as Other.[45]

The symbolic play of light and dark in *Medicine River* is more complicated than the simple reversals necessary and appropriate in *In Search of April Raintree,* yet King's novel, as much as Culleton's, still contests prior and long-held conventional white renderings of the Native as both uncivilized savage and nature's nobleman. Or more simply put, Will, in *Medicine River,* frames and takes completely different photographs than those framed and taken by Joe in *Contact Prints.*

Will also receives photographs, which is to say that the novel thematizes photography as much as it is thematized by it and does so, in both cases, to address large questions of representation. Both Will and his brother James early focus on techniques of representation—the one mostly through photographs, the other through drawings—as a means of figuring the white father missing in their lives, the man who married their mother but then permanently left her and his two sons but who occasionally writes promising his return or promising to send presents as a stand-in for his presence (promises that are never kept). The absence of the father also figures prominently in Will's adult foray into fiction, the stories he takes to telling to strangers, preferably on airplanes, about his father's mythical success and concern but real absence: "He's a photographer./He's a doctor./He's a lawyer./ . . . [he's] a rich opal miner in Australia" (80). A parody of the mythic Great White Father gives a concomitant portrait of Will as the son of that imaginary man: this is a self-portrait of the artist constructed not from a negative but from a complete blank. It is also an attempted resolution to Will's half-breed quandary. Married to a white man, his mother with her children was excluded from the world of the Reserve. But by racialist definitions Will is definitely Indian, even though biologically he is equally "white." Claiming a very successful white father (and in white terms the success of the father counts more than his success at fathering), Will represents himself in a way that might make him more acceptable within the dominant (i.e., white) culture.

Such dubious representation of father and son ends when Will's mother sends him a real photograph of his real father. "He was leaning against a fence with four other men. He had on a pair of jeans, a work shirt and a hat that was pulled down over much of his face" (86). He is just a common man but a man who cannot even be known as that. Having abandoned his wife and sons, his face, especially for the sons, will always be in the shadow. And equally significant is the other gift that accompanies this gift of a photograph and that literally and figuratively frames it:

> My mother normally sent me a shirt for my birthday. . . . Generally, they were used, shirts she had found at yard sales. Sometimes they were new. New or used, she would wash them, iron them, and pin them up in a neat rectangle. She didn't make a distinction between new and used. There were clean shirts and dirty shirts, and that was it. She never missed my birthday.
>
> She had pinned the photograph to the shirt pocket. "That's him," the letter said, as if knowing was an important thing for me to have. (87)

Knowing is important—knowing the father is an ordinary man, in jeans and workshirt; knowing that there are concerned fathers and unconcerned fathers, and that is it. But also knowing what can be counted on: the mother who never misses his birthday, and who doesn't make a distinction between old and new—some inflated idea of origins—but understands keenly that her son deserves a clean shirt, one that she has washed, ironed, and folded into a neat rectangle. The rectangle of the photo pinned to the rectangle of the pocket on the rectangle of the folded shirt: there is a larger picture here, and it takes Will a while to see it.

He begins to get that larger picture with another photograph that he takes later in the novel, one that he connects to his one photograph of his mother, not to the one of his father. Will advertises a family special. Joyce Bluehorn signs up, in a passage that, King notes, always elicits laughter when read to a Native audience that gets the "insider joke" a white audience misses:[46]

> "Does that special mean all the family?" she said.
> "Yes, it does."
> "I got a big family." (203)

By Native definitions, a big family is everyone—every cousin's cousin, every brother-in-law's ex-wife's new stepchild. The distinctions don't matter. Indeed, "Granny" wants to make Will her son because her own son has recently been killed and Will reminds her of him. Reason enough. Will takes twenty-four photographs of this large group of Natives, many generations, children running in and out of the photo, a changing and yet constant group, in which he is required to participate. Granny won't be satisfied unless he puts himself in every shot. Twenty-four times he sets up the camera, rushes to the place Granny has made for him next to herself, and then sits sweating and smiling into the camera among *his* family. This is a final act of self-representation but it is also a pointed contesting of the basic opposition of subject and object upon which photographic representation supposedly rests, a contesting of the notion that a photograph objectifies those it represents. The photographer becomes the photographic subject (which is to say the object of his own photograph).

Instead of managing the scene directorially, Will is *directed* by the photographic subjects, directed to become a subject (one of them) in order that, ultimately, he can share his/their subjectivity. Standard oppositions—white/Native, subject/object—are here superseded and division is undone. The photographer photographing himself also photographs "his people," or—more accurately—people who make him one of them: "I was smiling in that picture, and you couldn't see the sweat. Floyd's granny was sitting in her lawn chair next to me looking right at the camera with the same flat expression that my mother had, as though she could see something farther on and out of sight" (216).

As Will himself admits, the picture "turned out good" (215). He is in it. There is something beyond it—a revisioned past, an imagined future. Representation is ever provisional and problematic. However, it serves you better, especially if you are Native, when you are in it but not necessarily fixed by it and definitely not cropped, air-brushed, or otherwise edited out.

Epilogue: The One About "The One About Coyote Going West"

Story, of course, is the "one" in Thomas King's ingeniously traditional/experimental tale, "The One About Coyote Going West." Foregrounded by its absence through the frequent indirectness—"this one," "that one"—of Native discourse (here rendered in English), story both is and is not there in the naming of this story about story which is also about Coyote who is herself a storyteller. As with the title, so, too, with the tale. The narrative resonates with the prose rhythms of oral telling—sound and word repetitions, a phatic rhetoric of address, the sound poetry of spoken syntax—and is, at the same time, as postmodernly parodic and self-reflexive as anything written by Robert Kroetsch or considered by Linda Hutcheon.[1] A very old and new story indeed. But then that is the nature of story at its best.

In the story itself, a narrator, variously addressed as both "grandmother" and "grandfather" (each a term of respect), sets out to tell Coyote the story of how Coyote created the known world, and in particular the Indians. The storyteller trickily tweaks the trickster storyteller, looping around, mocking, straying from what seems the promised point, and protecting his/her toes and tea from Coyote. Coyote sits and sometimes stands on the edge of her chair, eager to hear of her exploits, anxious that the narrator is going to botch the telling, botch the creation of the story of creation. The narrator regularly reassures Coyote: "Calm down, I says. This story is going to be okay. This story is doing just fine. This story knows where it is going. Sit down. Keep your skin on," an admonition Coyote has a hard time following in the story itself.[2]

The process of story telling, the subject of the story, the teller, and the listener are all mixed and confused; as are sign, signifier, and signified; word and referent; representation and reality. "I'm going to see my friends," Coyote early observes. "Tell those stories. Fix this world. Straighten it up" (95). Telling stories/fixing the world. Does it amount to the same thing when nothing, in either the story or the world of the story, goes straight? And Coyote neither wanders nor recounts but is tricked into listening to another's tale of the troubles that occur when someone goes "fixing the world."

The creation story becomes a decreation story, a story of creation gone awry as told to the decreator. The first thing Coyote made, the narrator observes, was a big mistake. "That one is trying to think of everything to make at once. So she don't see that hole. So she falls in that hole" (97). The mistake is both falling in the hole and the big mistake as a separate entity already inhabiting the hole because Coyote has thought it and thus made it. It is a made mistake and not ready to be sung back to nonexistence. Coyote's creation/decreation song is graphically stopped by the big mistake. Having fallen into one hole, Coyote loses another, her mouth, which the big mistake "grabs" and "pulls off" (98). Stomped flat too, she must learn to sing herself whole again through a different hole, her anus. She becomes the butt (literally) of many comments about bad smells, all of which the narrator reiterates in gleeful detail and which Coyote tries to counter with indirect (third person) accolades about herself: "That one is sweet and kind," "very wise," "that brilliant one" (101–2).

The narrator further explains how Coyote took smooth, straight rivers and made them twist and turn, put in dangerous rocks and rapids and waterfalls, and made them run only one way, not two; how she took nice round mountains, lush with apples, peaches, and cherries, and made them high and craggy and barren; how much of the rest of the cataloged world comes from a catalog: "And there is some televisions. And there is some vacuum cleaners. And there is a bunch of pastel sheets. And there is an air humidifier. And there is a big mistake sitting on a portable gas barbecue reading a book. Big book. Department store catalogue" (102). Even before we get to the creation of the "Indians," we have material, modern objects, contemporary equivalents to twenty-four dollars worth of trinkets and glass beads, for the Indians to desire. As the big mistake observes, "We need these things to make up the world. Indians are going to need this stuff" (103).

After toaster ovens, finally come the Indians. White, green, red, and blue ducks lay eggs in colors different from themselves. But the eggs hatch only more ducks, and with "more ducks than we need" (105), the first ducks decide to go Indian:

And so they do that. Before Coyote or that big mistake can mess things up, those four ducks turn into Indians, two women and two men. Good-looking Indians. They don't look at all like ducks anymore.

But those duck-Indians aren't too happy. They look at each other and they begin to cry. This is pretty disgusting, they says. All this ugly skin. All these bumpy bones. All this awful black hair. Where are our nice soft feathers? Where are our beautiful feet? What happened to our wonderful wings? It's probably all that Coyote's fault. (105)

They take it out on Coyote, again leaving her "stomp[ed] all over" and "flat like before," like, adds the narrator, "some of these stories are flat" (105).

Flat, perhaps, but not without a moral. Indian-ducks lamenting what they are not. White men's Indians, wishing after golf carts or computers with a color monitor. Indians discovered in the story before they are discovered by "Christopher Cartier" and "Jacques Columbus," "wav[ing] and say[ing], here we are, here we are" (96). "That's what happens when you try to fix this world. This world is pretty good all by itself. Best to leave it alone. Stop messing around with it" (105), the narrator admonishes Coyote—and Christopher and Jacques.

With the story told, Coyote is released from her role as listener. She leaves to become again the creator, the storyteller, off to tell Raven this good Coyote story, heading West, out to fix the world again with her new story, having heard both that story and nothing at all. "When that Coyote's wandering around looking to fix things," the narrator concludes, "nobody in this world is safe" (106).

After such a cautionary tale of grand schemes gone awry, it would be foolish to end, here, with some overriding conclusion about the Canadian West and the Canadian Western. Suffice to say that the world in "The One About Coyote Going West" is not the world of Manifest Destiny and that Thomas King's story recapitulates the Canadian Western. Nothing is manifest. Destiny itself is overshadowed by the big mistake that haunts all attempts to overreach. The Turner thesis of Progress Going West to Invent America is inverted, overruled, parodied. "The One About Coyote Going West" is the one about the whole, long story of the West, fictional or historical. It is an endlessly repeatable and endlessly repeated story of story, in which Coyote is temporarily caught but always loose and wandering, and no one story is safe.

Notes

Introduction: Coyote Country

1   For the full story of Long Lance see Donald B. Smith's *Long Lance: The True Story of an Imposter* (Toronto: Macmillan, 1982). I will also here note that I follow the Canadian usage and refer to Natives, not Native Americans (a term that can hardly include Natives who are Canadians).

2   The standard biography is Lovat Dickson's *Wilderness Man: The Strange Story of Grey Owl* (Toronto: Macmillan, 1973).

3   Kenneth Brower, "Grey Owl," *Atlantic Monthly,* Jan. 1990, p. 74.

4   For a brief account of Will James's life, including his 1915 one-year sentence to the Nevada State Prison for rustling, see Blake Allmendinger, *The Cowboy: Representations of Labor in an American Work Culture* (New York: Oxford Univ. Press, 1992), pp. 99–103, 121–28. As Allmendinger also notes, James's "autobiography," *Lone Cowboy* (1930), particularly illustrates the cowboy's penchant for asserting "the *myth* of the orphan's autonomy" (123, emphasis in the original).

5   Grove's "cover" story, as set forth in *In Search of Myself* (1946), was accepted until twenty-five years after his death, when Douglas O. Spettigue, in *FPG: The German Years* (Ottawa: Oberon, 1973), ascertained just how fictional Grove's fictional autobiography actually was. I would here also note that both Will James's ostensibly autobiographical *The Lone Cowboy* and Grove's *In Search of Myself* contain substantial hints as to the real facts being suppressed by those proclaimed factual fictions.

6   William Bright, "Introduction" to *Coyote Stories,* ed. William Bright, International Journal of American Linguistics-Native American Text Series, Monograph No. 1 (Chicago: Univ. of Chicago Press, 1978), p. 1. A more substantial overview of Coyote as Native trickster can be found in Bright's "The Natural History of Old Man Coyote" in *Recovering the Word: Essays on Native American Literature,* ed. Brian Swann and Arnold Krupat (Berkeley and Los Angeles: Univ. of California Press, 1987), pp. 339–87. Bright's recent edited collection, *A Coyote Reader* (Berkeley and Los Angeles: Univ. of California Press, 1993) also conveniently provides a range of examples and assessments of both the tribal and the more contemporary literary use of Coyote, while Harry Robinson's *Write It on Your Heart: The Epic World of an Okanagan Storyteller,* ed. Wendy Wickwire (Vancouver: Talon-

books/Theytus, 1989) features a number of impressive and specifically Canadian Coyote narratives.

7   Gary Snyder, "The Incredible Survival of Coyote," *Western American Literature* 9 (1975), p. 266.

8   Dick Harrison, *Unnamed Country: The Struggle for a Canadian Prairie Fiction* (Edmonton: Univ. of Alberta Press, 1977), p. 51.

9   Dana D. Nelson, *The Word in Black and White: Reading "Race" in American Literature 1638–1867* (New York: Oxford Univ. Press, 1992), p. 68.

10   Catharine Maria Sedgwick, *Hope Leslie; Or, Early Times in the Massachusetts,* ed. Mary Kelley (1827; rpt. New Brunswick: Rutgers Univ. Press, 1987), p. 6.

11   James H. Maguire, "Fictions of the West," in *The Columbia History of the American Novel,* ed. Emory Elliott (New York: Columbia Univ. Press, 1991), pp. 439–40.

12   Ibid., p. 442.

13   Jon Tuska, *The American West in Film: Critical Approaches to the Western* (1985; rpt. Lincoln: Univ. of Nebraska Press, 1988), p. 235.

14   Ibid., pp. 257, 260.

15   Ibid., pp. 263–64.

16   Maguire, p. 441.

17   J. Arthur Lower, *Western Canada: An Outline History* (Vancouver: Douglas and McIntyre, 1983), pp. 118–19. Lower, incidentally, provides a good overview of the history of Western Canada. See also R. Douglas Francis's *Images of the West: Changing Perceptions of the Prairies, 1690–1960* (Saskatoon, Sask.: Western Produce Prairie Books, 1989) for extensive discussion and examples of how a different Canadian West has been differently imaged and imagined in Canada.

18   Herman J. Viola, *After Columbus: The Smithsonian Chronicle of the North American Indians* (Washington, D.C.: Smithsonian Institution, 1990), p. 182. Viola also notes, in this same passage, that "the Indians of Canada experienced little of the rancor or social and cultural deprivation that characterized relations with the tribes south of the international border." Canadian Natives (and others), however, would not all concur with this judgment. See, for example, Howard Adams, *Prison of Grass,* rev. ed. (Saskatoon, Sask.: Fifth House, 1989), and (focusing on one particular Western tribe) Terry Glavin, *A Death Feast in Dimlahamid* (Vancouver: New Star, 1990), or, on a more individual level, Maria Campbell, *Halfbreed* (Toronto: McClelland and Stewart, 1973), and James Tynan, *Inside Out: An Autobiography by a Native Canadian* (Saskatoon, Sask.: Fifth House, 1989).

19   Harrison, p. 162.

20   Tuska, p. 264.

21   Nelson, p. 55.

22   Paul Hiebert, *Sarah Binks* (1947; rpt. Toronto: McClelland and Stewart, 1964), p. 68.

23   For a fuller discussion of what I have termed the "paracolonial" implications of Canadian writing see my "Canada in Fiction" in *The Columbia History of the American Novel,* p. 584.

1   Reinventing the West

1   John G. Cawelti, *The Six-Gun Mystique* (Bowling Green: Bowling Green Univ. Popular Press, 1975), p. 57.

2   As Jane Tompkins concludes in *West of Everything: The Inner Life of Westerns* (New York:

Oxford Univ. Press, 1992), these imperatives operate for readers too, and the "pattern" of the Western works "to get the audience to the point where it can't wait until the hero lets loose with his six-shooters. . . . Vengeance, by the time it arrives, feels biologically necessary" (228).

3 John R. Milton, *The Novel of the American West* (Lincoln: Univ. of Nebraska Press, 1980), p. 40.

4 Ibid., p. 16.

5 Ibid., p. 203.

6 Dick Harrison, "Fictions of the American and Canadian Wests," *Prairie Forum* 8, no. 1 (1983), p. 97.

7 Dick Harrison, *Unnamed Country: The Struggle for a Canadian Prairie Fiction* (Edmonton: Univ. of Alberta Press, 1977), p. 73.

8 Rosemary Sullivan, "Summing Up," in *Crossing Frontiers: Papers in American and Canadian Western Literature,* ed. Dick Harrison (Edmonton: Univ. of Alberta Press, 1979), p. 152.

9 Quoted in Sullivan, p. 154.

10 Robert Kroetsch, "The American Experience and the Canadian Voice" (interview conducted by Donald Cameron), *Journal of Canadian Fiction* 1, no. 3 (1972), p. 49.

11 George Bowering, *Caprice* (Markham, Ont.: Penguin, 1987), p. 265.

12 Ibid., p. 266.

13 Margaret Laurence, *The Diviners* (1974; rpt. Toronto: Bantam, 1975), p. 302.

14 Barbara Godard, "Caliban's Revolt: The Discourse of the (M)other," in *Critical Approaches to the Fiction of Margaret Laurence,* ed. Colin Nicholson (Vancouver: Univ. of British Columbia Press, 1990), p. 212.

15 Ibid., p. 210.

16 Ibid., p. 225.

17 Ibid., p. 225.

18 Gabrielle Roy, *Where Nests the Water Hen,* trans. Harry L. Binsse (1951; rpt. Toronto: McClelland and Stewart, 1970), pp. 95–96. Subsequent references to this edition will be made parenthetically in the text.

19 Gabrielle Roy, *Windflower,* trans. Joyce Marshall (1970; rpt. Toronto: McClelland and Stewart, 1975), p. 4. Subsequent references to this edition will be made parenthetically in the text.

20 Robert Kroetsch, "The Fear of Women in Prairie Fiction: An Erotics of Space," in *Crossing Frontiers,* p. 82.

21 Robert Kroetsch, "Unhiding the Hidden: Recent Canadian Fiction," *Journal of Canadian Fiction* 3, no. 3 (1974), p. 43.

22 Robert Kroetsch in Robert Kroetsch and Diane Bessai, "Death is a Happy Ending: A Dialogue in Thirteen Parts," in *Figures in a Ground: Canadian Essays on Modern Literature Collected in Honor of Sheila Watson,* ed. Diane Bessai and David Jackel (Saskatoon, Sask.: Western Producer Prairie Books, 1978), p. 210.

23 Robert Lecker, "Haunted by a Glut of Ghosts: Jack Hodgins' *The Invention of the World,*" *Essays on Canadian Writing* 20 (1980–81), pp. 86, 89.

24 Robert Kroetsch, *Badlands* (1975, rpt. Don Mills, Ont.: Paperjacks, 1976), p. 45.

25 Walter Prescott Webb, *The Great Frontier* (1964, rpt. Lincoln: Univ. of Nebraska Press, 1986), p. 36. Subsequent references to this edition will be made parenthetically in the text.

26 Margery Fee, "Romantic Nationalism and the Image of Native People in Contemporary English-Canadian Literature," in *The Native in Literature: Canadian and Comparative Per-*

spectives, ed. Thomas King, Cheryl Calver, and Helen Hoy (Toronto: ECW Press, 1987), p. 30.

27   Ibid., p. 29.

28   Jane Tompkins, "'Indians': Textualism, Morality, and the Problem of History," *Critical Inquiry* 13 (1986), p. 109.

29   Shirley Neuman, "Unearthing Language: An Interview with Rudy Wiebe and Robert Kroetsch," in *A Voice in the Land: Essays by and about Rudy Wiebe,* ed. W. J. Keith (Edmonton: NeWest, 1981), p. 230.

30   W. J. Keith, *Epic Fiction: The Art of Rudy Wiebe* (Edmonton: Univ. of Alberta Press, 1981), pp. 80, 63.

31   Rudy Wiebe in Margaret Reimer and Sue Steiner, "Translating Life Into Art: A Conversation with Rudy Wiebe," in *A Voice in the Land,* p. 130.

32   Rudy Wiebe, "Where is the Voice Coming From?" in his *The Angel of the Tar Sands and Other Stories* (Toronto: McClelland and Stewart, 1982), p. 78. Subsequent references to the story will be made parenthetically in the text and will be to this collected volume of Wiebe's short stories.

33   Anne Cameron, *Daughters of Copper Woman* (Vancouver: Press Gang, 1981), pp. 7, 28.

34   Ibid., pp. 33, 145.

35   Katherine Govier, *Between Men* (Markham, Ont.: Viking, 1987), p. 303. Subsequent references to this edition will be made parenthetically in the text.

36   See note 20.

37   Daphne Marlatt, *Ana Historic* (Toronto: Coach House, 1988), p. 131. Subsequent references to this edition will be made parenthetically in the text.

38   Robert Harlow, *Scann* (1972; rpt. Toronto: McClelland and Stewart, 1977), p. 306. Subsequent references to this edition will be made parenthetically in the text.

39   Ross Chambers, *Story and Situation: Narrative Seduction and the Power of Fiction* (Minneapolis: Univ. of Minnesota Press, 1984), p. 51.

40   Robert Kroetsch, "Reading Across the Border," in *Canadian Literature: Introductory and Critical Essays,* ed. Arnold E. Davidson (New York: MLA, 1990), pp. 338, 341; and "The Fear of Women," p. 74. See also Davidson, "Canada in Fiction," in *The Columbia History of the American Novel,* ed. Emory Elliott (New York: Columbia Univ. Press, 1991), p. 566.

41   Thomas J. Ferraro, *Ethnic Passages: Literary Immigrants in Twentieth-Century America* (Chicago: Univ. of Chicago Press, 1993), p. 8.

42   Ethel Wilson, *The Innocent Traveller* (1949; rpt. Toronto: McClelland and Stewart, 1990), p. 92.

43   Arnold Harrichand Itwaru, *The Invention of Canada: Literary Text and the Immigrant Imaginary* (Toronto: TSAR, 1990), p. 37.

44   Toni Morrison, *Playing in the Dark: Whiteness and the Literary Imagination* (Cambridge: Harvard Univ. Press, 1992), p. 66.

45   Itwaru, p. 43.

46   For a full discussion of the historic and social background of the novel see Ken Adachi, *The Enemy that Never Was: A History of the Japanese Canadians* (Toronto: McClelland and Stewart, 1976).

47   Joy Kogawa, *Obasan* (1981; rpt. Markham, Ontario: Penguin, 1983), p. 2. Subsequent references to this edition will be made parenthetically in the text.

48   I assess much more fully the complex interplay of symbols and ceremonies and other

textual details whereby Naomi both tells and comes to terms with her story in my forth-coming *Writing Against Silence: Joy Kogawa's Obasan* (Toronto: ECW Press).

49   Sky Lee, *Disappearing Moon Cafe* (Vancouver: Douglas & McIntyre, 1990), p. 2. Subsequent references will be made parenthetically to this edition of the novel.

50   Aritha van Herk, "Writing the Immigrant Self: Disguise and Damnation," in her *In Visible Ink: Crypto-frictions* (Edmonton: NeWest, 1991), p. 174.

51   In Priscilla L. Walton's "An Interview with Thomas King," *Chimo* 21 (1990), p. 27, King notes that "I didn't start writing until I was here in Canada," and so "there's no question that I think of myself as a Canadian writer." But even though he has taken out Canadian citizenship, King also insists that "the line that divides Canada from the U.S. is a political line and it has damn little to do with Native people. It's a figment of someone else's imagination."

52   Thomas King, "One Good Story, That One," *Malahat Review* 82 (1988), p. 39. Subsequent references will be made parenthetically in the text.

53   Margaret Atwood, "A Double-Bladed Knife: Subversive Laughter in Two Stories by Thomas King," in *Native Writers and Canadian Writing*, ed. W. H. New (Vancouver: Univ. of British Columbia Press, 1990), p. 249.

54   Ibid., p. 250.

2   Untelling *Tay John*

1   Margery Fee, "Howard O'Hagan's *Tay John*: Making New World Myth," *Canadian Literature*, no. 110 (1986), p. 9, emphasis in the original.

2   Jack Robinson, "Myths of Dominance Versus Myths of Re-Creation in O'Hagan's *Tay John*," *Studies in Canadian Literature* 13 (1988), pp. 168–69.

3   Fee, p. 17.

4   Robert Kroetsch, "Unhiding the Hidden: Recent Canadian Fiction," *Journal of Canadian Fiction* 3, no. 3 (1974), p. 43.

5   Claude Lévi-Strauss, *The Raw and the Cooked*, tr. John and Doreen Weightman (New York: Harper and Row, 1969), p. 12.

6   Trinh T. Minh-ha, *Woman, Native, Other: Writing Postcoloniality and Feminism* (Bloomington: Indiana Univ. Press, 1989), p. 61.

7   As Ella Tanner, in *Tay John and the Cyclical Quest* (Toronto: ECW Press, 1990) points out, Tay John's first Salish name "actually does mean [in Salish] 'saviour with yellow hair'" (53), so even with the name itself something is definitely lost as Kumkleseem becomes Tête Jaune and then Tay John.

8   Both Michael Ondaatje, in "O'Hagan's Rough-Edged Chronicle," *Canadian Literature*, no. 61 (1974), p. 25, and Gary Geddes, in "The Writer that CanLit Forgot," *Saturday Night*, Nov. 1977, p. 86, have noted O'Hagan's indebtedness to Conrad.

9   Howard O'Hagan, *Tay John* (1939; rpt. Toronto: McClelland and Stewart, 1974), pp. 28, 262. Subsequent references to this edition will be made parenthetically within the text.

10   W. J. Keith, in *A Sense of Style: Studies in the Art of Fiction in English-Speaking Canada* (Toronto: ECW Press, 1989), has argued that it is "wrong" to see in *Tay John* such religious "parody as undermining and destroying the validity of a Christian or any religious viewpoint. The narrative voice here insists on our registering the Biblical parallels, but invites

us to hold the sacred and the profane in suspension" (35). But I would suggest that the "sacred" is undermined by any suggestion that it may be no different from the "profane."

11   Robinson also suggests the connection between these two acts: "Rorty's preaching has been a verbal rape, a paradigm for the taking of the land and the suppression of the indigenous cultures by the invading white culture" (167).

12   The hawk, I should note, might be particularly significant to me because, when my own mother was dying in a hospital, her Cree son-in-law looked out the window to see a circling hawk and told her that the hawk was flying, that she could go peacefully now.

13   For a fuller discussion of naming in the novel see my "Being and Definition in Howard O'Hagan's *Tay John*," in *Etudes Canadiennes* 15 (1983), pp. 137–47.

14   Denham notes that he first met one of the characters who figures in his tale "here in Edmonton, in this very bar" (166).

15   See Fee, pp. 14–20, for an overview discussion of the implications of Denham's mostly concealed European past.

16   Blackie's entrance into the novel need not be seen as the "irritating" flaw that Ondaatje suggests (30), but as Jackie's final separation—marked from the beginning by the mountain stream—from Tay John and his tale.

17   Ondaatje, pp. 29, 31.

18   Again it should be noted that the novel was written in the thirties, well before tests of existential honesty had become fictional clichés.

19   Keith observes that "the surely deliberate if sardonic use of Arthur as the husband's name" invokes a romance-triangle (36), and the whole Western tradition of romance thereby becomes another myth parodied in the novel.

20   As Fee observes, "the mythic ending balances and echoes the mythic beginning" and thereby sets forth a "hint of a possible return of the hero, of a cycle [that] is mythically irresistible" (16).

21   Robert Kroetsch in "The Veil of Knowing" in his *The Lovely Treachery of Words: Essays Selected and New* (Toronto: Oxford Univ. Press, 1989) makes much this same point when he argues that "not the raising of the veil but, rather, the lowering of the veil, the acknowledgement of the untellability of the story, is the generative moment, the enabling act" of this novel in which the protagonist "works often as a guide [but] works always to disappear," while the narrator "work[s] always to tell a story . . . he would tell us is untellable" (184).

22   Gerald Vizenor, "A Postmodern Introduction," in *Narrative Chance: Postmodern Discourse on Native American Literatures,* ed. Gerald Vizenor (Albuquerque: Univ. of New Mexico Press, 1989), p. 13. The trickster, Vizenor also points out in this challenging essay, is many other things as well.

3   Coyote at Dog Creek

1   Sheila Watson, *The Double Hook* (1959; rpt. Toronto: McClelland and Stewart, 1966), p. 19. Subsequent references to this New Canadian Library edition of the novel will be made parenthetically in the text.

2   Margery Fee, "Howard O'Hagan's *Tay John*: Making New World Myth," *Canadian Literature,* no. 110 (1986), pp. 22, 25.

3   Stephen Scobie, *Sheila Watson and Her Works* (Toronto: ECW Press, n.d.), p. 6.

4   Sheila Watson, "What I'm Going to Do," *Open Letter,* 3d series, no. 1 (1974), p. 183.

5   Watson, "What I'm Going to Do," p. 182.

6   Just how successfully Watson avoided the limitations of regionalism in *The Double Hook* can now be better appreciated by comparing that novel to her first, *Deep Hollow Creek* (Toronto: McClelland and Stewart, 1992), written in the thirties and also derived from her time teaching in the Cariboo country of British Columbia during the Depression. Perhaps the author delayed publishing this first novel for more than half a century because, unlike *The Double Hook,* it is both regional and overwritten in an attempt to transcend regionalism. Thus Stella, the visiting schoolteacher protagonist of *Deep Hollow Creek,* regularly records telling details of the place, such as her landlady showing off her one item of finery, a feathered pair of purple "boudoir shoes" bought from a catalog with money an aunt gave her years ago: "The only trouble, she said, the only thing—when they did send them they had to go and send a pair that didn't fit, and somehow I just never got time to send them back" (21). And just as regularly the protagonist-narrator attempts to load other details with literary reference as when she describes her dog, Juno, and her sleeping pups: "Juno and the Paycock—there you sit, your glory and your woe asleep behind you on the mat; here I sit, asking What are the stars, what is the moon" (135–36). These strained references to Sean O'Casey are in obvious contrast to Coyote who is totally at home in the text of *The Double Hook.*

7   Scobie, p. 20.

8   Watson, "What I'm Going to Do," p. 182, emphasis and ellipsis in the original.

9   Ibid., ellipsis in the original.

10 Scobie, p. 35.

11 Douglas Barbour, "Editors and Typesetters," *Open Letter,* 3d series, no. 1 (1974–75), reprinted in *Sheila Watson and "The Double Hook,"* ed. George Bowering (Ottawa: Golden Dog Press, 1985), p. 9.

12 As Angela Bowering, in "Figures Cut in Sacred Ground: *Illuminati* in *The Double Hook,*" *Line,* no. 2 (1983), p. 47, notes, with this opening scene, "narrative and imagery marry domesticity and death, doubling back on themselves."

13 Hugo McPherson, "An Important New Voice," *Tamarack Review* 12 (1959); Don Summerhayes, "Glory and Fear," *Alphabet* 3 (1961); Philip Child, "A Canadian Prose-Poem," *Dalhousie Review* 39 (1959); all reprinted in *Sheila Watson and "The Double Hook,"* pp. 24, 29, 32.

14 Margaret Morriss, "The Elements Transcended," *Canadian Literature,* no. 42 (1969), reprinted in *Sheila Watson and "The Double Hook,"* p. 87; and, Nancy J. Corbett, "Closed Circle," *Canadian Literature,* no. 61 (1974), reprinted in *Sheila Watson and "The Double Hook,"* p. 117.

15 Steven Putzel, "Under Coyote's Eye: Indian Tales in Sheila Watson's *The Double Hook,*" *Canadian Literature,* no. 102 (1984), p. 14.

16 Margot Northey, *The Haunted Wilderness: The Gothic and Grotesque in Canadian Fiction* (Toronto: Univ. of Toronto Press, 1976), p. 90.

17 Ibid., p. 88.

18 Beverley Mitchell, "Association and Allusion in *The Double Hook,*" *Journal of Canadian Fiction* 2 (1973), reprinted in *Sheila Watson and "The Double Hook,"* pp. 102, 111.

19 Ibid., pp. 105, 113.

20 Ibid., p. 104.

21 Ibid., ellipsis in the original.

22 As Bruce Nesbitt has argued in "Displacement in Patrick White and Sheila Watson: Musical and Mythic Forms," in *Australian/Canadian Literature in English: Comparative Perspectives,* ed. Russell McDougall and Gillian Whitlock (Melbourne: Methuen, 1987), pp. 151–69, there are hints of possible incest between James and Greta in the novel, which may partly explain the murder of the mother. Robert Kroetsch, in "The Veil of Knowledge" in *The Lovely Treachery of Words: Essays Selected and New* (Toronto: Oxford Univ. Press, 1989), also observes that the novel both conceals and reveals "the breaking of the incest taboo" (185).

23 Putzel, p. 13.

24 Scobie, p. 33.

25 Morriss, p. 93.

26 George Bowering, "Sheila Watson, Trickster," from *The Canadian Novel, Volume III: Modern Times,* ed. John Moss (Toronto: NC Press, 1981), reprinted in *Sheila Watson and "The Double Hook,"* p. 197.

27 As Glen Deer points out, in "Miracle, Mystery, and Authority: ReReading *The Double Hook,*" *Open Letter,* 6th series, no. 8 (1987), James, returning, "shuts his eyes and simply clings to the back of his animal"; thus it is "his remarkable horse" who is "responsible for [James's] own return" (32).

4 The Archaeology of *Badlands*

1 Robert Kroetsch, "On Being an Alberta Writer: or, I Wanted to Tell our Story," in *The New Provinces: Alberta and Saskatchewan, 1905–1980,* ed. Howard Palmer and Donald Smith (Vancouver: Tantalus Research, 1980). Reprinted in *Robert Kroetsch: Essays,* special issue of *Open Letter,* 5th series, no. 4 (Spring 1983), p. 71.

2 Ibid.

3 Ibid., p. 76.

4 *Labyrinths of Voice: Conversations with Robert Kroetsch,* ed. (and conducted by) Shirley Neuman and Robert Wilson (Edmonton: NeWest Press, 1982), p. 28.

5 *Labyrinths of Voice,* p. 10.

6 Kroetsch, "Alberta Writer," p. 76.

7 Linda Hutcheon, *The Canadian Postmodern: A Study of Contemporary English-Canadian Fiction* (Toronto: Oxford Univ. Press, 1988), p. 167, emphasis in the original.

8 Ibid., p. 168.

9 Robert Kroetsch, "Contemporary Standards in the Canadian Novel," in *Taking Stock,* ed. Charles Steele (Downsview: ECW, 1982). Reprinted in *Kroetsch Essays* issue of *Open Letter,* p. 42.

10 *Labyrinths of Voice,* p. 167.

11 Robert Lecker, *Robert Kroetsch* (Boston: Twayne, 1986), p. 79, emphasis in the original.

12 Mark Simpson, "The Found and the Unfounded: An Explosion of Authorship in *Badlands,*" *Alberta* 1, no. 2 (1989), p. 42.

13 Robert Kroetsch, "Unhiding the Hidden: Recent Canadian Fiction," *Journal of Canadian Fiction* 3, no. 3 (1974). Reprinted in *Kroetsch Essays* issue of *Open Letter,* p. 19.

14 Jeanette Seim, "Horses & Houses: Further Readings in Kroetsch's *Badlands* and Sinclair Ross's *As for Me and My House,*" *Open Letter,* 5th series, nos. 8–9 (1984), p. 101.

15 *Labyrinths of Voice,* p. 17.

16   Robert Kroetsch, "Beyond Nationalism: A Prologue," *Mosaic* 14, no. 2 (1981). Reprinted in *Kroetsch Essays* issue of *Open Letter,* p. 86.

17   R. H. Ramsay, "Questing for Origins," *Canadian Forum,* no. 657 (1975–76), p. 55; and Roy MacSkimming, review of *Badlands* in *The Toronto Star,* Sept. 27, 1975, p. F7.

18   Robert Kroetsch, *Badlands* (Toronto: New Press, 1975), p. 6. Subsequent references to this edition of the novel will be made parenthetically in the text.

19   Ann Mandel, "Uninventing Structures: Cultural Criticism and the Novels of Robert Kroetsch," *Open Letter,* 3d series, no. 8 (1978), p. 65.

20   Lecker, pp. 81–83.

21   Simpson, p. 52.

22   *Labyrinths of Voice,* p. 15.

23   Michel Foucault, *The Archaeology of Knowledge,* tr. A. M. Sheridan Smith (New York: Pantheon, 1972), p. 21.

24   Ibid., p. 23.

25   Hutcheon, p. 162. Hutcheon goes on to summarize the major critical "paradoxical formulations."

26   Margaret E. Turner, "Endings Be Damned: Robert Kroetsch's *Gone Indian," Canadian Literature,* no. 119 (1988), p. 57.

27   Simpson, p. 41.

28   Jane Tompkins, *West of Everything: The Inner Life of Westerns* (New York: Oxford Univ. Press, 1992).

29   Connie Harvey, "Tear-Glazed Vision of Laughter," *Essays on Canadian Writing,* no. 11 (1978), p. 29. Of course this structuring "duality" affirms the very sexual polarity that the novel ostensibly questions.

30   Ibid., p. 49.

31   Lecker, p. 80.

32   Ibid., p. 85.

33   Ibid., pp. 82–83.

34   Harvey, p. 49.

35   Lecker, p. 80.

36   For a full discussion of just how complex the interplay of different paradigms of gender are in this novel (and in all of Kroetsch's writing), see Susan Rudy Dorscht, *Women, Reading, Kroetsch: Telling the Difference* (Waterloo, Ont.: Wilfrid Laurier Univ. Press, 1991).

37   Rosemary Sullivan, "The Fascinating Place Between: The Fiction of Robert Kroetsch," *Mosaic* 11, no. 3 (1978), p. 175.

38   Charles R. Steele in "Dancing With Snowflakes: Monologue with the Silent Author," *Dandelion* 14, no. 1 (1987), perceptively assesses the associations between man and bear in the novel. As he points out: "Man and bear . . . man-like bear . . . meeting . . . miming. But who's miming whom? Which then is symbol? Both? and if both, then neither? Symbol symbolizing symbol" (77, ellipses in the original).

39   Arnold E. Davidson, "History, Myth, and Time in Robert Kroetsch's *Badlands," Studies in Canadian Literature* 5 (1980), pp. 127–37.

40   Peter Thomas, *Robert Kroetsch* (Vancouver: Douglas & McIntyre, 1980), pp. 94–95.

41   Robert Kroetsch and Diane Bessai, "Death is a Happy Ending: A Dialogue in Thirteen Parts," in *Figures in a Ground: Canadian Essays on Modern Literature Collected in Honor of Sheila Watson,* ed. Diane Bessai and David Jackel (Saskatoon, Sask.: Western Producer Prairie Books, 1978), p. 209.

42   *Labyrinths of Voice,* p. 170.

43   Aritha van Herk, "Biocritical Essay" in *The Robert Kroetsch Papers: An Archival Inventory* (Calgary: University of Calgary Press, 1986), p. xxviii.

44   Joseph Campbell, *The Hero with a Thousand Faces* (Princeton: Princeton Univ. Press, 1949), p. 206.

5   "Smile When You Call Me That,"
She Said Cuttingly

1   Jane Tompkins, *West of Everything: The Inner Life of Westerns* (New York: Oxford Univ. Press), p. 38.

2   Ibid., p. 41.

3   Ibid., p. 42.

4   Ibid., p. 45.

5   Frederick Philip Grove, *In Search of Myself* (Toronto: Macmillan, 1946), p. 259.

6   Aritha van Herk, "Woman Writers and the Prairie: Spies in an Indifferent Landscape," *Kunapipi* 6, no. 2 (1984), pp. 17, 15.

7   Dick Harrison, *Unnamed Country: The Struggle for a Canadian Prairie Fiction* (Edmonton: Univ. of Alberta Press, 1977), p. 111.

8   Martha Ostenso, *Wild Geese* (1925, rpt., Toronto: McClelland and Stewart, 1961), p. 237.

9   For a perceptive discussion of just how pervasive the gender role reversals are in this novel, see J. David Stevens, "The Gipsies of Shadow Point: Meg Merrilees, Murray Lees, and Laurence's *The Stone Angel,*" forthcoming in *Journal of Canadian Studies.*

10   Sharon Riis, *The True Story of Ida Johnson* (Toronto: Women's Press, 1976), p. 49. Subsequent references to this edition will be made parenthetically in the text.

11   van Herk, "Woman Writers and the Prairie," p. 23.

12   Coyote, I would here note, even more obviously figures duplicity and trickery in Riis's second novel, *Midnight Twilight Tourist Zone* (Vancouver: Douglas & McIntyre, 1989). Thus the narrator, at one point, "looked out the plate glass window into the night [and] saw nothing of course but myself . . . reflected back at me. And myself looking back, face to face, nose to nose, was a coyote" (72).

13   Aritha van Herk, *Judith* (1978, rpt., New York: Bantam, 1979), p. 166. Subsequent references to this edition will be made parenthetically in the text.

14   The working title of the novel, "When Pigs Fly," also emphasized these implications of the epigraphs.

15   For a detailed analysis of the structure of the novel see Reingard M. Nischik's "Narrative Technique in Aritha van Herk's Novels" in *Gaining Ground: European Critics on Canadian Literature,* ed. Robert Kroetsch and Reingard M. Nischik (Edmonton: NeWest Press, 1985), pp. 107–20.

16   It might be noted that pigs also originally supplied the narration of the novel in that the first draft was told from the animals' point of view. The change to the third person, van Herk has acknowledged, was made at the publisher's request but she still expects "the perceptive reader [to be] aware of the pigs' voice behind the narration." "Aritha van Herk" (interview conducted by Gyrid Jerve), *Kunapipi* 8 (1986), p. 75.

17   But both Freud and Lacan, I would note, are more likely to be encountered in a Canadian Western than in an American one. Thus the narrator of Kristjana Gunnars's *The Substance of Forgetting* (Red Deer, Alberta: Red Deer College Press, 1992) figures, from beginning to

end, her Québec separatist lover in terms of ladders and towers and her Okanagan home in terms of snippets from Lacan such as the following: "It is *pleasure as that which binds incoherent life together,* Jacques Lacan said. All my incoherent years are held up by the pleasure of being here" (117, italics in the original).

18 Jane Gallop, *The Daughter's Seduction: Feminism and Psychoanalysis* (Ithaca: Cornell Univ. Press, 1982), p. 39.

19 Ibid., p. 70.

20 Ibid., p. 76.

21 Ibid., p. 71.

22 One has to read the novel carefully to notice how much the mother is missing in the text and how much that absence goes without saying. Thus when the mother is killed in the same accident whereby the father also killed himself (running a stop sign, a law unto himself until the very end), the daughter explicitly mourns only for her father.

23 Gallop, p. 39.

24 Ibid., p. 96.

25 Ibid., p. 99.

26 Hélène Cixous, "Castration or Decapitation?" *Signs: Journal of Women in Culture and Society* 7 (1981), pp. 54–55. See also her "The Laugh of Medusa," *Signs* 1 (1976), pp. 875–93.

27 Aritha van Herk, *The Tent Peg* (1981, rpt., Toronto: Seal, 1982), p. 5. Subsequent references to this edition will be made parenthetically in the text.

28 Nischik, p. 115.

29 Cathy N. Davidson, *Revolution and the Word: The Rise of the Novel in America* (New York: Oxford Univ. Press, 1986). See especially her chapter "The Female Picaresque," pp. 179–92.

30 For a full theoretical assessment of cross-dressing see Marjorie Garber, *Vested Interests: Crossdressing and Cultural Anxiety* (New York: Routledge, 1992).

31 Davidson, pp. 181–85.

32 Nischik, p. 116.

33 See especially "A Meditation on Metaphor" in Annette Kolodny, *The Lay of the Land: Metaphor as Experience and History in American Life and Letters* (Chapel Hill: Univ. of North Carolina Press, 1975), pp. 148–60.

34 "Aritha van Herk" (Jerve interview), p. 70.

6 The Gynocentric *Journey*

1 That "long way," it must be admitted, is with respect to subject matter, not artistic sophistication. Of the Canadian Western writers I consider in some detail, Anne Cameron is the likeliest candidate for a "Literary Offenses" assessment. But even though Nicole Brossard's *Le Désert mauve* or Daphne Marlatt's *Ana Historic* or Jane Rule's *Desert of the Heart* are more literarily sophisticated lesbian Westerns, *The Journey* still better fits the design of my study, and I therefore use it as an ideologically paradigmatic text rather than an aesthetically exemplary one.

2 Anne Cameron, *The Journey* (San Francisco: Spinsters/Aunt Lute, 1986), n.p. Subsequent references to this edition of the novel will be made parenthetically in the text.

3 My focus here is on the popular-culture cowboy, not the working one. As Blake Allmendinger points out in *The Cowboy: Representations of Labor in an American Work Culture* (New York: Oxford Univ. Press, 1992), "cattlemen economically subordinated cowboys by

making them, in effect, sexually nonfunctional" (50). Indeed, in his whole chapter, "Frontier Gender: Livestock Castration and Square Dancing" (48–82), Allmendinger considers at length how and with what implications "cowboys were metaphorically castrated" (51).

4   Borrowing substantially from French feminist theory, Canadian women authors and critics have extensively queried the sexuality of textuality. See especially two recent anthologies of Canadian feminist criticism, *A Mazing Space: Writing Canadian Women Writing*, ed. Shirley Neuman and Smaro Kamboureli (Edmonton: Longspoon/NeWest, 1986), and *Gynocritics/La Gynocritique: Feminist Approaches to the Writing of Canadian and Québécoise Women/Approaches féministes à l'écriture des canadiennes et québécoise*, ed. Barbara Godard (Toronto: ECW Press, 1987).

5   Barbara Johnson, *The Critical Difference: Essays in the Contemporary Rhetoric of Reading* (Baltimore: Johns Hopkins Univ. Press, 1980), p. 13.

6   Barbara Johnson, *A World of Difference* (Baltimore: Johns Hopkins Univ. Press, 1987), pp. 40–41.

7   See Ann Douglas, *The Feminization of American Culture* (New York: Knopf, 1977). But the citing of Douglas's title does not imply that I agree with her views about the causes and consequences—or even the fact—of such feminization.

8   Annette Kolodny, *The Land Before Her: Fantasy and Experience of the American Frontiers, 1630–1860* (Chapel Hill: Univ. of North Carolina Press, 1984). See also Nina Baym, "Melodramas of Beset Manhood: How Theories of American Fiction Exclude Women Authors," *American Quarterly* 33 (1981), pp. 123–39.

9   Heather Murray, "Women in the Wilderness," in *A Mazing Space*, p. 77.

10   Elaine Showalter, "Feminist Criticism in the Wilderness," in *Writing and Sexual Difference*, ed. Elizabeth Abel (Chicago: Univ. of Chicago Press, 1982), pp. 30–31.

11   Murray, p. 82.

12   Ibid., p. 83.

13   Coral Ann Howells, *Private and Fictional Words: Canadian Women Novelists of the 1970s and 1980s* (London: Methuen, 1987), p. 18.

14   See Eve Kosofsky Sedgwick, *Between Men: English Literature and Male Homosocial Desire* (New York: Columbia Univ. Press, 1985). Jane Tompkins, in *West of Everything: The Inner Life of Westerns* (New York: Oxford Univ. Press, 1992), also explicitly extends Sedgwick's ideas to the sexual politics of the Western.

15   René Girard, *Deceit, Desire, and the Novel: Self and Other in Literary Structure*, tr. Yvonne Freccero (Baltimore: Johns Hopkins Univ. Press, 1972).

16   Sedgwick, p. 23.

17   Linda Hutcheon, *The Canadian Postmodern: A Study of Contemporary English-Canadian Fiction* (Toronto: Oxford Univ. Press, 1988), p. 3.

18   Ibid., pp. 3, 7.

19   Elaine Scarry, *The Body in Pain: The Making and Unmaking of the World* (New York: Oxford Univ. Press, 1985), p. 59.

20   Dianne F. Sadoff, "*Locus Suspectus*: Narrative, Castration, and the Uncanny," *Dickens Studies Annual* 13 (1984), p. 226.

21   Ibid., p. 227.

22   Terry Goldie, *Fear and Temptation: The Image of the Indigene in Canadian, Australian, and New Zealand Literatures* (Kingston and Montreal: McGill-Queen's Univ. Press, 1989), p. 215.

23   Bonnie Zimmerman, "Exiting from Patriarchy: The Lesbian Novel of Development," in

The Voyage In: Fictions of Female Development, ed. Elizabeth Abel, Marianne Hirsch, and Elizabeth Langland (Hanover, N.H.: Univ. Press of New England, 1983), p. 255.

7 Epic and Extinction

1   Earl F. Fitz, *Rediscovering the New World: Inter-American Literature in a Comparative Context* (Iowa City: Univ. of Iowa Press, 1991), p. 48.

2   Ibid., p. 69.

3   For brief overviews of recent reevaluations of the Columbus legacy see Garry Willis, "Goodbye, Columbus," *New York Review,* Nov. 22, 1990, pp. 6–10, and Kenneth Maxwell, "¡Adiós Columbus!," *New York Review,* Jan. 28, 1993, pp. 38–45.

4   Stephen Greenblatt, *Marvelous Possessions: The Wonder of the New World* (Chicago: Univ. of Chicago Press, 1991), p. 128.

5   Abdul R. JanMohamed, *Manichean Aesthetics: The Politics of Literature in Colonial Africa* (Amherst: Univ. of Massachusetts Press, 1983), pp. 4, 3.

6   Leslie Monkman, *A Native Heritage: Images of the Indian in English-Canadian Literature* (Toronto: Univ. of Toronto Press, 1981), pp. 5, 8.

7   Ibid., p. 8.

8   Gaile McGregor, in *The Wacousta Syndrome: Explorations in the Canadian Langscape* (Toronto: Univ. of Toronto Press, 1985), argues at length that "the theoretical wilderness/ civilization dichotomy does not operate in the Canadian book in the same way that it does in the American wilderness romance" (5) and that this difference is characteristic of Canadian literature.

9   Monkman, pp. 5, 6.

10   The quotation is, of course, from Joseph Conrad's "Heart of Darkness" in *Youth and Two Other Stories* (New York: Doubleday, 1924), p. 149.

11   Dana D. Nelson, *The Word in Black and White: Reading "Race" in American Literature 1638–1867* (New York: Oxford Univ. Press, 1992), p. 54.

12   Ibid., p. 39.

13   Ibid., p. 62.

14   Ibid., pp. 40–41, emphasis in the original.

15   Margaret Atwood, *Survival: A Thematic Guide to Canadian Literature* (Toronto: Anansi, 1972), p. 39.

16   John Moss, *Sex and Violence in the Canadian Novel: The Ancestral Present* (Toronto: McClelland and Stewart, 1977), p. 260.

17   Peter Such, Preface to *Riverrun* (Toronto: Clarke Irwin, 1973), p. viii. Subsequent references to the novel will be from this edition and will be made parenthetically in the text.

18   Sid Stephen, *Beothuk Poems* (Ottawa: Oberon, 1976), n.p. The quotation is from the Historical Note which precedes the poems in this unpaginated volume.

19   Ibid.

20   Frederick W. Rowe, *Extinction: The Beothuks of Newfoundland* (Toronto: McGraw-Hill Ryerson, 1977), p. 66.

21   Ibid., pp. 66–67. Rowe, incidentally, finds that, with the Beothuks, white good intentions always went somehow sadly amiss but is reluctant to consider that such regularly achieved ends might, perhaps, have been intended.

22   Ibid., p. 67.

23   Rowe's generally apologistic stance is early signaled by his claims that "hostility towards

the Beothuks did not involve the settlers generally"; that "only a relatively small number of fishermen-trappers of the north-east coast" perpetrated outrages; and that "white brutality, vicious and deplorable as it was, was only one of a number of factors that brought about the decline of the Beothuks" (7)—as if they well might have died out anyway, even had whites never arrived.

24 Ibid., p. 68.
25 Ibid., pp. 50–51.
26 Ibid., p. 51.
27 Greenblatt, p. 106.
28 Roy Harvey Pearce, *The Savages of America: A Study of the Indian and the Idea of Civilization,* rev. ed. (Baltimore: Johns Hopkins Univ. Press, 1965), p. 242.
29 Greenblatt, p. 99.
30 Quoted in Greenblatt, p. 101.
31 Greenblatt, p. 90.
32 Quoted in Greenblatt, pp. 101–2.
33 Greenblatt, p. 102.
34 Quoted in Rowe, p. 14.
35 As Diana Brydon in "The White Inuit Speaks," in *Past the Last Post: Theorizing Post-Colonial and Post-Modernism,* ed. Ian Adam and Helen Tiffin (Calgary: Univ. of Calgary Press, 1990), p. 196, rightly notes: "The current flood [an appropriate figure] of books by white Canadian writers embracing Native spirituality clearly serves a white need to feel at home in this country and to assuage the guilt felt over a material appropriation by making it a cultural one as well. In the absence of comparable political reparation for past appropriations such symbolic acts seem questionable or at least inadequate. Literature cannot be confused with social action." This quote also confirms what I noted earlier in the chapter, that *Riverrun* is not especially idiosyncratic in the Canadian tradition.
36 Quoted in Tzvetan Todorov, *The Conquest of America,* tr. Richard Howard (New York: Harper, 1984), pp. 36, 46.
37 Ibid., p. 49.
38 Monkman, p. 79.
39 Todorov, p. 49.
40 For a recent study of the theoretical implications of juxtaposing picture and text, see J. Hillis Miller, *Illustration* (Cambridge: Harvard Univ. Press, 1992). In the case of these illustrations, however, whatever Beothuk "story" they might tell to supplement the account of the white novel is beyond recovery. As Greg Sarris argues at length in *Keeping Slug Woman Alive: A Holistic Approach to American Indian Texts* (Berkeley and Los Angeles: Univ. of California Press, 1993), Native "texts" (narratives, artifacts, whatever) need to be "read across cultures so that intercultural communication is opened rather than closed" (3); this reading necessarily takes the form of a "record [of a] dialogue" instead of a "report [of an] outcome, what *they* [i.e., white readers] thought and concluded" (128, emphasis in the original). Such a dialogue is impossible when one party to it has been exterminated.

8   Lessons on Perspective

1 Annette Kolodny, *The Lay of the Land: Metaphor as Experience and History in American Life and Letters* (Chapel Hill: Univ. of North Carolina Press, 1975), p. 5.

2   Ibid., p. 4.
3   Caren J. Deming, "Miscegenation in Popular Western History and Fiction," in *Women and Western American Literature,* ed. Helen Winter Stauffer and Susan J. Rosowski (Troy, N.Y.: Whiston, 1982), p. 94.
4   Abdul R. JanMohamed, *Manichean Aesthetics: The Politics of Literature in Colonial Africa* (Amherst: Univ. of Massachusetts Press, 1983), p. 3.
5   O. Mannoni, *Prospero and Caliban: The Psychology of Colonization,* tr. Pamela Powesland (New York: Praeger, 1956), p. 21.
6   Sylvia Söderlind, *Margin/Alias: Language and Colonization in Canadian and Québécois Fiction* (Toronto: Univ. of Toronto Press, 1991), p. 5.
7   Marianna Torgovnick, *Gone Primitive: Savage Intellects, Modern Lives* (Chicago: Univ. of Chicago Press, 1990), pp. 228, 236.
8   Trinh T. Minh-ha, *Woman, Native, Other: Writing Postcoloniality and Feminism* (Bloomington: Indiana Univ. Press, 1989), p. 150.
9   Bill Ashcroft, Gareth Griffiths, and Helen Tiffin, *The Empire Writes Back: Theory and Practice in Post-Colonial Literatures* (London: Routledge, 1989), p. 59.
10 Natives are presently the fastest growing population in Western Canada and particularly in Saskatchewan and Manitoba. "It is estimated that . . . one in four people entering the labour force in Western Canada [is] of aboriginal ancestry; in Manitoba and Saskatchewan, the ratio is nearly one in two." From "Overview," in *Indian and Native Programs: A Study Team Report to the Task Force on Program Review* (Ottawa: Canadian Government Publishing Center, 1986), p. 28.
11 Indian men married to white women did not similarly lose their treaty rights, and this inequality in the law was not abolished until 1987, when legislation finally allowed all Native women with treaty rights to retain them instead of being subsumed under their husband's status.
12 Thus he can enjoy the "blanket marriage" (the Stony term) he and Victoria have already established, but he also decides that this union needs to be supplemented and affirmed by a Christian marriage ceremony.
13 Terry Goldie, *Fear and Temptation: The Image of the Indigene in Canadian, Australian, and New Zealand Literatures* (Kingston and Montreal: McGill-Queen's Univ. Press, 1989), p. 76.
14 W. O. Mitchell, *The Vanishing Point* (Toronto: Macmillan, 1973), p. 155. Subsequent references to this edition of the novel will be made parenthetically in the text.
15 Harold Bloom, *The Visionary Company: A Reading of English Romantic Poetry* (New York: Doubleday, 1961), p. 17.
16 Other codes are also present in this overcoding. For example, Paradise Valley can be seen as "an obvious and minimal disguise for the Eden Valley Reserve at which Mitchell himself taught," just as, as W. J. Keith also notes, in "W. O. Mitchell from *The Alien* to *The Vanishing Point,*" *World Literature Written in English* 27 (1987), p. 259, "clearly, there is irony in the name Paradise Valley," when the place "is both dirty and depressing."
17 This argument is further supported by the consideration that *The Vanishing Point* represents a substantial revision of *The Alien,* and that the first version, written some twenty years before the second, casts Sinclair as even more central to the text but is rather less concerned with Native problems and perspectives. Keith's previously noted article provides an excellent assessment of how the earlier novel was reworked into the later one.
18 Philip Kreiner, *People Like Us in a Place Like This* (Ottawa: Oberon, 1983), p. 66. Subsequent references to this edition will be made parenthetically in the text.

19   Dawn Lander, "Eve Among the Indians," in *The Authority of Experience: Essays in Feminine Criticism,* ed. Arlyn Diamond and Lee R. Edwards (Amherst: Univ. of Massachusetts Press, 1977), p. 201.

20   Deming, p. 95.

21   Sherry B. Ortner, "Is Female to Male as Nature Is to Culture?" *Feminist Studies* 1, no. 2 (1972), p. 24. See also Barbara Johnson's "Is Female to Male as Ground Is to Figure?" in *Feminism and Psychoanalysis,* ed. Richard Feldstein and Judith Roof (Ithaca: Cornell Univ. Press, 1989) for a more theoretically sophisticated discussion of the deployment of patriarchal narrative power that leaves "many . . . invisible men and women trapped in the wallpaper of the Western canon" and not "sufficiently" noticed by feminist or psychoanalytic theory either (268).

22   Ortner, pp. 24, 28.

23   For a full assessment of how differently sexual and gender paradigms could be drawn in Native societies see Walter L. Williams, *The Spirit and the Flesh: Sexual Diversity in American Indian Culture* (Boston: Beacon, 1986).

24   Valerie Sherer Mathes, "Native American Woman in Medicine and Military," *Journal of the West* 21, no. 2 (1982), pp. 45, 46. It might be noted that Frederick Manfred's *The Manly-Hearted Woman* (1975) does portray a Native woman who at first successfully leads a warrior's life. Yet, when the protagonist ends up "alone, without wife or husband, mourning [the real—i.e., male—warrior] whom she has grown to love," we have, as Barbara Howard Meldrum dryly observes in "Woman in Western American Fiction: Images, or Real Women?" in *Women and Western American Literature,* "a disappointing ending" to "a tale which started out by exploding the old myths about woman's place" (64).

25   Mathes, p. 47.

26   Deming, p. 97.

27   Lander, p. 211.

28   Frances Brooke, *The History of Emily Montague* (1769; rpt. Ottawa: Carleton Univ. Press, 1985), p. 49.

29   Anna Brewster Morgan as quoted in Leland S. Person, Jr., "The American Eve: Miscegenation and a Feminist Frontier Fiction," *American Quarterly* 37 (1985), p. 677. For a fuller discussion of the differences between white male and female accounts of female captivity consult Annette Kolodny, *The Land Before Her: Fantasy and Experience of the American Frontiers, 1630–1860* (Chapel Hill: Univ. of North Carolina Press, 1984), especially the section "From Captivity to Accommodation, 1630–1833," pp. 17–89. Kolodny's more recent "Among the Indians: The Uses of Captivity" (*New York Times Book Review,* Jan. 31, 1993) also provides an excellent overview of how "[f]rom the first, for both their authors and their readers, Indian captivity narratives have mirrored the aspirations and anxieties of successive generations, revealing new meanings and lending themselves to startling new interpretations over time" (26). See, too, June Namias's *White Captives: Gender and Ethnicity on the American Frontier* (Chapel Hill: Univ. of North Carolina Press, 1993) for a broad-based historical assessment of how "capture and its perceived threat shape[d] Anglo-American ideas of gender and culture from 1607 to 1862" (9).

30   Both Deming and Person cite various historical studies indicating that Indians rarely raped captive white women until they began to copy, in Deming's phrase, "the example [that] was set by white soldiers" (93). Namias also emphasizes how "little evidence" there is "for the rape of any white woman in early New England" but also points out that "although not one report even implied any truth to sexual misconduct among New England tribes," the

"'savage' Indian . . . ravishe[r]" nevertheless soon became "a fearful part of the colonial imagination" (89).

31   Two excellent discussions of the American construction of the Indian and particularly the "savage Indian male" are Francis Jennings, *The Invasion of America: Indians, Colonialism, and the Cant of Conquest* (1975; New York: Norton, 1976), and Robert F. Berkhofer, Jr., *The White Man's Indian: Images of the American Indian from Columbus to the Present* (New York: Vintage, 1979). Comparable Canadian studies are Leslie Monkman, *A Native Heritage: Images of the Indian in English-Canadian Literature* (Toronto: Univ. of Toronto Press, 1981); and Daniel Francis, *The Imaginary Indian: The Image of the Indian in Canadian Culture* (Vancouver: Arsenal Pulp, 1992). Terry Goldie's *Fear and Temptation: The Image of the Indigene in Canadian, Australian, and New Zealand Literatures*, as its subtitle suggests, also covers for Canada much the same topic but in a broader colonial context, while Terrence L. Craig incorporates the treatment of Natives into a general assessment of *Racial Attitudes in English Canadian Fiction, 1905–1980* (Waterloo, Ont.: Wilfrid Laurier Univ. Press, 1987).

32   James Fenimore Cooper, *The Last of the Mohicans: A Narrative of 1757* (1826; Albany: State Univ. of New York Press, 1982), p. 105.

33   Susan H. Armitage, "Women's Literature and the Frontier: A New Perspective on the Frontier Myth," in *Women, Women Writers, and the West*, ed. L. L. Lee and Merrill Lewis (Troy, N.Y.: Whitson, 1979), p. 6. Both this and the previous Cooper quotation can also be found in Person, p. 672, who effectively argues that the male literature of the frontier expressed mostly "male fantasies" (677) that were countered by a number of women writers who suggested as an "alternative to the Adamic myth," the "myth of an American Eve," with attendant "possibilities of marriage rather than antagonism between the races" (685). Glenda Riley, in *Women and Indians on the Frontier* (Albuquerque: Univ. of New Mexico Press, 1984), extensively sets forth the possible historical basis for seeing white women as freer from bias and more capable at negotiating enduring cross-racial relationships. This scholarship does, no doubt, have a certain feminist bias, but it still serves to suggest that earlier and more prevalent countering claims, such as Leslie A. Fiedler's contention, in *The Return of the Vanishing American* (New York: Stein and Day, 1968), that white women "always dreamed themselves and Indians irreconcilable enemies" (90), have long been mostly white male dreams.

34   For example, in Douglas Glover's *The Life and Times of Captain N* (Toronto: McClelland and Stewart, 1993), a novel set on the late eighteenth-century Niagara frontier, one of the white characters attempts to compile his "Book about Indians" but records mostly the contradictions of that endeavor: "Would it be possible for an Indian to dream me out of existence while I erase him with my pen?" (53); "The book about Indians is against the being of Indians" (109); "The book about Indians can't be a book at all. . . . It is an antibook meant to destroy all books" (121).

9   Representational Rites

1   Lenore Keeshig-Tobias, "Stop Stealing Native Stories," *Globe and Mail* [Toronto], Jan. 26, 1990, p. A7.

2   Ibid.

3   Ibid.

4   Stephen Godfrey, "Canada Council Asks Whose Voice Is It Anyway," *Globe and Mail*, Mar. 21, 1992, p. C15.

5   W. P. Kinsella, *The Miss Hobbema Pageant* (Toronto: Harper and Collins, 1989), p. 58.

6   Don Murray, *The Fiction of W. P. Kinsella: Tall Tales in Various Voices* (Fredericton, N.B.: York, 1987), p. 15.

7   Kinsella, pp. 62–63.

8   Gerald Vizenor, "Trickster Discourse," *The Wicazo Sa Review: A Journal of Indian Studies* 5, no. 1 (1989), p. 6.

9   Rudy Wiebe, "Proud Cree Nation Deserves Much More Than 'Funny' Stories," *Globe and Mail*, Feb. 17, 1990, p. C3.

10   "Kinsella 'Ripping Off' Indians," *Globe and Mail*, Dec. 8, 1989, p. A15.

11   Ibid.

12   Murray, p. 9.

13   Ibid.

14   Ibid.

15   See note 20 to chapter 7.

16   Godfrey, p. C1.

17   Ibid.

18   Ibid.

19   Philip Kreiner, *Contact Prints* (Toronto: Doubleday, 1987), p. 46. Subsequent references to this edition of the novel will be made parenthetically in the text.

20   For example, one character is, as an Inuk, an almost complete outcast in the Indian settlement, while Joe comprehends the feelings and actions of his French-Canadian colleague and roommate no better than those of his Cree or Inuk "friends."

21   For an excellent study of the long-term Western infatuation with indigenous art and the cultural implications of that infatuation see Marianna Torgovnick, *Gone Primitive: Savage Intellects, Modern Lives* (Chicago: Univ. of Chicago Press, 1990).

22   This use of "Indianism" is obviously indebted to Edward Said's comprehensive analysis of "Orientalism" and especially to his observation that "Orientalism depends for its strategy on [a] flexible *positional* superiority, which puts the Westerner in a whole series of possible relationships with the Orient without ever losing him the relative upper hand." Edward Said, *Orientalism* (New York: Random House, 1978), p. 7.

23   Joan Clark, *The Victory of Geraldine Gull* (1988; rpt. Toronto: McClelland and Stewart, 1989), p. 238. Subsequent references to this edition of the novel will be made parenthetically in the text.

24   E. M. Forster, *Passage to India* (1924; rpt. New York: Harcourt, 1952), p. 322.

25   For a Native reading of this tale and other Cree and Ojibway stories see Basil H. Johnston, *Ojibway Heritage* (Toronto: McClelland and Stewart, 1976).

26   Trinh T. Minh-ha, *Woman, Native, Other: Writing Postcoloniality and Feminism* (Bloomington: Indiana Univ. Press, 1989), p. 67.

27   Margery Fee, "Upsetting Fake Ideas: Jeannette Armstrong's *Slash* and Beatrice Culleton's *April Raintree*," in *Native Writers and Canadian Writing*, ed. W. H. New (Vancouver: Univ. of British Columbia Press, 1990), p. 169.

28   Jeannette Armstrong, *Slash*, rev. ed. (Penticton, B.C.: Theytus, 1988), p. 36.

29   Fee, p. 169.

30   As Fee points out, a first-person narrator and the consequent "construction of a Native 'I'" is "subversive . . . within the literary discourse of Canada" in that it offers Natives both a "voice that does not implicitly exclude them" and a "less contradictory subject position" (172).

31   The actual quotation, in Frederick W. Rowe, *Extinction: The Beothuks of Newfoundland* (1977; rpt. Toronto: McGraw-Hill Ryerson, 1986), p. 72, is "staggers one's credulity."

32   Beatrice Culleton, *In Search of April Raintree* (Winnipeg: Pemmican, 1983), pp. 116–17. Subsequent references to this edition of the novel will be made parenthetically in the text. I would also here note that the novel received little attention when it was first published and was redone in a young readers' version, *April Raintree* (1984), with the rape scene eliminated.

33   Lynn A. Higgins and Brenda R. Silver, "Introduction: Rereading Rape," in *Rape and Representation,* ed. Lynn A. Higgins and Brenda R. Silver (New York: Columbia Univ. Press, 1991), p. 1, emphasis in the original.

34   Mary Douglas, *Purity and Danger: An Analysis of the Concepts of Pollution and Taboo* (1966; rpt. London: Routledge and Kegan Paul, 1980), p. 128.

35   Margaret Atwood, *Survival: A Thematic Guide to Canadian Literature* (Toronto: Anansi, 1972), p. 207.

36   Thomas King, *Medicine River* (Markham, Ont.: Viking Penguin, 1989), p. 40. Subsequent references to this edition of the novel will be made parenthetically in the text.

37   Thomas King, "Godzilla vs. Post-Colonial," *World Literature Written in English* 30, no. 2 (1990), p. 12.

38   Ibid., p. 11.

39   Ibid., p. 12.

40   Ibid.

41   Ibid., p. 13.

42   Ibid., p. 14.

43   Ibid.

44   Thomas King in Priscilla L. Walton's "An Interview with Thomas King," *Chimo* 21 (1990), p. 25.

45   Percy [Priscilla] Walton, " 'Tell Our Own Stories': Politics and the Fiction of Thomas King," *World Literature Written in English* 30, no. 2 (1990), pp. 78–79.

46   Constance Rooke, "Interview with Tom King," *World Literature Written in English* 30, no. 2 (1990), p. 74.

Epilogue: The One About "The One About Coyote Going West"

1   I here refer to Linda Hutcheon as a theorist on parody, on the postmodern, and on English-Canadian fiction. See her *A Theory of Parody: The Teachings of Twentieth-Century Art Forms* (New York: Methuen, 1985), *The Poetics of Postmodernism: History, Theory, Fiction* (New York: Routledge, 1988), and *The Canadian Postmodern: A Study of Contemporary English-Canadian Fiction* (Toronto: Oxford University Press, 1988).

2   Thomas King, "The One About Coyote Going West," in *All My Relations: An Anthology of Contemporary Canadian Native Fiction,* ed. Thomas King (Toronto: McClelland and Stewart, 1990), p. 99. Subsequent references will be made parenthetically in the text.

Index

Arnold E. Davidson is Research Professor of Canadian
Studies at Duke University. He has edited or authored
seven other books including *The Art of Margaret Atwood:
Essays in Criticism, Studies in Canadian Literature: Intro-
ductory and Critical Essays,* and *Writing Against Silence: Joy
Kogawa's "Obsan."*

Library of Congress Cataloging-in-Publication Data
Davidson, Arnold E., 1936–
Coyote country : fictions of the Canadian west / Arnold E.
Davidson.
Includes index.
ISBN 0–8223–1453–3 (cl).—ISBN 0–8223–1469–X (pa)
1. Canadian fiction—Canada, Western—History and criti-
cism. 2. Frontier and pioneer life in literature. 3. Western
stories—History and criticism. 4. Canada, Western—In
literature.
I. Title.
PR9198.2.W4D38   1994
813.009'32712–dc20   93–43231   CIP